Undoing
DEPRESSION

Also by Richard O'Connor, PhD

Happy At Last: The Thinking Person's Guide to Finding Joy

Undoing Perpetual Stress: The Missing Connection
Between Depression, Anxiety, and 21st-Century Illness

Active Treatment of Depression

Undoing DEPRESSION

What Therapy Doesn't Teach You *and* Medication Can't Give You

SECOND EDITION

RICHARD O'CONNOR, PhD

Little, Brown and Company
New York   Boston   London

Little, Brown and Company
Hachette Book Group
237 Park Avenue, New York, NY 10017
www.hachettebookgroup.com

Second edition, January 2010
Originally published in hardcover by Little, Brown and Company, April 1997

Little, Brown and Company is a division of Hachette Book Group, Inc. The Little, Brown name and logo are trademarks of Hachette Book Group, Inc.

The author is grateful for permission to include the following previously copyrighted material: "Daily Record of Dysfunctional Thoughts" from *Cognitive Therapy of Depression* by Aaron T. Beck, A. J. Rush, B. F. Shaw, and G. Emery. Copyright © 1979. Reprinted by permission of Guilford Press. The figure on page 239 is based on "Why the Complexity of Consciousness..." (adapted) from *Flow: The Psychology of Optimal Experience* by Mihaly Csikszentmihalyi. Copyright © 1990 by Mihaly Csikszentmihalyi. Reprinted by permission of HarperCollins Publishers, Inc. Exercise 2, "Your Dirty Laundry," is reprinted with permission from Richard O'Connor, *Happy at Last*. Copyright © 2008, St. Martin's Press, New York. Exercise 3, "A Simple Mindfulness Meditation," is adapted with permission from *Undoing Perpetual Stress* by Richard O'Connor. Copyright © 2005, Berkley Press.

Library of Congress Cataloging-in-Publication Data
O'Connor, Richard, Ph. D.
    Undoing depression : what therapy doesn't teach you and medication can't give you / Richard O'Connor. — 2nd ed.
      p. cm.
    Includes bibliographical references and index.
    ISBN 978-0-316-04341-0
    1. Depression, Mental.   2. Depressed persons—Life skills guides.   I. Title.
    RC537.O326 2010
    616.85'27—dc22   2009024016

10 9 8 7 6 5 4 3 2 1

RRD-IN

Contents

Preface to the Second Edition

As I write in 2009, I find myself alternately pleased and dismayed to find that so much of *Undoing Depression* remains quite relevant eleven years after it was first written. Pleased that I can pat myself on the back for giving useful advice that has stood the test of time; dismayed because there has been so little progress in achieving deeper understanding or developing more effective treatment for this devastating condition. Indeed, it seems sometimes that progress has only been backward. Medications are now understood to be considerably less effective than we'd hoped for. The assumption that depression is caused by a deficiency in serotonin in the brain has proved false. And depression keeps growing in epidemic proportions. The World Bank and World Health Organization estimate that depression soon will be the single most costly disease there is—more costly than AIDS, cancer, or TB.

Yet there is hopeful news for this new edition. Previously, I was out on a scientific limb in arguing that the "skills of depression"—the habits that make it so hard for us to recover—are essentially neural pathways that can be replaced by more effective ways of living. Now the new neuroscience has confirmed that is indeed what happens in the brain; old pathways wither when we stop our habits, to be replaced by new connections that are learned through changes in our behavior. *We can change our own brains* through focused attention and practice. At the same time, new developments in psychology and behavioral medicine have given us much more specific, proven methods to help us escape the habits of depression and learn new ways out of our misery. Thus it's even more imperative that people with depression be encouraged and enabled to take effective action for themselves — which is the goal of this book.

Author's Note

TWO PARTICULAR PROBLEMS with language occur throughout this book. One is the difficulty of what to call someone with depression. In different contexts, this person may be called a patient, a client, a victim, a sufferer, or a consumer. Each term says more about the assumptions of the person applying the label than the recipient. The only descriptive term I know of, which is to call someone with depression a "depressive," will suggest to some the concept of a "depressive character," a loaded concept suggesting that there is something in the personality that causes depression. I disagree with the implication that there is a depressive character, yet I argue that depression does affect one's character and personality, so I opt for the term "depressive" as descriptive of what can become a way of life. Since I count myself among this number, I can plead the right to use the term without its implicit value judgment.

The second problem is the use of "he" or "she" to refer to a person when gender really doesn't matter. In this book in particular, since depression is much more commonly diagnosed among women, and since that phenomenon is a subject of some heated debate in gender politics, the issue becomes ticklish. For a male writer to refer to depressed individuals as "she" may appear to perpetuate what, to some, is an artifact of male-dominated science and culture. For me to refer to depressed individuals as "he" exclusively, however, may appear to gloss over the apparent greater suffering of women. For me to write "he or she" and "himself/herself" every time just becomes too awkward. I have, therefore, decided to try to intersperse male and female pronouns in instances when gender really doesn't matter, but there are times when this becomes labored, and I revert to using "he" to refer to an individual of either sex.

Undoing
DEPRESSION

Introduction

THE ESSENTIAL QUESTION that patients and therapists ask themselves over and over is: why is it so hard to get better? Once we understand the hidden meanings and motives behind our behavior, and see how we keep repeating behaviors that prevent us from feeling good about ourselves and getting to where we want in life, *why don't we just stop?* Once we have the right medication to prevent us from sinking back into the blackest depths, once we can start feeling a little more optimistic about the future and ourselves, why do we remain shy, passive, and withdrawn? Why do people persist in self-destructive behavior when they can see that it does them no good? Freud had to invent theories as elaborate and arcane as the death instinct to answer this question—the idea that as a counterpart to a desire to create, enjoy, and live we have an equally strong desire to destroy, suffer, and die. All my experience tells me that there is a much simpler answer. People persist in self-destructive behavior because they don't know how to do anything else; in fact, all these depressed behavior patterns become written into the brain itself. How do we undo that?

I'm convinced that the major reason why people with depression stay depressed despite therapy, medication, and support from loved ones is that we are simply unable to imagine an alternative. We know how to "do" depression. We are experts at it. Our feelings about ourselves and the way we see the world have forced us over the years to develop a very special set of skills. We become like those who are blind from birth. They become very attuned to sounds, smells, and other senses that sighted persons take for granted. They can read Braille as well as anyone else can read printed matter. They get very good at memorization. But asking them to imagine a sunset, or a flower, or a Van Gogh is pointless—they have no reference; it's beyond their experience. Expecting us to stop being depressed is like expecting a blind person to suddenly see the light of day, with one important difference: eventually, we can do it. There are also unconscious forces at work, primarily fear, that oppose change. We develop defense mechanisms that distort reality so that we can put up with being depressed, or sustain the unconscious belief that we don't deserve to feel better. People learn and grow through experience, but the depressed person, out of fear, avoids the curative experience. I think that by practicing, by taking big challenges in small steps, by learning gradually that fears can't kill you and impulses don't overwhelm you, the depressed person learns alternatives to depressed behavior, and enough nondepressed behavior means you're not depressed anymore.

Depression becomes for us a set of habits, behaviors, thought processes, assumptions, and feelings that seems very much like our core self; you can't give those up without something to replace them and without expecting some anxiety along the way. Recovery from depression is like recovery from heart disease or alcoholism. The good heart patient knows that medication isn't enough; lifelong habits of diet and exercise, how one deals with stress, must change. The recovering alcoholic knows that abstinence is not enough; ways of thinking, relating to others, and dealing with emotions have to change. We depressives become shaped by our disease as well; the skills that we develop with depression in a vain effort to save ourselves pain—skills like swallowing our anger, isolating ourselves, putting others first, being over-responsible—prevent our recovery. We have to give up the depressed habits that keep us down and make us vulnerable to relapse.

In the ten-plus years since the first edition of this book came out, there have been some startling developments in what we know about depression, thanks to the new technology that allows scientists to see into the brain as it's working. First the bad news: *Depression causes brain damage.* Then the good news: *We can undo that damage* with focused practice and attention. In fact, we may be able to move beyond what was normal for us and feel better than we ever have. Science knows now that our brain does not simply store our experiences. Each experience changes the brain, structurally, electrically, chemically. The brain *becomes* the experience. If we are careful about the experiences we give our brains, we can change the brain itself.

One thing we can take away from all the new brain science: *Practice is essential to change.* We can spend years in therapy so that we have a pretty good understanding of what led us to this dark place, but if we don't get out of bed in the morning, we're still going to feel depressed. Medications, when they work, do so partly by giving us enough energy to get out of bed. But it's practice that leads to change in the brain. Practice in anything new develops networks between brain cells that previously weren't connected to each other. The networks in your brain that support depressed behavior are so well-used, they're like the interstate highway system. You have to get off the highway and explore some new paths, but with enough practice, going down these new roads becomes automatic to you as new connections develop in your brain.

Overcoming depression requires a new set of skills from us. But now we are recognizing that happiness is a skill, willpower is a skill, health is a skill, successful relationships require skills, emotional intelligence is a skill. We know this because practice not only leads to improvement but also to changes in the brain. This is a much more empowering and adaptive way of understanding life than assuming that these qualities are doled out from birth in fixed quantities and that there's nothing we can do to change our fate. The skills required to undo depression will permeate your entire life, and if you keep practicing, you can go far beyond mere recovery.

My goal is to present a "program" for depression. People in AA know from experience that not drinking is not enough; they have to "live the program." Like alcoholism, depression is a lifelong condition that can be cured only by a deliberate effort to change our selves. Later chapters explain how in key elements of our personality—feelings, thoughts, behavior, relationships, how we treat our bodies, and how we handle stress—depression has taught us certain habits that have come to feel natural, a part of who we are. But we don't realize that those habits just reinforce depression. We have to unlearn those habits and replace them with new skills—which I'll explain in detail—for real recovery to take place. Practicing the exercises described later can be a way for people with depression to "live the program"—and live a vital, rich existence again.

I believe very strongly that people can recover from depression but that medication and conventional psychotherapy don't go far enough—and now the research bears me out. The terrible irony of depression is that we come to blame ourselves for our own illness; I hope to show that this belief is a symptom of the disease, not a matter of fact. People need new tools, and practice in using them, in order to make a full recovery. In putting these techniques together, I've had the benefit of being able to draw on a great deal of research and clinical experience developed over the last thirty years, which have suggested new ways of thinking, acting, relating, and feeling to replace the old ways of being that have never worked and often made things worse. I've also had the benefit of working in clinics in the real world to help me understand how these methods can be applied in everyday life. Further, my own experience with depression and recovery has helped me learn firsthand what's helpful and what's not.

When I was fifteen I came home from school one day to find that my mother had committed suicide in the basement. She had bolted the doors and taped a note to the window saying she was out shopping and I should wait at a neighbor's. I knew something was wrong and was climbing in a window when my father came driving in after work. We discovered her body together.

She had put a plastic bag over her head and sat down at the table where I played with my chemistry set. She ran the gas line from my Bunsen burner into the plastic bag and turned on the gas. Later we learned that she had also taken a lethal dose of a sleeping pill that my father sold in his job as a pharmaceutical representative. Her body was cold, so she must have started to set things up soon after we had left the house in the morning. This was no cry for help; she went to a great deal of trouble to make sure she would end her life.

Until two years before, my mother had seemed happy, confident, and outgoing. I remember her joy getting ready to go out to a party, or singing forties songs with my father on evening car rides. When I look back at the course of my life, I realize now how much it has been shaped by my need to understand what happened to her.

To understand also what was happening to me, because I've had my own depression to contend with. I didn't recognize it for a long time, though I'm a reasonably well-trained and experienced psychotherapist. I've been a patient myself several times, but I never put a label on my problems; I always told myself I sought help for personal growth. This was despite the fact that there were long periods in my life when I drank too much, when I alienated everyone close to me, when I could just barely get to work, when I would wake up each morning hating the thought of facing the day and my life. There were many times I thought of suicide, but if I couldn't forgive my mother, I couldn't forgive myself, either. And I have children and family, patients, and colleagues I couldn't bear to do that to. But for many long periods life seemed so miserable, hopeless, and joyless that I wished for a way out. Everyone who has ever been depressed knows it's impossible to be sure, but I think those days are finally behind me now. I don't hit the deepest depths, but I live with the aftereffects. I still struggle with the emotional habits of depression. But accepting the fact that it's going to be a long struggle has made me more able to deal with the short-term ups and downs. And I see progress.

I've worked in mental health for thirty years, as a therapist, supervisor, and agency director. I've studied psychoanalytic, family

*systems, biochemical, cognitive, mindfulness-based, you name it,
ways of understanding people. I've worked with some wonderful
teachers and had some wonderful patients. I won't pretend to have
all the answers on depression, but you won't find many people with
more experience, both personal and professional.*

I believe now that depression can never be fully grasped by mental health professionals who have not experienced it. I've repeatedly seen "comprehensive" theories of depression develop, flourish, and dominate the field for a time, only to be rejected because new, contradictory evidence is found. Many psychologists and psychiatrists seem to prefer theory-building—making their observations fit with some preexisting theory or developing a new theory that will explain it all—rather than trying to figure out practical ways to help their patients. They get too far away from experience. I realize now that no simple, single-factor theory of depression will ever work. Depression is partly in our genes, partly in our childhood experience, partly in our way of thinking, partly in our brains, partly in our ways of handling emotions. It affects our whole being.

Imagine if our medical knowledge was such that we could reliably diagnose heart disease but knew nothing about the effects of exercise, cholesterol, salt and fat, stress, and fatigue. Patients who were diagnosed would be grasping at all kinds of straws that might help them recover. Some would stop all exercise, some would exercise furiously. Some would withdraw from stressful situations. Some would take medication to reduce blood pressure without knowing that their unhealthy diet undoes any beneficial effect of medication. Many would die prematurely; some would get better accidentally; without good, controlled scientific studies, doctors would not learn what was causing some to die, some to recover.

This is where we are with depression. We get all kinds of advice, some of it helpful, some of it not, most of it unproven. Some of it simply designed to sell a product. The depressed patient is in the dark about what exactly he or she needs to do to help recovery. But in fact a great deal is known about how people recover from depression. It doesn't all fit into a neat theoretical package, so it's hard to pull together, but the knowledge is there to be used.

Depression is a complex condition that blurs our Western boundaries between mind and body, nature and nurture, self and others. Many people with depression seem to have been primed for it by trauma, deprivation, or loss in childhood. Most people with depression describe difficulties in their childhood or later in life that have contributed to low self-esteem and a sensitivity to rejection, an uncertainty about the self and an inability to enjoy life. But these observations are not true for everyone with depression: some people who have no history of stress, who appear very stable and well integrated, develop it suddenly, unexpectedly, in response to a life change. There is clearly a biochemical component to depression, and medication can be helpful for many people, but medication alone is not sufficient treatment for most. The truth is that whether the roots of depression are in the past in childhood, or in the present in the brain, recovery can only come about through a continuous act of will, a self-discipline applied to emotions, behavior, and relationships in the here and now. This is a hard truth, because no one deserves to feel this way, and it doesn't seem fair that the blameless have to work so hard to help themselves. Besides, the depressed are always being told to snap out of it, pull yourself together, don't give in to weakness, and it's the cruelest, most unfeeling advice they can be given. What I want to do here is to give guidance and support, along with advice, to help the depressive find the resources he or she needs for recovery.

People who are depressed are in over their heads and don't know how to swim. They work very hard at living, at trying to solve their problems, but their efforts are futile because they lack the skills necessary to support themselves in deep water. The real battle of depression is between parts of the self. Depressed people are pulled under by shadows, ghosts, pieces of themselves that they can't integrate and can't let go. The harder they work, the more they do what they know how to do, the worse things get. When their loved ones try to help in the usual ways, the commonsense ways that only seem natural expressions of caring and concern, they get rejected. The depressed person then feels more guilty and out of control.

People with depression have to learn new ways of living with themselves and others—new emotional skills. These skills take practice, coordination, and flexibility. Instead of flailing at the water in panic, they have to learn emotional habits that are much more like swimming: smooth, rhythmic, learning to float, learning to be comfortable in the water. Depressed people are great strugglers, but to struggle is to drown. Better to learn how to let the water hold you up.

Obviously this is an intensely personal book for me. I want to keep would-be suicides alive, I want to spare people the useless pain of depression. There is a great deal more that can be done now than was available for my mother or for myself when I was younger. Psychotherapy and medication offer hope to everyone. Learning techniques of self-control, skills of communication and self-expression, and challenging one's assumptions about the self and the world, can give people who literally don't know anything other than depression the chance for a rewarding life.

Something that touched me deeply when I worked at our community mental health clinic was the great number of people who didn't know they were depressed. People are usually prompted to call for help not because they simply feel rotten, but because something is going wrong in their lives: their children won't listen, there is a marital problem, they are having trouble at work. But it often doesn't take much digging to find that the caller has been depressed for some time; the family conflict, the job problem, is a manifestation, not a cause, of the depression. If we had been able to help them sooner, their lives wouldn't be the train wrecks they are now. These are people who now feel almost no joy in life, who have no hope, no ambition, who feel stuck, powerless, and perennially sad—*and who think this is the normal way to feel.* It's not.

Part 1

What We Know About Depression

1

Understanding Depression

WE ARE LIVING in an epidemic of depression. Every indication suggests that more people are depressed, more of the time, more severely, and starting earlier in their lives, than ever before. Depression is not going to go away no matter how much we ignore it, scorn it, or neglect it. We need to attend to it as a major public health problem. But that's difficult to do because the idea of depression frightens us all — we think of a descent into madness — and thus we avoid the subject. We have a natural wish to forget about depression, to hope that we are immune. Can you make yourself remember the sensation of pain? Most people react to the question with a cringe but really can't describe pain or evoke the sensation in their memory. We repress it, push it away, so that most of the time we don't think about it and we can get on with life. But when we hear the dentist's drill, we suddenly remember exactly what it's going to feel like. We do the same mental trick with depression. We've all felt it, but we believe we have to shut out the memory. We want to think of depression as something that happens to somebody else.

But it strikes closer to home now, because the incidence is increasing. For each generation born since 1900, the age of onset of depression is younger and younger, and the lifetime risk has increased.[1] According to the most official, conservative estimates, approximately

6.7 percent of Americans will experience an episode of major depression in their lifetimes.[2] When you add in the so-called milder forms of depression, I believe the rate goes up well past 25 percent. Every fourth person you meet is likely to have a serious encounter with depression at some point in their lives. And every fifth person is depressed right now: researchers estimate that almost 20 percent of the population meet the criteria for some form of depression at any given time—and that does not mean people who are temporarily feeling the blues and will be better next week, but people who are having real difficulty functioning in life.[3]

This epidemic is not merely a result of growing awareness of depression, but a true growth in hard numbers.[4] Nor is it only a phenomenon of American, or even Western, culture. A recent study comparing incidence of depression in Taiwan, Puerto Rico, and Lebanon, among other countries, found that for each successive generation, depression was likely to begin at earlier ages, and that over the course of a lifetime, the risk of depression kept increasing.[5] Of all people with major depression, 15 percent will end their lives by suicide.

Clinical depression is a serious, often fatal illness that is so common it's hard to recognize. But health economists consider it just as disabling as blindness or paraplegia.[6] In terms of overall economic burden to our society, depression is the second most costly disease there is. This surprising news comes from the World Bank and World Health Organization, which measured the lost years of healthy life due to disease.[7] The cost, in terms of direct treatment, unnecessary medical care, lost productivity, and shortened life span, was estimated at $83 billion dollars a year in the United States alone for the year 2000.[8] Depression is second only to cancer in terms of economic impact, and approximately the same as the cost of heart disease and AIDS. The number of deaths from suicide in the United States each year (33,000) is approximately twice the number of deaths from AIDS,[9] and shows no sign of declining. And the impact will only get worse: if current trends continue, children today will develop depression at the average age of twenty, instead of the thirty-plus we are used to.[10] Yet only a third of people with long-term depression have ever been tried on antidepressants, and only a small number of them have ever had adequate treatment.[11]

If this is all true, if depression is as dangerous and prevalent as I'm saying, you may well ask: Where's the big national foundation leading the battle against depression? Where's the Jerry Lewis Telethon and the Annual Run for Depression? Little black ribbons for everyone to wear?* The obvious answer is the stigma associated with the disease. Too much of the public still views depression as a weakness or character flaw, and thinks we should pull ourselves up by our own bootstraps. And all the hype about new antidepressant medications has only made things worse by suggesting that recovery is simply a matter of taking a pill. Too many people with depression take the same attitude; we are ashamed of and embarrassed by having depression. This is the cruelest part of the disease: we blame ourselves for being weak or lacking character instead of accepting that we have an illness, instead of realizing that our self-blame is a symptom of the disease. And feeling that way, we don't step forward and challenge unthinking people who reinforce those negative stereotypes. So we stay hidden away, feeling miserable and blaming ourselves for our own misery.

This is a dirty little secret of mental health economics: if you're depressed, you don't think you're worth the cost of treatment. You feel guilty enough about being unproductive and unreliable; most likely your family members have been telling you to snap out of it, and you believe you should. You're not likely to shell out a hundred dollars an hour to see a therapist, and if your insurance won't pay, you're not likely to put up a fight. Yet your therapist needs his fee, and insurance carriers often require you to be very determined before they will pay their share. They will play on your own guilt

---

* An encouraging development is the American Foundation for Suicide Prevention's "Out of the Darkness" walks, which seem to be attracting more notice, little by little.

about your condition to make it difficult for you to get anything more than the absolute minimum treatment. They count on discouraging you from pursuing your claims in order to save themselves money; and, in doing so, they reinforce your depression. There are hopeful signs about "parity" for mental health services, but until the laws are changed and new regulations published, managed care plans still will find ways of drastically restricting coverage for outpatient care.

The decade between 1987 and 1997 brought extraordinary changes in how depression was treated in the United States, trends that have very likely continued since. The percentage of people being treated for depression tripled in that time, from less than one percent to 2⅓ percent (while the percentage of people receiving healthcare treatment of any kind actually declined slightly). But all that growth was due to the appearance of new drugs on the market. In 1987, 37 percent of people being treated for depression were taking an antidepressant; in 1997, it was 75 percent. Meanwhile, the proportion receiving psychotherapy declined from 70 to 60 percent, and the average number of therapy sessions declined as well.[12] SSRIs (selective serotonin reuptake inhibitors; the new class of antidepressants — Prozac, Zoloft, Paxil, Celexa, Lexapro) were not generally available in 1987, but within ten years they were being prescribed to almost 60 percent of patients. By 1998, more than 130 million prescriptions for antidepressants were written each year in the United States, and Prozac, Paxil, and Zoloft were among the six best-selling drugs of any kind.[13] By 2004, fully one-third of U.S. women's doctor visits resulted in a prescription for an antidepressant.[14] By 2005, 10 percent of the American population was taking an antidepressant.[15] Here you have the intersection of two factors: the direct-to-consumer advertising of (and all the media hype about) the newer antidepressants, and the advent of managed care, which often requires treatment by a physician (not a psychiatrist), and reimburses less for psychotherapy. Most experts agree that treatment with medication and psychotherapy combined is best, but very little research is being conducted on combined treatment because in the U.S. drug companies fund research, and they're not interested in supporting that conclusion. So psychotherapy for depression became the exception, and a scrip from your GP became the norm. Depression became chemical, and there was no need to look at the stresses in your life.

Then the news began to trickle out that medications weren't so effective after all. We learned that in their testing, they had proved only slightly better than sugar pills, that the testing used measures that were designed to exaggerate the success of the meds, and that over the long haul, most people using them relapsed. We learned that the side effects were far more pervasive and serious than we had been led to believe, and subsequently realized that depression can't be brushed off as a chemical imbalance.

Despite greater awareness and all the pills prescribed, depression remains amazingly underdiagnosed. That same study showing the remarkable expansion in treatment still notes that most people with depression get no treatment at all. Many people don't realize they have it. When I worked at our community mental health center in rural Connecticut, we would see two or three new people every week who had trouble sleeping and other physical symptoms, felt anxious and overwhelmed, had lost ambition and hope, felt alone and alienated, were tormented by guilt or obsessional thoughts, may even have had thoughts of suicide — but they wouldn't call it depression. They just concluded that life stinks and there was nothing they could do about it. They would go to their doctors for aches and pains, sleeplessness, lack of energy, and get a useless prescription or medical procedure or be dismissed as hypochondriacs. They might medicate themselves with alcohol and drugs. Their families didn't know how to help; neither sympathy nor moralizing seemed to have any effect. In this way, the depressed person gets caught up in a vicious circle from which there seems to be no escape. Life like this does stink, especially when you blame yourself and don't realize you have an illness.

Untreated depression will damage the course of your life. Men with early onset (before age twenty-two) major depression are only half as likely to marry and form intimate relationships as men with late-onset (or no) depression. Women with early onset depression are only half as likely to obtain a college degree as their female counterparts, and their future annual earnings will be substantially lower.[16]

The real tragedy is that in mental health, where there is so much we can't help, depression is one thing that can usually be treated effectively and efficiently. Many good, unbiased research studies have shown that treatment works. Most people improve quickly; though total recovery is often a slow, challenging process, it's well within our grasp.

Janet was admitted to a psychiatric hospital in an acute state of depression. She was extremely upset and confused, could not organize her thoughts, could not drive to the store or take care of her children. She was obsessed with thoughts and impulses of suicide, though she did not consciously desire to kill herself. She couldn't sleep, felt hopeless and helpless, and had lost all interest in ordinary activities. She was convinced she was losing her mind.

This all seemed to start recently when Janet found out her husband had had an affair. Although he seemed ashamed of himself and assured her it would never happen again, her world seemed to collapse. Within a few weeks, her ability to function had deteriorated dramatically. Her husband brought her to the family doctor, and together they arranged for an emergency admission.

After a week in the psychiatric ward, Janet felt much better. Just before she was ready to be discharged, she went home on a weekend pass. Her visit went smoothly until Janet discovered a letter her husband's girlfriend had written to him while Janet was in the hospital. Again he tried to reassure Janet that the affair was over. But her condition took a dramatic turn for the worse, and she spent several more weeks in the hospital.

Depression is a fascinating condition. There is a great deal of value in thinking of it as a disease. The brain chemistry of depressed people is different from that of other people, and it is possible to find the same biochemical differences in the brains of animals that appear "depressed." Over the long term, depression seems to result in loss of brain cells and shrinkage of certain parts of the brain (see Chapter 4). On a human level, helping people understand that they have a disease can free them from much of the guilt and self-blame that accompanies depression. They can learn different ways of reacting to stress and learn to take steps so that the danger of future episodes is greatly reduced.

But if it's a disease, how do we catch it? If Janet's husband hadn't had his affair, would she ever have come down with depression? There was nothing about her to suggest susceptibility to depression before she got sick. Janet now thinks she has had a "breakdown," she now thinks of herself as a mental patient — but isn't this because her husband is a jerk? Is the depression in Janet, or in her marriage? If it's in her marriage, how can the pills Janet takes help her feel more competent and capable? If it's in Janet, is it the part of herself that sees the truth more clearly than she and her husband can admit to?

Most people who have had a true experience with depression have no trouble at all believing that something biochemical in nature has happened to them. The change in mood, in how the self and the world are perceived, seems so profound and overwhelming that it makes intuitive sense to feel that the self has been invaded by something alien. We do not feel like our selves. Something very powerful, something from outside us, has invaded and changed us.

But most people going through their first experience of depression also recognize that this feeling that seems so foreign is also eerily familiar. They remember many times from their childhood and adolescence when they felt the same way — alone, helpless, and friendless. They may remember their parents as kind and loving, but they wonder why they felt so unloved. They may have believed that they had to be perfect, and they may have tried very hard, but failed, and felt again the futility of their efforts. As adults, they may have thought they'd grown out of it, but here it is again. Winston Churchill referred to his depression as the "black dog"—the familiar beast that quietly pads in in the evening and settles down at your feet.

Depression is a disease both of the mind and of the body, the present and the past. In psychiatry now we have pitched battles going on between opposing camps, those who want to treat the brain and those who want to treat the mind—and those interested in the mind are losing the fight.[17] The side that wants to treat the brain has all the support of Big Pharma, traditional medicine, and the gee-whiz media. But their research is almost always flawed. Unfortunately, the patient is caught in the middle. The family doctor, supported by the pharmaceutical industry, is likely to say, "Take this pill"—but when it doesn't work, the patient just has another in a long line of failures to add to his baggage. The mental health professional is likely to say, "Let's talk about it"—and the patient is likely to feel patronized, misunderstood, because how can simply talking lift such terrible pain?

It's not an either-or question. Both ways of thinking are true. Psychotherapy and medication both produce similar changes in brain functioning.[18] There is a biochemical process in depression, but the individual has been made susceptible to depression through life experiences. The current episode may be precipitated by an external event, but the event has set in motion a change in the way the brain functions.

When he was in his thirties, Robert went to bed for fourteen months. He was profoundly depressed, though he didn't acknowledge it. A highly intellectual man, his mind was preoccupied with questions about the meaning of life. Unable to find a reason for living, he saw no reason to get up. He didn't consciously feel depressed, he just felt empty. His wife did everything she could to get him out of bed—brought in doctors, family members, appealed to his duty to their child. It became a bitter power struggle between them. Finally, one day long after his wife had given up, Robert decided to get up and go back to work.

I got to know Robert fifteen years later. He had had other epi-sodes in which he took to his bed for weeks, but never for so long. He and his wife had been separated for a few years, when she finally tired of his coldness.

Robert came in for treatment because he feared slipping back into his old ways. He lived alone now, in a house literally crammed with junk. There were days when he just couldn't get out of bed. When he did, he procrastinated and couldn't accomplish anything. He was troubled by his wife, who seemed bent on a nasty divorce battle. He still saw absolutely no purpose in living, but he wanted to resolve the divorce. He was dead set against medication of any kind, and since he never went into a major depressive episode while we worked together, I didn't push it.

Robert had exactly the family background that is so common among depressed men: a critical, distant, hostile father and a shal-low, narcissistic mother. He felt he could never satisfy his father or interest his mother. Because children can't see their parents objec-tively, they make the way their parents treat them part of themselves; if you are treated like dirt long enough, you begin to feel like dirt. Instead of understanding that Father is too critical, the child experi-ences himself as inadequate; instead of understanding that Mother is cold, the child experiences himself as unlovable. These feelings persist into adulthood as the basis for a characterological depres-sion, an existence without hope or joy.

I decided to try to go with Robert's strengths: his intelligence, his intellectualized curiosity about the meaning of life, and his recogni-tion that the world of feelings was foreign territory. I suggested that he do some reading so that he could better understand his own con-dition. Robert was fascinated with Alice Miller's book Prisoners of Childhood,[19] *understanding that she was describing his parents and childhood with perfect accuracy. He learned that depression is not a feeling, but the inability to feel. He began to learn that when he felt like taking to his bed, it was in response to some interpersonal event. He wanted to learn better ways of responding.*

Eventually Robert began a relationship with Betty. With Robert's permission, Betty came in to see me; her devotion to him was obvious, but I was especially pleased with her "tough love" approach. She helped educate Robert about feelings. When he got mad at her, she wouldn't let him withdraw. She teased and joked him out of his coldness. For his part, he was so moved by her evident love for him that he wouldn't let himself act like the aloof, self-absorbed iceberg he used to be. Instead of ruminating about the meaning of life, for the first time he began to enjoy living.

The crisis in therapy came after a few months. Betty decided to move away from our small town, which had no jobs available. She had family in another state that would help her make a new start. Robert could come too. But he got caught up in obsessional thinking. He became terrified that his wife would break in and steal something he didn't want her to have. But Robert knew intellectually that these worries were really trivial in proportion to the opportunity he had. With his new understanding of depression, he could see that he was displacing his anxiety about change and commitment to seemingly simpler things. Still it was very difficult for him to let go; I had to make him imagine in detail what his life would be like without Betty.

I saw Robert again, three years later. He was in town for another hearing on his divorce, which continued to drag on. He and Betty were living together, and he was working and happy. For at least three years, there was no sign at all of his depression.

What helped Robert so much? Was it the therapy, his relationship with Betty, or something else? How destructive was his marriage? His withdrawal into bed was at least partly a retreat from his wife's nagging. Would medication have helped him sooner, or helped him even more effectively?

To understand depression, we should ask ourselves, what was it about Robert and Janet that made them respond to life stresses in the way they did? This is what sets them apart from other people.

Many wives in Janet's situation would have questioned their marriage, not themselves. Others might have shrugged off a husband's affair. What made Janet so vulnerable? How could Robert become so immobilized for so long, and then one day snap out of it? To what extent did his coldness, his inability to feel, which seemed so much a part of him, contribute to his depression?

William Styron, author of *Sophie's Choice* and winner of the National Book Award, wrote *Darkness Visible* to describe his own bout with depression. He referred to his experience as "madness," feeling that the word "depression" is simply an inadequate expression of the experience—"a true wimp of a word for such a major illness.... Told that someone's mood disorder has evolved into a storm—a veritable howling tempest in the brain, which is indeed what a clinical depression resembles like nothing else—even the uninformed layman might display sympathy rather than the standard reaction that 'depression' evokes, something akin to 'So what?' or 'You'll pull out of it' or 'We all have bad days.' "[20]

Styron was right. People feel ashamed of being depressed, they feel they should snap out of it, they feel weak and inadequate. Of course, these feelings are symptoms of the disease. *Depression is a grave and life-threatening illness, much more common than we recognize.* As far as the depressive being weak or inadequate, let me drop some names of famous depressives: Abraham Lincoln, Winston Churchill, Eleanor Roosevelt, Sigmund Freud. Terry Bradshaw, Drew Carey, Billy Joel, T. Boone Pickens, J. K. Rowling, Brooke Shields, Mike Wallace. Charles Dickens, Joseph Conrad, Graham Greene, Ernest Hemingway, Herman Melville, Mark Twain.

Depression accounts for a large part of the business in most outpatient practices. At our clinic, we could see a big difference between self-report and diagnosis; only 12 percent of people told us when they first called that depression was their primary problem, but 45 percent of our patients ended up with a diagnosis of some form of depressive disorder. People usually called not because they were aware they were depressed, but because the depression had reached the point where their lives were in crisis—marital problems, drug or alcohol problems, trouble at work. But we would see someone who looked sad, tired, and defeated, couldn't sleep, was irritable, hopeless, and blamed himself for the situation. Depression often grows in us so slowly that neither we nor those close to us notice the change, while an objective observer detects it right away. When I first decided to try medication and consulted a psychiatrist who knew me socially, I asked if he thought I might be depressed. He was amazed that I didn't know.

Depression most often strikes young adults, but 10 percent of all children suffer an episode before age twelve, and 20 percent of the elderly report depressive symptoms. Both children and the elderly are amazingly undertreated. Estimates are that six million elderly persons suffer from some form of depression, but that three-quarters of those cases are undiagnosed and untreated, despite regular routine medical care. Depression in the elderly tends to get dismissed as inevitable, but in fact it is caused more by poor health and poor sleep than grief, loss, and isolation. Among the elderly who commit suicide, almost three-quarters visit a doctor within a week before their death; but only in 25 percent of those cases does the physician recognize a depression.[21] In long-term care facilities, most of the patients are given some form of antidepressant, but is this because they are depressed, or to make them less sensitive to their living conditions? Do we call it depression if they are correctly seeing that the world treats them as useless and forgotten?

Twenty-five percent of all women and 11.5 percent of all men will have a depressive episode at one time in their lives. But this reported lower incidence among men may really be a mistake arising from the way we diagnose. Men are socially prohibited from expressing or even experiencing the feelings associated with depression. Instead, they act them out through substance abuse, violence, and self-destructive behavior. Across the United States, four men commit suicide for every woman who does, a dramatic reversal of the differences in reported depression.[22] In Amish culture, where macho acting out is frowned upon, the incidence of depression is the same for both sexes. See Chapter II for a more thorough discussion of these sex differences.

Suicide, the "worst case" outcome of depression, is officially the tenth most common cause of death in America.[23] There are 33,000 documented suicides annually, but the true incidence is probably double that (because police and medical examiners prefer not to label ambiguous, solitary deaths as suicide). One out of every two hundred people will eventually take their own lives. And although I personally think that suicide can sometimes be a rational choice for people who are in intractable pain or facing great disability, the vagueness of the boundary lines means that we have no reliable data on how many suicides are people who are really depressed, versus how many are "rational." My experience is that far, far more suicides are truly depressed. Among adolescents, the suicide rate has quadrupled in the past twenty-five years. A few years ago in a small city near where I work, there were eight suicides among young people in one year. These were usually young men just out of school, often intoxicated, usually with no "warning signals" beforehand. An angry, bitter kid who has an unexpected disappointment, gets drunk, and has a gun close at hand is a disaster waiting to happen.

When I still worked in Chicago, I got to know Jane, whose twenty-year-old son had shot himself while she slept in the next room. This was a young man no one would have described as depressed; rather he was a troublemaker. With a history of arrests for minor offenses as a juvenile, he had been sent to a reform school when he was fifteen. Since being discharged, he had lived off and on with Jane and with friends. He worked occasionally, drank a lot, and got into fights.

On the night he took his life, Jimmy had two pieces of bad luck that probably put him over the edge. First he met his ex-girlfriend at a local hangout; she went out of her way to be snotty to him. Then he ran into his father at another bar. A true town drunk, the father barely recognized his son; when he did, it was to ask him for money.

Jimmy came home about midnight. His mother woke, got up and spoke to him, asking him if he needed anything. He was drinking a beer and reading a magazine, and as far as Jane could see, he was his usual self. She went back to bed. Jimmy went to his room and wrote a brief note, more a will than a suicide note. He wanted his brother to have his motorcycle, snake, and hunting rifle. Then he shot himself with the hunting rifle.

Jane kept asking me why. I couldn't tell her what I thought was the true answer to that question, because I thought it was too cruel, but in my opinion she and her son were as much victims of chance as anything else. If you take any sample of impulsive, alcoholic young men whose lives are going nowhere, get them drunk, expose them to rejection, and leave them alone with a gun, some of them will shoot themselves. Which ones take their lives on any given night is just the law of averages. Are they depressed? They sure are, but they can't admit it or show it.

Jane is like most survivors of suicide I've known. You certainly don't get over it, but you learn to live with it. She was depressed herself for over a year, had terrible headaches (a psychosomatic symptom mimicking her son's injury), was unable to work, became overwhelmed with stress, and went from doctor to doctor seeking relief from her pain. Antidepressant medications didn't help; all I could do was listen while she grieved. Eventually her headaches became less frequent and she began to have a little more energy to put into her life. I think of her every time I hear of an adolescent suicide.

2

The Experience of Depression

EVERYONE HAS HAD A TASTE of what depression feels like. Everyone feels the blues at times. Sadness, disappointment, fatigue are normal parts of life. There is a connection between the blues and clinical depression, but the difference is like the difference between the sniffles and pneumonia.

Depressive disorders are "whole person" illnesses; they affect the body, feelings, thoughts, and behavior. The depression itself can make us feel it's useless to seek help. The good news is that 80 to 90 percent of people with depression can be helped significantly, but the bad news is that only one sufferer in three seeks treatment. More bad news is that almost half the American public views depression as a character defect, rather than an illness or emotional disorder.[1] Still more bad news is that only half of all cases of depression are accurately diagnosed, and only half of those receive adequate treatment.

We confuse depression, sadness, and grief. However, the opposite of depression is not happiness, but vitality—the ability to experience a full range of emotions, including happiness, excitement, sadness, and grief.[2] Depression is not an emotion itself; it's the loss of feelings, a big heavy blanket that insulates you from the world yet hurts at the same time. It's not sadness or grief, it's an illness. When we feel our worst—sad, self-absorbed, and helpless—we are experiencing what people with depression experience, but they don't recover from those moods without help.

The hallmark of depression is a persistent sad or "empty" mood, sometimes experienced as tension or anxiety. Life lacks pleasure. People with mild depressions may go through the motions of eating, sex, work, or play, but the activities seem hollow; people with more severe depressions withdraw from these activities, feeling too tired, tense, or bitter to participate. There is often a nagging fatigue, a sense of being unable to focus, a feeling of being unproductive.

Grieving the loss of someone or something important to you hurts like depression, but people with depression usually experience a lowered self-esteem, feel hopeless, and blame themselves, which is not common with grief. In a depression, you may feel that you are a helpless victim of fate, but you also feel that you don't deserve any better. In grief, you usually don't lose sight of the fact that you will someday recover.

There are often a host of physical symptoms with depression, and sleep disturbances are key. People may have difficulty falling asleep, or may awaken early without feeling refreshed. Others may sleep excessively, again without feeling rested. Obviously, lack of sleep leads to fatigue, emotional withdrawal, difficulty with clear thinking — more symptoms of depression. Appetite may increase or decrease. There may be difficulty in sexual functioning. There may be nagging aches and pains that don't respond to medical treatment. But there are physical illnesses that cause symptoms like depression — Lyme disease, diabetes, thyroid conditions, anemia — and depressions can cause physical symptoms that look like other diseases. If you are feeling depressed, it's important to be sure that an underlying health problem does not exist, and you should see your physician for a checkup. At the same time, if you know you have a health problem and are feeling depressed, don't assume your depression will lift once the health problem is under control.

Suicidal thoughts and impulses are often present, and suicide may be a real risk. Some people are repeatedly tormented by these impulses, which they experience as frightening and painful, while others have them appear as if out of the blue, detached from emotions. The impulse to spin the wheel and drive suddenly into oncoming traffic is horribly common, though no one ever talks about it.

Alcohol and other drugs may be used to give relief from the depression. But the relief is only temporary, at best, and usually the person just hates himself more for giving in to temptation. Alcohol itself is a depressant, and long-term alcohol abuse may lead to chronic depression—it certainly doesn't help you make the right decisions in life, and that is enough to be depressed about.

From all these symptoms, it might seem that a depressed person is easy to recognize. It is often easy, when the person recognizes it himself. When it's a distinct change from a more normal state of mind, the depression is experienced as something foreign to the self, something to be overcome. But very often, depression has gradually become part of the self: the person doesn't remember and can't imagine anything other than this depressed state.

The Depressed Life

The symptoms of depression are very painful and debilitating, but what makes recovery most difficult is the effect depression has on our world. Depression makes us see life differently; it changes how we think; it makes us feel inept and weak; it robs us of social skills and damages our relationships; it depletes us of all self-confidence. Depression pervades our entire being, like a metastatic cancer. And because it affects how we see, we become blind to the changes that are taking place in ourselves. Only rarely, if at all, do we remember that at one time we were happy, confident, active.

All of us weave stories together to make sense of our experience in the world, to help us predict the future and make sense of the past. A very simple story is "Mary likes me." If I think Mary likes me, I may assume that she will be happy to see me in the future, enjoy spending time with me, may understand my point of view. This story is in words, but it's also going to affect how I feel, my behavior, even my body. If I think Mary likes me, I will probably feel good around her; I will treat her with more attention than I give other people; I may feel safe and relaxed around her, and my body will cut down on the stress hormones it emits. It also affects my expectations: under normal circumstances I will expect Mary to continue liking me, that she will enjoy some of the things I enjoy, that she will agree with my opinions. So these stories we create become self-fulfilling prophecies: in this case, I treat Mary as if I like her, I'm more open and relaxed around her, and our affection for each other will grow.

People with depression, however, share a whole set of stories about the world that are highly distorted, and because their stories are self-fulfilling prophecies, they maintain and reinforce the depression. We differ from others in how we perceive the world and ourselves, how we interpret and express our feelings, and how we communicate with other people. We think of ourselves as unable to live up to our own standards, we see the world as hostile or withholding, and we are pessimistic about things ever changing. In our relationships with others, we have unrealistic expectations, are unable to communicate our own needs, misinterpret disagreement as rejection, and are anxious and unassertive in our presentation. Finally, we are in the dark about human emotions. We don't know what it's like to feel normal. We fear that honest feelings will tear us apart or cause others to reject us. We learn what I call the "skills of depression"—denying or stuffing our feelings, putting up a false front for the world, being satisfied with less, not making demands. Our stories become so detailed and intertwined that we create a world of depression, of sadness and no hope, of disappointment and self-blame, of lethargy and self-absorption.

The thesis of this book is that we can repair and restore ourselves through learning new ways of thinking, feeling, and doing—self-constructive behavior. When we try these new skills they will at first seem forced and artificial, but they can become a habit, part of ourselves, replacing our old ways of being with new skills. As we do this, our expectations and perceptions will change. We can go from thinking *I can't do anything right* to *I'm as good as the next guy*. There is a lot of new, exciting research that suggests we can reprogram our own brains through focused practice of any new skill, through attending to ourselves in a mindful, noncritical way. As we practice new behaviors, they become easy and more natural. And because depression is such a big, intertwined ball of string, we can start anywhere to change — just getting out of bed in the morning, for example — and expect that pulling that one thread will have good consequences in other areas of our lives.

Before we move on, however, let me explain what I mean when I refer to the skills of depression. Depressed people work harder at living than anyone else, although our efforts bring us little joy. But in the course of our hard work, we become very good at certain skills. We are like weight lifters who concentrate exclusively on upper body strength — resulting in massive muscles in the arms and trunk but little spindly legs underneath — easy to knock down. People get good at depression — they overadapt and develop skills that, at best, just keep them going, and often make things worse.

Many people who have had severe depression report that they suffered for years, sometimes for decades, before they told anyone. They felt so isolated and so self-blaming that they assumed there was nothing to be done, nothing that anyone else would understand. Meanwhile they "passed" as normal — they went right ahead with life, putting on a happy face and achieving success in school, in careers, in the family. This ability to maintain a false front is a primary skill of depression. Not everyone with depression is so good at fooling everyone so consistently, but we all try it every day. Of course, this just makes us feel even more alienated. Often the meaning of a suicide attempt, a breakdown, or a psychiatric hospitalization is *Look! I can't keep up this charade. I feel terrible and I need help.* It becomes a transforming experience, a clear message to the self and others that there is terrible distress below the appearance of competence and good cheer.

We learn the skills of depression out of necessity. They served a purpose at one time, but they've become stuck in our brains. They are part of the vicious circle that perpetuates the depression, and they make recovery difficult. The self-destructive element of many of these skills is obvious, or will be explained shortly, so I will just comment briefly on a few at this point.

Depressed Emotional Skills

• *Isolation of affect.* "Affect" is simply another term for emotion. Isolation drives a wedge between the experience and the feeling. We are aware of what's happening around us, but we don't experience the emotion that we would expect to accompany the event. Isolation is useful for surgeons, rescue workers, police officers, and others who have to remain calm in very stressful situations. But people with depression learn not to show, or even feel, their feelings because it has only worked against them in the past. In some families, in some situations, to let others know how you feel is dangerous; it gives people ammunition to be used against you. But turning off your feelings makes you a cold fish, and people who might become friends are warned off before they get to know you.

• *Somatization.* This is the use of the body to express feelings or an interpersonal message. We all know people like this, who have pain they can't relieve, fatigue that isn't helped by rest, who are irritated by multiple stimuli, or easily nauseated, or have an irritable bowel. Their bodies are saying *You can't do anything to help me,* or *My suffering gives me special privileges,* or *My suffering means you can't expect me to do my share.* Somatization allows people to communicate feelings without having to take responsibility for them.

• *Denial.* One example: A depressed father whose adult son has lost his driving privileges because of a DUI conviction drives the son around town, absorbing his abuse: "You're just a lousy driver. Can't you drive a little faster? You're always late. You can't do anything right." Telling me about this, he is more embarrassed about his son's bad behavior than he is about his own passivity in the face of abuse. When I ask him how this makes him feel, he is completely unaware of feeling angry—but remains depressed. The old saw that depression is anger turned inward is often quite true.

• *Repression* has two meanings now, both important for depression. One meaning is the opposite of isolation: it's experiencing the feeling, but not recognizing the experience that stimulates the feeling. The depressive gets suddenly sad without knowing why—but the objective observer sees the event that led to the feeling. This may be a criticism, a disappointment, a snub that passes quickly in and out of the depressive's consciousness. The event itself is quickly forgotten—repressed—but the feeling lingers. This leads us to the other, more common, meaning of repression, that of "forgetting" events that are too painful to remember. This is not an uncommon phenomenon with trauma—sexual abuse, combat, disasters. The events are not really forgotten, of course; they come back as nightmares or in other manifestations. The depressive who has been through traumatic experiences will use repression to help keep the feelings associated with the event out of consciousness.

Other depressed emotional skills include *intellectualization; projection, externalization,* and *internalization* (an old stereotype with some truth: men blame others, women blame themselves; neither can be objective); *rageaholism* (ranging from tantrums to physical abuse; the individual doesn't take responsibility for his behavior and expects to be quickly forgiven); and *anhedonia* (the loss of all joy), *hopelessness,* and *apathy,* which can insulate you from feelings. I discuss these more fully in Chapter 6.

Depressed Behavioral Skills

• *Procrastination.* This can be considered a skill because it protects you from ever having to put your best self on the line. You always have an excuse: *if only I'd had more time.*

• *Lethargy.* Keeping yourself in a haze of television or sleep or fatigue will mean you miss out on a lot of opportunities. But for the depressed person, opportunities can be a challenge to be avoided.

• *Work till you drop, inability to prioritize, pushing yourself mindlessly*—and never checking to see if you're going in the right direction, thus not taking real responsibility for the decisions you make.

• *Obsessive and compulsive behavior.* Psychologists understand these patterns as ways of attaching some real fears about life to behaviors or thoughts that can be more or less controlled. As we'll see, depression and fear are closely related, each causing the other in a potentially endless feedback loop.

• *Victimizing, violence, and acting out.* Violence is often a response to shame. It can make you feel powerful again without facing what made you ashamed in the first place. Unfortunately, it usually leads to more shame.

• *Victimization and self-mutilation.* Treating yourself sadistically—or allowing others to—can make you feel real again, and provide a sense of focus, calm, and control during times of great distress. This process, and the other behavioral skills of depression, are the focus of Chapter 7.

Depressed Cognitive Skills

• *Pessimism.* Expecting the worst protects you from disappointment. Many depressed people have been traumatically disappointed by abandonment, faithlessness, or abuse from loved ones. Other experiences, like the failure to reach goals, can also turn you sour on hope.

• *Negative self-talk.* Thoughts like *I can't, I'm hopeless, I'll never succeed, I'm repulsive, I'm trapped,* which run through the depressive's mind like too-loud background music. I discuss more about the Inner Critic in Chapter 9.

• *Passivity.* People with depression tend to see themselves as acted upon by powerful outside forces, not in charge of their own lives, and thus not truly responsible for their fate.

• *Selective attention.* By selectively paying attention only to what confirms our expectations, we avoid stress and feel more secure in the world we've built for ourselves. This becomes an automatic, unconscious process in which we are blind to opportunities to excel, the affection and respect of others, the beauty of the physical world, and so on. This helps the depressed person to maintain an even keel.

• *Depressed logic.* I discuss this in Chapter 8.

Depressed Interpersonal Skills

• *Recruiting accomplices*—restricting your social world to those who don't expect much of you.

• *Social isolation*, avoiding contacts that might challenge your depressed thinking.

• *Dependency*, putting someone else in charge of your life.

• *Counterdependency,* acting as if you don't need anyone. A kind of phony independence when in reality there is a great fear of any need at all, masked by coldness or a feigned superiority.

• *Passive aggression.* I discuss this at length in Chapter 7.

• *Porous boundaries.* Not deciding how others' actions, feelings, and expectations should affect you, just letting yourself be influenced.

Depressed Treatment of the Self

• *Impossible goals, low expectations.* We believe we should be able to attain great things, at the same time as we believe we're incompetent and inept. But we keep trying to hit a home run: *This time will be different, this time I'll make it, and then I'll be happy.*

• *No goals, lots of guilt.* Conversely, we may avoid setting goals for ourselves entirely, to avoid disappointment. But depressed people are not the laid-back, happy sort who can coast through life without feeling guilty about not doing our best.

• *Passive aggression against the self.* When I make a mess in the kitchen and deliberately leave it for myself to clean up later, feeling too oppressed and overwhelmed in the present, I'm going to be angry at myself later. The future me is going to be mad at the past me who left this mess behind. Plus, the future me is going to feel hopeless and helpless, reconfirmed in the belief that I'll never change and never catch up with life. Chapter 12 has much more on how depressives abuse themselves.

Depressed Treatment of the Body

- *The cycle of exhaustion/collapse.*
- *Lack of exercise.*
- *Neglecting medical care/succumbing to quacks.*
- *Defensive eating*—stuffing your feelings with food.
- *Abuse of drugs and alcohol.*

All of these ways of neglecting or abusing our physical selves are skills of depression in the sense that they keep us from having to face reality. They are direct expressions of our belief that we don't deserve to be treated well. See Chapter 11 for more on this theme.

Depression is the replacement of parts of the self that are natural, spontaneous, and honest with these self-destructive skills. It's the loss of parts of the self, the gradual numbing of feelings and experiences that we gradually come to believe are unacceptable and banish from experience. Cure comes from recovery of the missing pieces. *"The true opposite of depression is not gaiety or absence of pain, but vitality: the freedom to experience spontaneous feelings."*[3] The ability to experience the full range of human feelings in response to what's happening to you—to be joyful when good things happen, angry when your toes are stepped on, sad when you're disappointed, warm and loving with your family—instead of the dull gray curtain that separates the depressive from reality. As patients learn from their experiences in psychotherapy and in real life that the breakthrough of suppressed emotions, however painful or upsetting, can be counted on to lift depression, they begin to change how they handle feelings. Specifically, painful or upsetting feelings are no longer avoided, but experienced. This leads to a reconnection with the lost parts of the self, a reintegration, and recovery. Now that we know that destructive emotional habits are learned and are mediated by new connections in the brain, we also understand that we can unlearn these habits and replace them with healthier ways of living. And through practice, these new skills, which may seem awkward and self-conscious at first, become etched in our nervous systems, parts of ourselves.

3

Diagnosing Depression

RECOGNIZING AN emotional problem and giving it a psychiatric diagnosis are very different processes. At what point does
the depressed mood that everyone experiences from time to time
become an illness that requires treatment?

Diagnosis in psychiatry is currently based on the *Diagnostic and
Statistical Manual of Mental Disorders, Fourth Edition*, commonly
known as DSM-IV.[1] The process of arriving at a standard nomen-
clature for emotional conditions and mental disorders has been
complex, partly because so many of the conditions are themselves
controversial topics in contemporary culture: Is alcoholism a disease,
a habit, or a weakness? Is bulimia a disease, or a cultural conflict
about what the female body should look like? Why do Vietnam vets
apparently suffer from post-traumatic stress disorder at such higher
rates than soldiers in previous wars? Should rebellious adolescents
be hospitalized against their will because they can't get along with
their parents? Should people with chronic substance abuse problems
be considered disabled, and thus entitled to Social Security benefits?
These questions require answers that make us question our deepest
values — do we have the ability to make our own decisions in life, or
are our decisions programmed by our heredity, nervous system, or

early childhood experiences? If our decisions are determined, what happens to the social contract, guilt, crime, and punishment?

Depression as a diagnosis has not pushed quite so many of society's hot buttons, but it is subject to the same controversies. For instance, until the third DSM came out in the seventies, many psychiatric diagnoses were strongly influenced by Freudian theory. Because the theory held that depression was caused by a harsh, strict superego, and because a superego was not thought to be developed until a child was twelve or so, it was assumed that children could not be depressed. Subsequent versions of the DSM addressed that, and many other blind spots in the diagnosis business, by taking a phenomenological approach: if a symptom cluster was observed commonly enough to be a problem perhaps worth addressing, and if objective observers could reliably identify the same symptom cluster with the same patients, that symptom cluster was given a name. There might or might not be a good explanation, a theory, for why that particular group of symptoms seemed to occur reliably together. Certainly the compilers of the new DSM hoped that a reliable classification system, in which we could all be sure we were counting and observing the same things, might lead to better explanations for the underlying mechanisms beneath the symptoms, and to improvements in treatment.

But this approach has also had its drawbacks. It has certainly contributed to the medicalization of complex emotional/behavioral states, like alcoholism, depression, or post-traumatic stress disorder. It led insurance companies to permit X treatment for this diagnosis, Y for that, regardless of the individual's needs. It has led to absurd legal strategies by defendants who eschew responsibility for their actions. Most tragically, it has led to patients hoping that the cure for their condition will come about from a new pill, and that until the pill comes along there is nothing they can do to help themselves.

In the case of depression, the phenomenological approach has led to some hairsplitting in diagnosis that emphasizes artificial distinctions, minimizing commonalities and contributing to the trivialization of research. Currently, the DSM-IV recognizes several distinct depression-related diagnoses, which we will describe along with what we know of their frequency and prevalence. But keep in mind that some of these distinctions are quite arbitrary. The DSM was designed to be a research tool leading to further refinement of diagnosis, not the bible it has become to many people.

Major Depression

Major depression is a very serious condition. Usually the patient and family recognize that something is gravely wrong, but they often can't name it. In the simplest case, the patient feels, looks, and acts depressed, and tells people about it.

Nancy has major depression. Although she is able to hold down a responsible job and has raised a family successfully, most of the time she is miserable. She looks tense and sad. She is thin, shy, and worried. She's hesitant to say what's on her mind, though she is caring and intelligent. She constantly puts herself down. She believes she can't handle any stress; in fact, she copes very well, but constantly fears that she's messing up. She has recurrent migraines that force her to bed several times a month. She has to take a medication for these that costs $80 a dose, and her antidepressant medication costs $8 a day. Her family is on a tight budget, and her insurance doesn't pay for medication, so she feels guilty for having to spend so much money on treatment.

Nancy describes her depression as a well. When it's at its worst, she is stuck down in the mud at the bottom of the well. The mud is full of worms and rats, and it's all she can do to keep from being eaten alive. The best she can feel is to be at the top of the well, her elbows perched on the wall, able to see life but unable to truly engage in it. Most of the time, she's partway down the well. She remembers what it's like to feel alive and good, but she can't quite reach it.

The formal criteria for a diagnosis of major depression include a depressed mood or a loss of interest or pleasure in ordinary activities for at least two weeks, accompanied by at least four of the following symptoms:

1. Significant weight loss when not dieting, or weight gain, or change in appetite
2. Insomnia or hypersomnia (sleeping too much) nearly every day
3. Activity level slows down or increases
4. Fatigue or loss of energy
5. Feelings of worthlessness or excessive guilt
6. Diminished ability to think, concentrate, or make decisions
7. Recurrent thoughts of death or suicide, or suicidal ideation, or a suicidal plan or attempt

The symptoms must not be due to the direct effects of medications, drugs, or a physical condition, and must not be a simple grief reaction. The depressed mood is usually self-reported as a feeling of sadness, hopelessness, or discouragement, although it is sometimes denied and may be elicited by a professional interview (the therapist says "You sound sad," and the patient starts to cry), or inferred from facial expression or body language. Some people emphasize physical complaints or report irritability more than sadness.

The percentage of people estimated to be suffering from major depression at any given time (the "point prevalence") in Western countries is roughly 3 percent for men, 8 percent for women. The lifetime risk (the chance that any one person will develop the condition at some point in his or her life) is 7 to 12 percent for men, 20 to 25 percent for women.[2] Risk is not affected by race, education, income, or marital status. The dramatically higher incidence among women raises questions of a gender bias in the diagnosis, since men are generally considered to be socially prohibited from self-reporting feelings of sadness, worthlessness, or hopelessness, a primary criterion for the diagnosis. On the other hand, women may be constitutionally more vulnerable to depression, or simply have more to be depressed about than men. I explore these issues in greater depth in Chapter 19.

There is good statistical evidence that recent stress may precipitate the first and/or second bouts of major depression, but that it may take much less stress to set off later episodes. I find that patients can usually pinpoint what made them depressed the first time, but it's not so easy for subsequent episodes.

Dysthymic Disorder

Major depression is an acute crisis; dysthymic disorder is a long-term illness. The essential criterion for diagnosis of dysthymia is a depressed mood for most of the day, for more days than not, for at least two years (!). In addition, there must be at least two of the following symptoms while feeling depressed:

1. Poor appetite or overeating
2. Insomnia or hypersomnia
3. Low energy or fatigue
4. Low self-esteem
5. Poor concentration or difficulty making decisions
6. Feelings of hopelessness

Note that the secondary symptoms are very similar to those for major depression, except that changes in activity level and thoughts of death or suicide are not listed, and low self-esteem is. Clearly the distinction between major depression and dysthymia is rather arbitrary, a matter of degree rather than kind. Yet since the distinction is made, we have researchers testing interventions on one population or the other, with little attention paid to the possibility of error or overlap in the diagnosis. All the newer antidepressants have been tested with major depression, few with dysthymia, because research on dysthymia would be time-consuming and expensive.

Chris fits the picture of dysthymia. A bright, intelligent woman with a forceful manner and a terrific sense of humor, she has been unhappy most of her life. Raised by an alcoholic mother and a critical father, as a child she tried to make them both happy—an impossible task. She rebelled in adolescence, getting in all kinds of trouble. Her first marriage was to a man who was alcoholic and abusive. Having found a lot of strength through Al-Anon, Chris is determined to get her life together. But she and her present husband can't communicate. Chris is very quick to anger and her husband withdraws. She struggles constantly with her sense of having a grievance against life—she knows this, along with her angry expression, drives people away, but she can't control herself.

Chris speaks of her depression as a big, soft comforter. It's not really comforting, but it's safe and familiar. Sometimes she feels as if she's entitled to be depressed, to quit struggling, to snuggle down and watch old movies and feel sorry for herself.

The point prevalence for dysthymic disorder is estimated at 3 percent, while the lifetime risk is estimated at 6 percent. Again, female gender is associated with higher risk, but race, education, and income are independent.[3]

People with dysthymia are sometimes dismissed as the "worried well," but nothing could be further from the truth. Imagine spending the better part of two years feeling depressed, having trouble functioning, unable to enjoy life, feeling lousy about yourself, sleeping poorly, and feeling powerless to do anything about it. These people are more accurately described as "walking wounded." They get through life, but life tends to be nasty, brutish, and short. They are not the Woody Allen stereotype of the self-absorbed neurotic, but rather long-suffering and self-sacrificing.

We often see the effects on children of having a mother who functions like this. Frequently, the children are anxious, tense, and have difficulty getting along with their peers and keeping up with schoolwork. They know all too well that something scary is going on with

Mom, and they feel that they should be able to do something about it. These children often adapt and become "pseudoadults," who appear tough and independent. They may actually take care of Mom by assuming adult responsibilities—meals, housecleaning, babysitting the younger siblings. Often when Mom recovers, there is a backlash. With a functioning mother again, the child is able to feel the anger he has suppressed at having been emotionally abandoned. He becomes rebellious and tests Mom to see if she can really be relied on. Mom, still vulnerable, has difficulty understanding why her child isn't grateful to see her functioning again and may revert to her depressed stance. Depression becomes a vicious circle in the family.

Depressive Disorder Not Otherwise Specified (DDNOS)

This is a catchall term in the DSM used for all patients who show some symptoms of depression but do not meet the criteria for one of the more restrictive diagnoses. Their symptoms may be less severe, or of shorter duration, or they may meet most of the criteria, but not all, for major depression or dysthymia. This category also includes women suffering from depression associated with the menstrual cycle and people with schizophrenia or other psychotic disorders with an associated depression. But it still excludes people who are grieving, those who are depressed as a result of a loss or change in their lives, and those dealing with a medical problem and depressed as a result. In other words, the diagnosis includes a wide variety of people who suffer from depression that has no clear external cause, but is serious enough to interfere with their ability to function.

Estimates are that, at any given time, 11 percent of the population meets the criteria for DDNOS. This is an astounding number, making DDNOS easily the single most common disease in the United States.[4] The combined incidence of major depression, dysthymia, and DDNOS approaches 20 percent at any given time. This does not mean that 20 percent of the population will have depression at some time in their lives, but that 20 percent have it *right now*. One in five of your friends, family members, coworkers. There is simply no other disease that approaches this kind of prevalence.

A Distinction Without a Difference

If you are now a little confused and can't see much difference between major depression, dysthymia, and DDNOS, don't worry about it. These precise distinctions have some use in science, but also have been misused to confuse and scare the public. The bottom line is that with major depression, you feel intensely horrible, confused, listless or agitated, guilty, and suicidal, and your sleep, appetite, and sex life are affected, and it hits you rather quickly. To qualify as dysthymic, you feel some or all of the same symptoms, but not as intensely, for at least two years. DDNOS simply means you feel many of the same symptoms, but not as intensely as in major depression, and not for as long as dysthymia.

Some scientists have pushed the idea that these conditions are separate entities, as if your sniffles might be caused by a cold, an allergy, or a deviated septum. For instance, prominent researchers have advocated for the concept of "double" depression[5] — dysthymia and major depression — giving the idea that there are separate disease processes at work and an individual has been unlucky enough to catch both, rather than simply stating that a person who has been depressed for some time has recently gotten worse.* But most patients don't see these distinctions; they just know they feel bad most of the time, and occasionally they feel absolutely terrible. Most patients know, and an increasing number of researchers and psychiatrists admit, that DDNOS is usually either the early stage of or a slightly milder case of dysthymia, that dysthymia is what people with major depression feel when they get a little better, that major depression is a more severe

---

* It was later revealed that at least one of those researchers, Dr. Martin Keller, had received over $500,000 in under-the-table payoffs from Big Pharma (see Chapter 13). Perhaps double depression was part of an effort to legitimize use of two drugs at the same time.

version of dysthymia, and that whatever it is you have at present, complete recovery is a long way away.

For instance, a study that followed 431 patients for twelve years after a major depressive episode found that they continued to experience major depression, on average, about 15 percent of the time. But that doesn't mean that they were symptom-free 85 percent of the time. On the contrary, they experienced dysthymia 27 percent of the time and DDNOS 17 percent of the time.[6] The more time they spent in these states, the more likely they were to relapse into major depression.[7]

Bipolar Disorder

Bipolar disorder is another type of depression of great concern, and seems to be qualitatively different from major depression, dysthymia, and DDNOS. Bipolar disorder type I (manic depression) typically features episodes of major depression interspersed with periods of mania. A manic episode must meet the following criteria:

A. A discrete period of abnormal, persistently elevated, expansive, or irritable mood
B. At least three of the following in the same period:
   1. Inflated self-esteem/grandiosity
   2. Marked decrease in need for sleep
   3. Pressured speech
   4. Flight of ideas (racing thoughts)
   5. Marked distractibility
   6. Increased goal-directed activity or psychomotor agitation
   7. Excessive involvement in pleasurable activities without regard for negative consequences
C. Symptoms must be severe enough to cause marked impairment in functioning or place self or others in danger
D. Symptoms must not be caused by schizophrenia or substance abuse

Walt has bipolar disorder. A big man, a truck driver, who seems pleasant and good-natured in his normal state, Walt has had trouble holding down a job for the past few years because of his erratic behavior. Sometimes he becomes sexually obsessed. He can't get sex off his mind. If an attractive woman is anywhere near, he can't concentrate on anything but his sexual fantasies. Sometimes he loses touch with reality enough to start believing that she returns his fantasies. When he's in this state, he'll spend money he doesn't have on prostitutes, on gambling junkets, on anything to impress women. He believes he's attractive, powerful, and charmed, and he feels he can do no wrong. Nothing bothers him. He can stay up for days, talking nonstop. He once showed up at my house, unannounced, to show me his new car — the only time I've ever had a client violate a boundary like that. But Walt just wanted to share his joy.

At other times, Walt is severely depressed. He doesn't believe he's capable of anything. He hardly has the energy to get out of bed. He tries to go to work, but his lack of confidence makes his employers distrust him. He develops obsessive anxiety symptoms — going back into the house ten times to make sure the coffee pot is unplugged. He's constantly apologizing for himself.

The mean age of onset for bipolar disorder is the early twenties. It affects men and women equally; it's reported that over the course of their lifetime, between 0.4 and 1.2 percent of men and women will develop bipolar disorder. At any given time, between 0.1 and 0.6 percent of the population are suffering from an episode. I suspect that the actual incidence of bipolar disorder, or the more severe forms of bipolar II, are really much higher than these formal statistics. There is a high genetic correlation: first-degree relatives of bipolar patients have a 12 percent lifetime incidence, while another 12 percent will experience major depression.[8]

Untreated, a manic episode will last an average of six months, and a major depressive episode eight to ten months; over time, the manic episodes become more frequent. There is a high mortality rate, due to suicide (15 percent of untreated patients), accidental death due to risky behavior, and concurrent illness. Many people with untreated bipolar disorder will die from alcoholism, lung cancer, accidents, or sexually transmitted disease; feeling so invulnerable during an episode, they simply do not take the precautions that most of us have come to accept as part of a sensible lifestyle.

There are other subtypes of bipolar disorder. Bipolar disorder type II features episodes of major depression alternating with hypomania (an abnormally elevated or expansive mood that does not interfere with your ability to see reality objectively; "hypo" = "less than" mania). These people make up a distinct subcategory; anyone who can go from the depths of major depression to a giddy, excited, or highly focused and productive state, and repeat this cycle over and over, is not your usual depressive.

Then there are bipolars type III, III ½, IV, and IV ½. (I'm not kidding, and researchers squabble about these distinctions, though they might seem petty.) One definition of type III, for example, refers to people with depression who take an antidepressant (or switch to another) that suddenly triggers a full-blown manic episode, a phenomenon that is not that rare. Other people define bipolar type III in an entirely different way, so I'll just leave the subject alone. If someone gives you one of these diagnoses, be sure you get a very clear understanding of what they're talking about, especially before taking an antidepressant.

I said in the first edition of this book that bipolar disorder (type I) seemed to be a different kettle of fish from other kinds of depression, though the depressive episodes may look and feel the same as major depression. I argued that bipolar type I has such a high degree of genetic loading, the manic episodes are so distinctive and limited to the disease, and the disease itself has such a unique response to a specific medication (lithium) that it makes sense to think of it as primarily a biogenetic disease causing a chemical imbalance in the brain that leads to the unique mood swings.

But the unexplained fact that sometimes taking an SSRI may send a garden-variety depressive off on a full-blown manic episode suggests that there may be more connections than meet the eye. And I keep running into people who think of themselves as bipolar type I who have all the childhood history—emotional neglect, loss, abuse—that goes with major depression or dysthymia. Many clinicians expect that within the next few years, we will see a breakthrough in understanding the connections in the brain and the genes between mania and depression—and anxiety, attention deficit hyperactivity disorder (ADHD), and post-traumatic stress disorder (PTSD)—which may lead to better medications and improved treatment for all.

Time *magazine's Man of the Year in* 1992, *Ted Turner, may have been the first to come out of the closet regarding his psychiatric treatment. His story is fascinating for those who are interested in the problems men have with success and intimacy, and for those who are interested in the mix of genetics, biochemistry, and family dynamics that underlies depression and bipolar disorder.*

For many years Turner was troubled by the obsessive thought that he would not live longer than his father had, because his father had killed himself at age 53. *(This is a common fear among suicides' children.) Ted talked of suicide rather often, and drove himself mercilessly to succeed in joyless pursuits. After all the time he put in sailing, including winning the America's Cup, he told a friend repeatedly that he never enjoyed the sport. "I got cold and I got wet." His eye was always on the finish line, always looking for some achievement that would finally be enough to make him feel good about himself.*

Turner's father, Ed, by all accounts was a tortured man who inflicted psychological torture on his son. Young Turner was beaten with a coat hanger when he let his father down; when Ted did something really bad, his father had Ted beat him with a razor strap. When Ed served in the navy during World War II, he had his wife and daughter move from base to base with him but left Ted, only six, behind at a boarding school. From fifth grade on, Ted was sent to military academies. No grade he ever got was good enough, no achievement great enough, to please his father. Ed shot himself when Ted was in his early twenties, leaving Ted to rescue the family billboard business, which had sunk into debt. By working feverishly and gambling recklessly, he not only rebuilt the business, he began the communications empire that became CNN.

But with his father dead, Turner had no yardstick to measure his success against. He drank, womanized, alternately neglected and bullied his own children, and apparently was sheer hell as a boss. Finally, in 1985, he sought help, and began to work with a psychiatrist in Atlanta.

The psychiatrist first put Turner on lithium, a reliable treatment for bipolar disorder. Because in this disorder patients may have great self-confidence and energy, may go without sleep, may believe they are capable of great achievements, may enjoy taking risks, for someone like Turner it can be hard to tell where disease ends and personality begins. It can also be hard to get the patient to accept treatment for symptoms that in many ways have paid off. But Turner was a cooperative patient.

As Turner began to be stabilized by the lithium in his system, therapy helped him deal with the shadow of his father. Like most men with critical, emotionally rejecting fathers, Turner had developed no internal mechanism for feeling good about himself. Like most family members of suicide victims, he was haunted by the idea that the suicide had the truly accurate perspective on life: that it's not worth the trouble. Time could not get the psychiatrist to talk about the details of Turner's case, but it's clear that Turner had to work hard to make peace with his own children and with the women in his life.

Turner is a classic example of the observation that achievement doesn't mean happiness; instead, it's how we live rather than what we do that leads to peace.[9]

Depression, Anxiety, and Stress

Before we move on to address other types of depression, I want to touch on the relationship between depression and anxiety. The fact is that most depressed and bipolar patients also experience a great deal of anxiety; often it's difficult to tell which should be the primary diagnosis. A very common scenario: a young person in college or their twenties will have a mini-breakdown, with anxiety the most troubling symptom. If they get help quickly, this is as far as it goes. But if they don't get good treatment, the anxiety wears them down, they feel out of control and hopeless about getting better, they drop out of school, and depression begins to be the primary problem. The mania associated with bipolar disorder is often thought of as a defense against anxiety, a total reversal: *I can do anything, nothing can hurt me.*

Though most people can recover substantially from an episode of severe depression, they remain more vulnerable to stress and anxiety than others. That is why most patients who suffer from depression have poor outcomes in the long run. Clinical trials generally run for two to three months, with "recovery" measured at the end of treatment and little if any follow-up conducted; but this is like arguing that ice is a cure for fever. The STAR*D trial, a huge research program still under way that is run by the National Institute of Mental Health instead of a drug company, found that only 30 percent of patients were significantly better after the first phase of treatment.[10] Why such a low number? Because these were real patients in the real world, not paid volunteers carefully screened in a clinical study. Thus we need to educate the public and the health insurance industry about the fact that depression is a chronic disease that waxes and wanes over a lifetime, especially if inadequately treated.

Adequate treatment for depression increases the likelihood of complete recovery, but most patients still remain vulnerable. The best predictor of long-term outcome is the duration of the initial episode, from before treatment begins until the patient recovers; thus early detection and effective treatment should be a priority.[11] Recurrence becomes more likely over time; three-quarters of patients can expect to have another episode within five years.[12] The major risk factors for recurrence are psychosocial: the patient's level of anxiety and self-destructive behavior, as well as lack of self-confidence, areas that are much more likely to be improved by psychotherapy than by medication.[13]

The largest study of co-occurring illnesses in the United States found that among those who had suffered a major depressive episode within the past year, 51 *percent had also suffered an anxiety disorder* during the same time, 4 percent had experienced dysthymia, and 18.5 percent had also suffered a substance abuse disorder.[14] The STAR*D study much more recently found that 53.2 percent of their 2,876 participants with major depression also met their rather strict criteria for "anxious depression." They found that people with anxious depression reported more frequent and more intense side effects from medication, were less likely to achieve remission, and took longer to achieve it.[15] Depression and anxiety are always closely interrelated; most patients have a combination of symptoms that could be diagnosed either way, depending on rather small changes in emphasis.[16] Most studies have found that anxiety and depression are likely to be found together at rates from 51 to 68 percent of the time.[17] Medicine and psychiatry increasingly agree that the two conditions are, if not the same, at least siblings.[18] I think of anxiety and depression as fingers of the same hand, peaks of the same mountain.[19]

We could note other fingers of that hand as well: PTSD, stress-related physical illness, perhaps cognitive disturbances like attention deficit disorder. It makes most sense to believe that people suffer from a general distress syndrome that causes symptoms that manifest themselves as depression, anxiety, PTSD, autoimmune disease, cognitive impairment, and what I call "nonspecific illness."[20] I think we need to make a little leap here and presume that all these conditions are interrelated, the effects of current stress on a mind and body that have been made susceptible because of genetic vulnerability and the scars of stress and trauma in childhood and adolescence.[21] Most people with depression have a combination of symptoms from all of these diagnoses, just as the others usually have some symptoms of depression. It may be that anxiety is the initial response to too much stress—our panicky attempts to escape an inescapable situation—while depression represents the damage done to the nervous system, and the mind, when the stress goes on too long.[22] Anxiety and depression can wear out the body and the immune system, resulting in physical disease. The distinction between acute PTSD and anxiety and depression may be a matter of degree—how dramatic and intense the trauma is. Your diagnosis depends partly on which symptoms are most painful or most in the way. It also depends on which doctor you see, as his or her training and personal biases will certainly make a difference in your diagnosis.

It's also important to emphasize that there is precious little research going on in the United States about how we can prevent depression, anxiety, or other serious mental illnesses. Research in other parts of the world shows the effects of childhood experience on development of adult depression. In a British study of 1,142 children who were followed from birth to age thirty-three, it was found that factors like poor mothering, poor physical care, parental conflict, overcrowding, and social dependence were all highly linked with development of adult depression.[23] Findings like these have been unwelcome in the United States; the emphasis on mental illness as "brain disease" suggests that developmental factors and the social environment are irrelevant. At a recent conference, the director of a major national depression foundation told me she does not believe that mental illness can be prevented.

But adult patients continue to come into our offices and tell us that their depression feels related to past experiences of trauma and deprivation. Do we dismiss that? Are there not ways to help people improve their parenting so that their children will be less vulnerable to depression? Or ways to structure our society so that we all have less chance of becoming depressed?

Other Types of Depression

Adjustment Disorder

Adjustment disorder with depressed mood or with anxiety and depression is diagnosed when the depression is clearly a response to an external stress. This is not the same as grief. Grief is a state that looks and feels a lot like depression, but people normally recover from grief without formal help. There is also some question of degree. Most people who are grieving are still able to feel that life will go on and hold some future rewards for them, and are able to experience enjoyment when the occasion merits. They don't feel decreased self-esteem or irrational guilt. But people with an adjustment disorder with depression are in worse shape than this. They feel hopeless and helpless, empty and joyless. They can point to exactly what made them feel this way — a setback, the death of someone close, an illness, a blow to their self-esteem of some sort — and they don't yet meet the criteria for dysthymia or major depression. Unfortunately, this diagnosis has almost no predictive value; we can't tell if you're going to recover next month or if this might be the first episode in a lifelong career of depression. My advice: if you don't feel like you're getting better within a month after the stress that started you going downhill, or if you're unable to take effective action to remove the stress, consult a therapist.

Major Depression with Psychotic Features

Some depressions are so severe that the patient begins to experi-ence schizophrenia-like symptoms — hallucinations or delusions, which frequently take the form of an accusatory voice condemning the patient. When depression becomes this severe, it is urgent to get to a good psychiatrist immediately. Treatment is difficult, as most antipsychotic drugs make you feel so sedated and lethargic that you have trouble doing what you need to do to address your depression; and psychotherapy is difficult because you're not in solid contact with reality.

Atypical Depression

This refers to a small subset of patients who display some unique symptoms. Instead of the insomnia that usually goes with depression, these people sleep too much; they also eat too much and put on weight. They experience "leaden paralysis," a feeling of being weighted down, usually in the arms and legs. There is also a high degree of rejection sensitivity, which makes some people avoid relationships, while for others all relationships become stormy and dramatic. People with this condition apparently are highly responsive to MAOIs (monoamine oxidase inhibitors), particularly Nardil.[24]

Depression, Panic, and Phobias

While the other forms of depression we discuss are recognized by the DSM, I want to address a common and dangerous phenomenon that doesn't have a formal diagnosis. Very frequently, especially in the first one or two episodes of major depression, patients also feel extreme anxiety and panic attacks. As mentioned earlier, depression and anxiety are closely related, perhaps two aspects of the same stress reaction. But if out-of-control anxiety is not addressed early in the treatment, it often develops into a phobia, or multiple phobias. Phobias have a life of their own and can be very difficult to treat if they get entrenched, so it's vital to address the panic and anxiety early.

Anyone who has ever had a panic attack knows how terrifying this state is. But the terror can be relieved if patients can learn to understand and control their own reactions. Major depression, when it develops suddenly, feels like an invasion by aliens; you no longer feel like yourself. People who are prone to phobias often experience depression just this way, because they are good at compartmentalizing. The bottom suddenly drops out, and they feel transformed almost overnight into a new person, caught in a panic attack — scared, thoughts racing, pulse pounding, unable to breathe or calm down. Naturally enough, there is a fear that this unbearable tension will never end. A therapist or psychiatrist at this point has to help the patient regain a sense of control by explaining what's going on — *This is a panic attack. I know it's horrible but it does end, and you will feel better. It happens to a lot of people. It's a reaction to stress* — and then go on to talk about the patient's own individual situation, how perhaps it's really not surprising that he couldn't take it anymore. It can be framed in terms of burnout, which is not a stigmatizing label and suggests that recovery is possible.

The free-floating anxiety that the patient is experiencing can easily attach itself to a specific object or situation: driving; going to work; making phone calls; crowds, heights, enclosed spaces, eating. A phobia like this is actually a defense mechanism at work, the patient's mind trying to make the panic more bearable by confining it to a particular situation. But because phobias, once established, can be so difficult to overcome, it's really best to keep confronting the patient with the situation he fears. Anxiolytic medications (minor tranquilizers) can be a tremendous help at this point, because they can give almost instant relief, while antidepressants and psychotherapy work to gain control of stress. Patients also can be helped greatly by learning relaxation methods like breath control or mindfulness techniques. That flood of stress hormones will respond to repeated practice of relaxation skills. It won't happen overnight, and the patient is likely to be uncomfortable for a while; but in the long run it's best not to let the patient be dominated by his fears and depression, and expect him to go on with his normal responsibilities just as much as he can. I have seen too many times the lifelong damage that happens when someone doesn't get the intense, urgent care that this situation demands.

Postpartum Depression (PPD)

Many women develop a serious depression after delivery of their child. While the "baby blues" are quite frequent, but mild and temporary, postpartum depression (PPD) is a serious complication of pregnancy that happens to almost 15 percent of mothers.[25] PPD includes all the symptoms of major depression—the insomnia, loss of appetite, guilt, self-blame, obsessive thoughts—but this is usually focused on the baby and motherhood. You feel like a bad mother, unable to care for your child; you feel that you don't love the baby, or the baby doesn't love you; you feel that you made a terrible, irrevocable mistake and you're hopeless about things ever getting better. In the terrible irony of depression, your mental state, if it continues without treatment, may have a real effect on your relationship with your baby. In the worst cases, PPD can become postpartum psychosis, and a new mother may develop delusions, such as the belief that her baby is a child of the devil and must be destroyed.

Fortunately, things rarely get that bad. But being a new mother should be a time of great joy for you, and if it's not, you should do something about it. If you feel you might have PPD, see a *good* therapist as soon as possible. Note that I emphasize *good*. I have seen too many examples of damage done by well-meaning professionals trying to help new mothers than almost any other group. I think this is because moms are extremely sensitive and vulnerable, and the professionals feel an urgent need to fix the problem, so they rush in with advice that just gives Mom more to blame herself about.

PPD seems to be another example of stress acting on a vulnerable person. In this case, the stress includes both the sudden hormonal changes associated with giving birth (which we still don't fully understand) and the equally sudden extra workload, lack of sleep, and confinement that new mothers experience. Vulnerabilities include a previous history of depression, trouble in the marriage, and a lack of social support—though again, we all know mothers who have been hit by PPD "out of the blue." In many cases, the depression begins during pregnancy, for some of the same reasons—hormonal changes and stress. Often the pregnancy reveals faults in the marriage that have always been there but become more obvious. Sometimes the husband will have a negative reaction to the pregnancy. Friends and relatives can be jealous or insensitive.

The question of using antidepressants during pregnancy and breastfeeding is unfortunately complex. There is increasing evidence that use of SSRIs, both early and late in pregnancy, is associated with birth defects, primarily cardiovascular; but the increase in risk is rather small—on the order of 2 percent compared to 1 percent among mothers with no SSRIs.[26] But of course, other risks may show up later, as has tended to happen with SSRI research. There are risks to the fetus associated with mood stabilizers, as well. So for a depressed and pregnant woman, there is no easy answer. Going off SSRIs can be very difficult, and of course increases the risk of another depressive episode, but there is reason to be concerned about the effects on the baby. Please refer to my discussion of the pros and cons of antidepressants in Chapter 13. We have to balance the severity of the mother's depression, and all the effects that it can have on a child, against the increased risk of birth defects.

Seasonal Affective Disorder (SAD)

This remains a controversial diagnosis for people who regularly become depressed in response to changes in daylight or the seasons. The DSM compilers feel enough confidence to say that there are people who become depressed regularly, usually in winter, and recover in the spring, and that this is not related to lack of exercise or opportunity to socialize or to stimulus deprivation, but appears to be related to absence of sunlight. In the depressive phase, patients feel sad, anxious, irritable, and socially withdrawn. They become lethargic, sleep too long, gain weight, and crave carbohydrates. Four times as many women as men are affected; over half the women complain of premenstrual mood problems as well. Symptoms often improve if the patient moves nearer to the equator during winter. Light therapy, using a powerful fluorescent light regularly, was initially thought to be helpful, though later studies can't show it adds any benefit.[27] But sitting quietly in a good light, reading a book or practicing mindfulness, will do anyone some good.

I was always skeptical about this condition, simply believing that every depressive in New England just feels worse in the winter, until I met Noah, who has a distinct pattern of seasonal bipolar disorder. In August, he begins to be anxious about his upcoming classes (he's a teacher at an upscale prep school in New York), and by October is in a state of major depression. He believes he's doing a lousy job at work and that everyone sees this. He can't sleep, loses interest in food, and gets into an obsessive negative-thinking cycle. He looks like a different person—tense, uncomfortable, and ill at ease. He feels that he can barely express himself, despite the fact that his students give him positive feedback. Then, about January 12—we have tracked this for several years—he starts to feel better. By March he is in a definite hypomanic state, energetic, confident, outgoing, and full of ideas. Students flock to his classes to be entertained, but they actually rate his teaching lower than they do in the fall. In his hypomanic state, he has real trouble focusing, and sometimes makes decisions he regrets very much later on. Early summer is the best time of year for him.

Explaining Depression

SINCE THE FIRST EDITION of this book came out, the news about depression has become both more disturbing and more hopeful. Here's the really scary news: *Depression causes brain damage.* After enough depression, the brain loses its resilience, so when good things happen to us, they have no impact on the brain. We lose the ability to produce dopamine, one of the primary neurotransmitters in the pleasure system. The receptor sites for endorphins, those happy hormones associated with chocolate, sex, and the runner's high, wither away. The hippocampus, a central processor for all emotional messages, appears to shrink with each new episode of major depression—to a total of up to 20 percent, according to some studies.[1] This probably explains the difficulty in concentration and memory that accompanies depression, because the hippocampus is essential in moving memories from short-term into long-term storage. It is also one place where we now know that new brain cells are formed, a process that seems to be associated with learning. Treatment with some antidepressants helps the hippocampus regain the ability to generate new cells, at least in lab animals. One recent study demonstrated that cognitive-behavior therapy also results in hippocampal growth.[2] Still, it seems that repeated episodes of depression result in an overall shrinkage of the brain.[3] Depression seems to lead to specific changes in brain activity that remain as a vulnerability when sad or stressful events happen to recovered patients.[4] And we know from other lines of research that people with depression *are* more likely to react with self-blame, helplessness, and confusion when faced with stress or loss than other people are.[5]

Ready for the hopeful news? More and more research shows that *with focused attention and practice we can change and repair our own brains.* Scientists have begun paying attention to the fact that repeated practice affects the brain. London cabbies' brains are enlarged in the areas that have to do with navigation and orientation.[6] Violin and guitar players' brains are enlarged in the area corresponding to the hand that does the fingering.[7] One study that I particularly enjoyed involved teaching a group of college students to juggle. After three months of daily practice, the investigators, using advanced imaging techniques, were able to see growth in gray matter in the areas associated with hand-eye coordination. Then, after three months in which the students weren't allowed to juggle, that growth disappeared.[8] Now, for the first time in the history of psychology, researchers are looking into whether there is anything we can do to make ourselves feel good, not just recovered. Research into mindfulness meditation shows that regular practice actually rewires the brain. Meditation practice results in an increase in activity in the prefrontal cortex, which many scientists consider the physical location of our own self-awareness. It also seems that meditation helps form a new brain circuit that takes what Daniel Goleman refers to as the "high road" through the wise, self-controlled part of the brain, instead of the "low road" connection that leads from the fear center to immediate, impulsive relief seeking.[9]

The new notion of a "plastic" (changeable) brain resolves much of the long-standing controversy about whether depression is caused by early childhood experiences or neurochemical imbalances: stressful experiences can cause the imbalance, which can become a chronic condition. But whatever the cause in the past, the patient has to recover in the present. Depression, like agoraphobia—another disorder that we now know how to treat—develops a "functional autonomy." Once begun, it continues even after the immediate cause is removed. The patient can have all the insight in the world, but the symptoms have a life of their own. In agoraphobia, you provide medication and teach relaxation skills so the anxiety diminishes, but the patient still doesn't leave the house. You use a metaphorical crowbar or dynamite to get the patient out of the house, the patient experiences the outdoors without experiencing the symptoms, and with a little more practice the disorder is "cured." In depression, you can try medication to help alleviate the pain and suffering, but the patient may still feel a lack of confidence, be painfully shy, lack assertive skills, have a distorted self-image, ruminate and procrastinate, abuse alcohol, be stuck in a loveless marriage or a dead-end job. The patient must address these kinds of issues—in psychotherapy or, as this book proposes, through a deliberate skill-building program—in order to achieve complete recovery.

The Disease That Causes Itself

In my book *Active Treatment of Depression* (Norton, 2001), I presented a model of how depression works that encompasses much of our current knowledge. Let me describe that model and its elements briefly, then talk about what it means for patients, friends, and families.

The basic assumption behind this and most other ways of thinking about depression is that it is a result of a current stress acting on a vulnerable individual. That stress is enough to push the individual over a threshold—an invisible cliff—into the vicious circle of depression. The vicious circle is made up of elements such as depressed thinking, self-destructive behavior, guilt and shame, neurochemical changes, and discrimination and stigma, all of which keep the cycle spinning. These elements both cause and reinforce each other: Depressed thinking causes more guilt and shame, which can lead to self-destructive behavior, which will elicit more guilt and shame—it can go on forever, continually getting worse unless something is done about it. The patient now is trapped; he can't climb back over that invisible cliff without help—medication, therapy, and the removal of some of his sources of stress.

These are some of the factors that seem to contribute to a person's vulnerability to depression:

- *A genetic predisposition.* There is some inheritable component to depression. When one identical twin has depression, chances are two in three that his or her sibling will develop it as well.[10] One study shows a significant degree of thinning of the cortex in the families of those with depression, which the researchers suggest may indicate an inherited genetic vulnerability.[11]
- *Difficulty in early relationships with parents.* We learn more and more every day about how early childhood experiences affect the developing brain and thus lead to trouble in adulthood. If the primary caregiver is emotionally out of tune with the child—perhaps because of her own depression—the child may never develop a healthy sense of self-esteem, of being worthy of love; or may be unable to trust others or unable to control his own impulses.[12]
- *Poor interpersonal skills.* Shyness and social phobia are highly linked with depression. Feeling awkward or embarrassed in social situations will lead you to avoid them, which drives you further into your own head, where all your negative thinking can nibble you to death.
- *Lack of social supports.* Many of my patients are isolated not only by their depression, but also by circumstances. Only children, working in jobs with little or no social contact, divorced, estranged from family, living in the middle of nowhere. Others are married, but stuck in a loveless relationship, just as isolating and damaging. Having no one to rely on in a crisis results in loneliness and insecurity.
- *Unstable self-esteem.* A hallmark of depression is that rejection seems to hurt terribly and corrode your self-image, while good things only result in a temporary and weak pleasant feeling. I like the

analogy of a car's oil system. Oil lubricates the engine by reducing friction between moving parts. It helps the engine run smoothly and efficiently. The oil needs to be changed at regular intervals because it accumulates dirt, but for the most part the system requires little maintenance. However, when there is a leak, like a cracked oil pan or blown gasket, the oil runs out or burns up and we have to keep replenishing the supply. The depression-resistant person has the equivalent of a good, tight oil system; he can function well in life with only occasional support from others, and isn't thrown for a loop by loss or reversal. But many people with depression have a "crack in the pan"—a leaky oil system—and need more or less continual affirmation, love, or success to function, even though their behavior may get in the way of achieving these things.

• *Pessimistic thinking.* There is solid evidence that people with depression think in characteristic negative, self-critical ways that are quite different from other people. I discuss this further in Chapter 8.

• *Early loss or other traumatic experiences in childhood and adolescence.* Death of a parent may be terribly stressful to a child. The world he counted on is gone forever. Some children reject comforting because they feel they have to be brave, or they fear the intensity of their feelings; a surprising number feel guilty and responsible. Other childhood trauma is horribly frequent. In one study of 17,000 largely white, middle-class adults, 22 percent reported childhood sexual abuse.[13] More than a quarter said their parents drank to excess or used drugs, problems that suggest child neglect. Those who reported childhood experiences like these were much more likely to have adult depression, suicide attempts, substance abuse, anxiety problems, and other health issues such as stroke or cardiac problems. In all my experience with patients over the years, most of those with serious depression have told me about experiences of being abused or neglected as children. It's not usually the horror stories of beatings or incest, although those are frequent enough. Much more often, it's emotional abuse: one or both parents seem to consistently undermine the child by criticizing harshly or cruelly, name-calling, emotionally battering the child when he expresses needs or wishes that are upsetting or inconvenient to the parents, yelling at the child just because the parent is in a bad mood (or intoxicated, or hung over), or withdrawing attention or affection because the child has displeased the parent.

• *Childhood problems with siblings also are linked to adult depression.*[14] Many of my depressed patients have felt that a sibling was favored, or that a sibling rejected or bullied them, sometimes to the extent of physical or sexual abuse.

Stresses

These are some of the acute stresses that might push a vulnerable person over the edge into depression.

• *Illness.* Some illnesses, like migraine, MS, and heart attack, seem to precipitate depression much more than their pain, stress, and disability alone would account for, suggesting that the illness itself is physically linked to depression. But any major illness can set off a depressive cycle because of the fear of long-term consequences, lack of energy, difficulty concentrating, and the whole new stress of getting good medical care and paying for it.

• *Failure.* We live in a very competitive society, where status is determined by wealth, not by what you contribute or how well people love you. In these conditions, losing your job or position can be devastating. Most of us depend on our jobs to help us feel competent and useful, and knowing that your layoff is just one example of a worldwide economic meltdown doesn't really make you feel much better.

• *Loss of an important relationship.* Grief feels very much like depression and indeed can lead to depression unless we can move on. The loss of the relationship also means the loss of an important source of love, validation, and comfort.

• *Loss of role status.* We can lose our status, for example, when we are no longer the big breadwinner, the star athlete, the sex symbol, the mom. Some of these changes are an inevitable fact of life; but some of us have built our precarious self-esteem on a particular role, and the adjustment is a major letdown.

• *Other blows to self-esteem.* These can be highly individual, such as an injury that means no longer being able to run, or the trouble remembering that comes with aging.

• *Social stress,* like serious economic uncertainty or the threat of terrorism, can lead to depression.

The Vicious Circle

These are some of the things that happen to you as part of depression, each of which strongly supports and reinforces all the others.

• *Preoccupation with the self.* People who are asked to do tasks like perform an activity in front of a mirror or video camera often experience a loss of self-esteem, unrealistic standards for their own performance, increased self-blame, and feelings of inadequacy.[15] People with depression often turn their focus inward like this, developing a harsh Inner Critic (see Chapter 9), who tells you that anything that goes wrong is your fault.

• *Depressed thinking.* All the research tells us that depressed people have some distinct differences from other people in how they think, which I explore further in Chapter 8.

• *Self-destructive or self-sabotaging behavior* is a hallmark of depression. Drug and alcohol abuse, procrastination, disorganization, shyness, unassertiveness, lethargy, passivity — all these patterns resonate throughout the vicious circle of depression. They provide ammunition for depressed thinking and for feelings of guilt and shame. They tell you that you're not in control of yourself. They have lasting consequences because you're not able to take advantage of school, training programs, or other opportunities. They drive away people who are mature and well functioning and attract others who are equally dysfunctional. Lack of exercise and self-care will result in long-term damage to the body. I discuss this in more detail in Chapter 7.

• *Guilt, shame, and diminished self-esteem.* There is a pervasive sense of guilt, inadequacy, unworthiness, or unlovability that can't be erased no matter how loving or self-sacrificing you are, nor by reassurance that others love you and do not blame you.

• *Feared loss of emotional control.* This is something that patients report all the time, although there's not much attention paid to it in the professional literature; it's the fear that you're losing your mind, that you're having a "nervous breakdown," that the men in white coats are coming to take you to the hospital. There is a sense that some awful, nameless, and permanent change to the self is taking place. This dread is often the key motivation in suicide. And the mere experience of this kind of fear *does* result in lasting change in how you feel about yourself—you may never again feel the kind of naïve self-confidence that you've relied on.

• *Impaired functioning in most aspects of living.* Depression makes us think less effectively; we have trouble concentrating, making decisions, remembering, and taking in new information. This can have lasting consequences, sometimes referred to as "collateral damage." You can make decisions in the midst of depression that will ruin your future: dropping out of school, turning to drugs, running away from or spoiling a good relationship. The damage to your social skills can mean that you lose people that you love. Children with depression have trouble learning and may suffer real educational deficits that will have lasting effects. They also suffer socially; they can become the target for bullying, and have difficulty making friends. Damage to their self-esteem can last a lifetime. "It is bad enough that the depressed person feels terrible, but worse still that the depression can ruin his or her life."[16] Some of these cognitive deficits may remain even after successful treatment and require a specific rehabilitation program.[17]

• *Development of a stable, dysfunctional interpersonal world.* Since you drive away people who expect a lot from you, who challenge you, you may be left with people who support your depression. In the worst case, you can slip into a role where you are expected to be self-sacrificing, hard-working, and uncomplaining, to take care of others, and to be satisfied with the smallest piece of the pie. When you start to recover, you begin to find out that people around you took advantage of your depression. A mother of four, who never let on that she was feeling depressed but one day tried to gas herself in the garage, found out as soon as she got home from the hospital that her husband and children expected her to step right back into the role of domestic manager, schlepping, cooking, and cleaning up after everyone. When she tried to take a part-time job, there was a lot of talk about how she was inconveniencing them all. When she tried to talk about her feelings, no one would listen.

• *Assumption of the sick role.* The "sick role" is a concept from sociology; it means that because you're sick, you're temporarily let off the hook from taking your share of responsibility. If depression lasts long enough, you and the people around you will stop expecting you to act like an adult or be responsible for yourself. The family may have a special name for it—nervous breakdown, delicate, weak. I don't know if there's anything worse than pity, but some long-term depressed people will take it as the best they can get.

• *Physiological symptoms.* Many patients develop chronic physical or pain conditions that are on a vague borderline of recognized diseases (see Chapter 10). Years of stress, lethargy, and insomnia caused by depression take a real toll on the brain, endocrine, and immune systems. Depression actually shortens the lifespan and increases the risk of other medical problems. Patients with depression visit their MDs more frequently, are operated on more frequently, and have more nonpsychiatric emergency room visits than the general population.[18]

• *Neurochemical changes.* We've already talked about the effects of depression on the brain. These changes are powerful factors in the vicious circle, perhaps especially responsible for the disturbed sleep, lack of ability to feel good, low self-esteem, and intrusive negative thought patterns of depression.

• *Somatic changes.* We expect to see certain physical problems as part of depression—that's why they are part of a diagnostic interview. Disturbed sleep is primary, and the research shows that depressed people have different REM patterns than other people. It's terribly demoralizing to be unable to get a good night's sleep. There are also disturbances of appetite—in either direction. There's often a loss of interest in sex, or performance problems. All these symptoms add to the patient's sense of being out of control: that something is happening to him and he doesn't know what it is.

• *Discrimination and stigma.* People with depression are ashamed of having it, and most of our efforts to change public attitudes have been in vain, so the patient's shame is validated by society. Depression is not only a result of biochemistry, genetics, faulty thinking, or self-destructive behavior. It is also a result of how society treats the patient. I sometimes need to point out to people when they're being discriminated against—for instance, by charging a higher co-pay for "mental illness," or by being treated like a workhorse, or left out of social events. If therapists don't acknowledge stigma and discrimination when their patients experience it, we are in essence telling them they are merely imagining it.

I'm far from the first to point out that depression is inherently circular. Observers from many different points of view have commented on the irony of depression, the fact that the sufferer's behavior so often has unintended negative consequences that just make the situation worse.[19] Once we have crossed over the threshold into a depressive cycle, the door slams shut behind us. We can't return to a state of health merely by an act of will, because we are caught in a process that repeats itself over and over; a vicious circle that creates the very conditions that sustain it. The ways we adopt to seek love drive others away; the ways we have of chasing success guarantee our failure. We actually generate disappointments, rejection and low self-esteem, and experiences that reinforce our sense of hopelessness. These "skills" of depression become the default circuitry in the brain. And since we can only look at things from our depressed viewpoint, we can't see a way out.

Trauma, Stress, and Depression

One of the things I like about my model is that it helps explain the current epidemic of depression. Like all epidemics, this one just keeps on accelerating — but it's not because each person with the disease will infect two or three more. Rather, it seems that more and more people are made vulnerable, chiefly because their childhood experiences don't enable them to build a resilient self; then they have to face a much more stressful and difficult adult world than we were designed for. Let me explain.

After almost a century during which Freudian theory, with its focus on the mind alone, dominated psychiatry, the Vietnam War reminded everyone that there was a physical structure called the brain as well. Soldiers came back with symptoms that we eventually recognized as post-traumatic stress disorder (PTSD): nightmares and flashbacks so vivid that the person believes he's right back in combat, the avoidance of anything related to the experience, danger of violent behavior, hypervigilance, dissociation. We now understand that these symptoms are caused at least partly by the effects of overwhelming emotional trauma on the physical brain. In any trauma where the person suddenly fears for his life, or that of someone close to him, excess cortisol (a stress hormone, part of the fight-or-flight response) is secreted by the brain. Normally, when the stress stops, the stress hormones stop as well. But when we continue to experience fear and flashbacks, too much cortisol can damage the hippocampus. This is part of the short-term memory system, where memories of events up to about two weeks ago are temporarily stored, waiting until they are woven into part of our story about ourselves. A lot of cortisol in the hippocampus means we have especially vivid memories for highly emotional events, like remembering exactly where we were on 9/11. But too much cortisol short-circuits the hippocampus and interferes with the process of weaving together short-term memories so they can be put in long-term storage. Thus, the PTSD sufferer relives, rather than remembers, traumatic experiences. It's like the difference between remembering and dreaming. When I remember something, I'm aware that I'm in the present, looking back on the past. But when I'm dreaming, the only "I" there is is back in the dream. So in PTSD, you have nightmares while you're awake. No wonder you're hypervigilant. No wonder you want to sleep with your KA-BAR knife, and your wife is scared of you.

But it doesn't take combat experience to leave you with PTSD: any situation in which you feel terrorized and fearful for your life can do it. The longer the experience lasts, the more likely a PTSD response. Currently the incidence of PTSD in the United States is estimated at about 5 percent for men, 10 percent for women — the higher rate for women because the experience of victimization and helplessness that goes with rape and abuse may make the difference between PTSD and a normal stress reaction. But clearly this is a continuum; there are many, many cases of "mild" PTSD that don't meet all the diagnostic criteria but can make for miserable lives. Rape, abuse, battery, victimization, and helplessness all can lead easily to trauma reactions — which takes us to our next subject, chronic stress and complex PTSD.

Judith Herman, in her now-classic book *Trauma and Recovery,* opened clinicians' eyes to see that the result of exposure to prolonged, repeated abuse and the experience of being subjected to totalitarian control, which she labeled "complex PTSD," is in many ways worse than simple PTSD.[20] And she pointed out that the experience of battered wives and abused children is not that different from POWs — the learned helplessness, the hopelessness, the constant fear, the brain damage that goes with physical or sexual abuse. After adding up all the data I know about domestic violence and child abuse, I estimate conservatively that about 30 percent of Americans are suffering from complex PTSD. As I've said, most of my patients, even those from "good families," tell me of experiences amounting to abuse or neglect. Not necessarily beatings or sexual abuse, but emotional abuse: treating the child harshly or sadistically, micro-managing the child, expecting perfection, yelling, name-calling, shaming, stripping the child of dignity, making the child toe the line just to show who's boss, or scaring or humiliating the child in sadistic "fun." And then perhaps acting as if nothing had happened the next day; or having an elaborate emotional scene where the parent tearfully asks for forgiveness while unloading on the child all his or her own problems. Yet most adult patients are shocked when I tell them that in my opinion childhood experiences like this amount to abuse. They know it wasn't right, they feel alienated from their parents now because of it—but depression makes them believe that they themselves are somehow culpable, rather than that their parents are child abusers. Remember Robert, from Chapter 1: *If you're treated like dirt long enough, you begin to feel like dirt.*

It's really the enormous body of work by Allan Schore, a highly respected neurological scientist,[21] that has shown us the connections between childhood experience, the child's brain development, and the adult's mental health. Schore is able to account for and explain many of the observations that alert psychotherapists had discovered independently: for instance, that most adults labeled borderline personality disorder had been abused as children, or experienced severe disruptions in early attachment; or that many adults with addictive problems seemed to have cold or emotionally unavailable caregivers; or that many adults with autoimmune disorders were sexually abused as children. Since these were only anecdotal data, responsible therapists held back from suggesting that child abuse "caused" borderline personality or autoimmune disease, or that parental rejection was linked to substance abuse. Schore, with his encyclopedic knowledge of the literature from diverse fields, has been able to provide strong support for these causative links at work. His bottom line: *Childhood experience—not only trauma and neglect, but also simply a poor relationship between caregiver and child—results in damage to the structure of the brain itself.* This damage to the brain in turn results in things like a reduced ability to experience and control emotions; an unstable self-concept; damage to our immune system; difficulty in forming relationships; reduced ability to focus, concentrate, and learn; and damage to our capacity for self control.[22]

When I state these conclusions in presentations, more than a few people are incredulous: *Do you mean that what happens in childhood can cause brain damage that lasts into adulthood? That affects our health, our ability to think, our relationships?* Perhaps I shouldn't use the term "brain damage" because it's so inflammatory, but I want to get their attention. Of course childhood experience affects the physical brain. Everything we think, feel, and remember is somewhere in the structure of the brain itself. Our brains embody our experiences. If your childhood is full of bad experiences, it leaves its scars on the brain. If the scars weren't there, it would be easy for us to just stop self-destructive behavior when it's pointed out to us. But instead, we have to find ways to undo, heal, or grow new circuits to replace those old scars.

What Good Is Depression?

Some scientists believe that the reason depression exists in the first place is that it is an adaptive response, hard-wired into us because it has survival value. When dogs are trained that they can't escape from a shock, they stop trying to escape, even when the way out is obvious.[23] Human infants cease activity, become lethargic, and thereby conserve energy when their cries go unanswered too long. Getting depressed may be adaptive for the species if it gets us to retreat in the face of overwhelming obstacles, or stop our misguided efforts to get what we want when the cost is too high.[24]

I've never known anyone with a serious depression who hadn't earned the right to feel that way; after being kicked in the teeth for a long time, you begin to realize that it's best to keep your head down. But most of us, unfortunately, blame ourselves instead of taking a cold look at our upbringing, the stresses of living in contemporary society, and the damage done to our brains and bodies as a result. We have to forgive ourselves for not being able to do the impossible. Then we can stop the blame cycle and remind ourselves again of the good news: *we can change our own brains.* But it takes hard work, and it requires us to learn to see things as they really are. We have to change our own bad habits and the ways we see the world.

Part 2

Learning New Skills

5

The World of Depression

HEART DISEASE is a good analogy to major depression. Heart disease is "caused" by a complex of factors, including a genetic predisposition, emotional factors like how we handle stress, and habits like diet and exercise. You don't catch heart disease from an infection. You develop it gradually, over time, as plaque builds up in your arteries. Once you cross an invisible threshold marked by standards of blood pressure and cholesterol levels, you have heart disease, and you have it for the rest of your life. Yesterday you were normal, today you have heart disease. You don't feel any different, but now you have to change your life. Depression may be a similar threshold disease — genetic and biochemical factors may determine a different level of stress for each of us that, once reached, puts us over the edge into depression. Childhood trauma, stress, and loss bring us closer to the edge.

Some stress pushes us over into our first real depression. Once over the line, we can't go back. We "have" depression. We can recover from episodes, we can modify our lifestyles to prevent or moderate future episodes, but we "have" depression. Except for a few lucky people who get the best care the first time around, for most people there's a low-grade dysthymia always there in the background that wasn't there before — unless we undertake a serious rehabilitation program.

Unfortunately, we know a lot more about treatment and prevention of heart disease than we do about depression. By changing your eating habits, exercise habits, and stress level, you can reduce your risk of heart disease. No one seems to know how to reduce your risk of depression. In fact many psychiatrists have argued that there is nothing you *can* do to reduce your risk.[1] There are many effective medications and surgical procedures that can reverse the effects of heart disease, restore you to near-normal functioning, and reliably reduce your incidence of another attack. Although there are medications and treatments that help depression, only a few have been shown to effectively reduce the risk of future episodes, and only a lucky few patients feel back to normal again.

Since no one seems to really understand depression, everyone feels entitled to an opinion. You have no way of knowing if your physician's advice is any better than that of your wife, your clergyman, a mental health professional, or a random self-help website you stumble on. But the truth is that experienced, open-minded therapists know a great deal about what helps people recover from depression. This "practice wisdom" of therapists rarely filters out to the public, not because it contains trade secrets, but because much of it is tied to theoretical points of view that themselves get in the way of exchanging knowledge and experience. When it comes down to what we do, effective therapists have a great deal in common, but we are hopelessly divided in how we explain it.

I want to briefly summarize here how good psychotherapy works to facilitate recovery from depression. The purpose at this point is not to sell psychotherapy, but to use it as a model to explain recovery; how people can learn to stop the self-defeating behavior that seems to them to be the only possible response to their desperate inner state.

One of the essential elements in effective psychotherapy is trust. The patient is open and honest with the therapist in return for an implicit contract that the therapist will use his special knowledge only to help, never to harm, the patient. For many adults, the therapeutic relationship is the only one in which they can let their gua... Depressed patients are almost always full of guilt and shame. ...haven't lived up to their own standards. They feel like failures. The... feel that they've let their loved ones down. When the therapist hears the guilty secrets and doesn't run screaming from the room in revulsion, or castigate the patient for being the moral leper he thinks he is, healing begins. Accepting the patient as a worthwhile individual, even though he's not perfect, is crucial for the patient to begin to overcome his pervasive guilt and shame.

Another essential element is emotional engagement and support. The patient doesn't usually communicate the depth of his pain and fear to those closest to him, out of shame or fear of rejection; he "stuffs" his feelings, to borrow an AA term. He bites back on his feelings and tries to pretend they aren't there. If he shows them at all, he usually gets advice from those around him, when he really needs understanding. Others are quick to give advice because they, like the patient, are afraid of the need and pain. They want to move on, as quickly as possible. The good therapist, at this stage, doesn't give advice. She shows by example that the feelings are not to be feared; in fact, she probes and goes deeper. She lets the patient know that depression is a process that has a life of its own, that there is good reason for hope because depression does end, but that feelings are important. Sometimes all the therapist can do is hold the patient's hand, metaphorically, while they wait together for the worst storms to blow over. Often there is no one else in the patient's life who can do this.

Once trust and support are relatively stable, the healing work of psychotherapy can begin. Many aspects of the individual's functioning can change with treatment. I have grouped these into seven major areas:

Emotions. People with depression usually have learned ineffective or self-defeating ways of handling emotions. Some, like Robert, seem to be frightened by all emotions and come across as cold, intellectual, and avoidant of human contact. When he got better and recognized this, Robert liked to joke about himself as "emotionally challenged." Others, by contrast, feel so close to the edge that they fear bursting into tears in public. Many depressed people have particular trouble with anger. We feel we should never get angry, so we bite back on it until we can't take any more, and then explode. Those nearby can't understand the explosion because they don't know all the little frustrations that led up to it. The depressive gets even more depressed because he feels he's lost control. In therapy, the patient must learn to see these patterns and then learn that intimacy doesn't lead to being engulfed and that anger doesn't end relationships. This is often played out in the relationship between therapist and patient, where the patient feels safe enough for the first time to experience trust and anger without running away or being destroyed.

Behavior. The patient often must also change patterns of behavior that lead to a depressed lifestyle. Most depressed people are perfectionists. We feel that if we don't do a job perfectly, our entire self-esteem is endangered. Often this leads to procrastination, so the job is never really begun. Outright failure is avoided, but the depressive knows he's let himself down. Our perfectionism makes us want to make ourselves over from the ground up: we want to lose thirty pounds, run five miles a day, quit smoking and drinking, get our work completely reorganized, and have time for relaxation and meditation. It seems like there is so much to do that we never start; or we may start one day in a burst of energy that gets dissipated in so many directions that nothing really gets accomplished, and we are again confirmed in the belief that there's no point trying. We have to learn that attaining more limited, realistic goals is much more satisfying than building castles in the air.

Thought processes. We have to change the way we think. Jerome Frank talked about our unique "assumptive world," the idiosyncratic set of beliefs we all have that explain to us how life works.[2] We get some assumptions from our parents, we develop others as we grow up, and we continue to add to and revise our beliefs about what makes things tick into adulthood and old age. Depressed people tend to have certain assumptions in common, assumptions that are self-perpetuating and not corrected by experience. We think that we are responsible for the bad things that happen to us, while the good things are just accidental. We are pessimists, thinking that things left alone will usually go to pieces rather than working out for the best. We think that we have to be in control of things at all times, and if we're not, disaster will happen. These habits of thinking are largely unconscious. They must be brought out into the open, challenged, and changed for recovery to start.

Stress. Here I have added a new chapter in this revised edition, because so much more is known now about the effects of psychological stress on the body and mind. Twenty-first-century living conditions have us constantly in fight-or-flight response, pouring out stress hormones—adrenaline and cortisol—which are very useful in emergencies but over time have devastating effects on the body, brain, and mind, including but not limited to depression. The only way I know how to cope with this kind of stress is to learn to be more mindful. Mindfulness—learning to be more conscious, aware, in the present moment—has been shown to be a very effective road to recovery from stress, anxiety, and depression. It also has preventive value. Mindfulness means being very aware of but a little detached from your experience; learning to watch yourself as a loving parent would, with greater objectivity but also greater acceptance. Mindfulness meditation is a practice that has shown itself to be effective with many emotional and physical problems. There's exciting new research suggesting that meditation practice can actually reverse some of the brain damage that depression entails.

Relationships. Relationships with other people are always difficult for the depressive. We walk around with a vast hurt inside and long for someone to heal it, but we're also ashamed of feeling that way, so we don't let anyone know. We care too much about how others feel and think about us, but we're afraid to let them know we care; consequently we're almost always disappointed. Always expecting rejection, we may reject first as a defense. Our boundaries are too porous, so that we often assume others know how we feel, and that we know how they feel. Despite the fact that we're wrong about this so often, we don't learn from experience and stop making these assumptions. We have to learn specific techniques of communication that will establish boundaries and stop the confusion.

The body. Depressed people tend to be insensitive to messages from our bodies. We often overwork ourselves, then collapse with exhaustion, not realizing that this cycle is damaging. Simple things like eating become loaded issues, so we don't eat well and are prone to weight gain or undernourishment or both. We've forgotten how to sleep. We don't exercise. We can easily come to abuse alcohol or other drugs, both legal and illegal, to try to regulate our moods and bodies.

The self. Depressed people don't have inner resources of self-esteem that help them get through trying times. We look to others to replace those resources but know that such wishes are unfair and unrealistic; consequently we are consumed by shame and guilt. We want desperately to be loved, but feel we are unlovable. We haven't been able to determine principles and values for ourselves, nor to guide our lives by rational priorities, because we lack confidence in our own judgment. We can't feel good when we accomplish a meaningful goal because all goals are the same; burning dinner feels as if it can undo our pride about graduating from college. We need to learn how to set priorities, to trust our decisions, and to take pride in our accomplishments.

The next chapters review how depression affects our functioning, and how our altered functioning in turn reinforces depression, in each of these areas of living. By stepping back from ourselves and seeing how we *do* depression, we can also perhaps see how to *undo* it. The reader may not need any more from this book than an altered perspective. But most people with depression need more — they need specific advice about how to change, they need specific techniques, skills, or habits that they can learn to replace the self-defeating skills of depression. So I'm providing these as well. Remember that the brain itself is changed by what we think and what we do. We can rewire ourselves so that depressed behavior is no longer our first, automatic response to new situations. The work of rewiring is difficult at first, but change happens gradually, so that healthy behavior, thinking, and feeling gain momentum and become more and more natural to us.

The depressed reader might be overwhelmed by Part 2, concluding, "Oh Lord, I have to remake myself from the ground up. I'll never be able to do all this. I'd better just go back to bed." What I want to say is: Relax; take it easy. You don't have to do it all at once. You can start anywhere to undo depression. Any chapter, any suggestion, may be enough to get you started on a self-reinforcing cycle of healthy behavior. But you *do* have to start.

Emotions

ALEX WAS an extremely introverted man. An only child, his parents deceased, he had lived by himself since college. He worked in a job that most people would consider boring. Though he did not appear shy or self-conscious — he had a pleasant smile and talked easily when spoken to — he seemed to avoid most human contact.

He told his therapist how lonely and depressed he was. He was envious of people who had others to be close to. He identified himself as gay, though he had had little sexual experience of any kind. His only outlet was to go to gay bars. There he would always find someone who became his imaginary lover. These affairs in Alex's mind lasted for months. Alex would interpret every look and gesture made by his imaginary lover in the bar as a secret signal to him, confirming their love. During these times, Alex was euphoric. He often missed his therapy appointments, and when he did come in, he was hard-pressed to think of things to talk about. Inevitably, however, the imaginary lover would make some gesture that Alex interpreted as a betrayal. Then his bubble would burst, and Alex would be plunged into the depths of depression, feeling for all the world as if a real lover had rejected him cruelly and thoughtlessly.

Alex's therapist finally talked him into trying Prozac. It had a miraculous effect. Within a few weeks, Alex was talking realistically about his life for the first time. He realized he was kidding himself with these imaginary affairs. Also, he saw that he was going nowhere in his career. He and the therapist excitedly began to make plans for how Alex could meet real people. They considered his going back to school, or asking for more responsibility at work. Alex seemed like a changed man, and the therapist was much heartened.

Then Alex dropped out of therapy for a few months. When he called again, it was because he had been spurned by a new lover. Her heart sinking, the therapist realized this was another imaginary affair. She asked Alex if he was still taking his Prozac. "Oh, that," said Alex. "That wasn't good for me. I didn't feel like myself on that. This is me."

When his therapist and I talked about Alex, we found that psychotherapy had many ways of explaining why he'd gone back to his old ways, but they all centered around fear: *Alex was simply afraid of feelings he couldn't control.* When the affair was taking place only in his imagination, he wrote the script. Everything that happened, including the final rejection, was a product of his own mind. But if he got close to a real person, he wouldn't be in charge anymore. He placed himself in danger of feeling real feelings. What if someone else really loved him? To be loved is heady stuff. Alex spent his life avoiding extremes of emotion.

In order to learn any new skills that will help overcome and prevent depression, we have to start with emotions. *Depressives fear feelings.* Other self-defeating habits that will be explored in the following chapters—in how we think, act, communicate, and view ourselves—are essentially ways we have developed to help us not feel certain things. Understanding that emotions are not to be feared will free us up to change our other habits.

Most people, depressed or not, have some fear of feeling. One of the central insights of psychodynamic therapy is that "anxiety"—the fear of being torn apart, consumed by our emotions—is the underlying problem in most human situations. And one of the central truths is that there is really nothing to fear. It is our fear itself, and the habits we develop to control or avoid it, that leads to most of our suffering. If we stop running and turn around and face the demons, they usually turn out to be no threat at all.

People with depression have a special talent for stuffing feelings. They can pretend to themselves and the world that they don't feel normal human emotions. They are very good at the defenses of repression, isolation, and intellectualization. They raise self-denial and self-sacrifice to the point where the self seems to disappear.

One of Freud's greatest but least-understood contributions is the notion of unconscious guilt. Any child will, at times, get angry and frustrated by even the best, most loving parents. He may have fantasies of running away or daydreaming that he doesn't belong to these people, that someday his "real" parents will come and take him away. He can get angry and have fantasies about murdering his parents. But because he loves them and depends on them, he tries to stuff away those fantasies. In repressing his feelings this way, they become lost to consciousness. Yet the child still feels guilty.

This process of repressing our feelings yet still feeling guilty or ashamed about them is one of the most fiendish aspects of the human mind: we don't let ourselves imagine the desire, to indulge it in fantasy, to relish the thought of seduction or revenge, but we still get to feel guilty about it.

I once had a patient who had already filed for divorce when his wife was struck with a terminal illness. The marriage had been horrible, the wife had been a sadistic harridan. The illness seemed to make her more so. But my patient couldn't leave her at this stage. He never expressed a desire that she might die, even though I told him it might be normal under the circumstances—but he still felt horribly guilty. All his tender ministrations and self-sacrifice during her illness couldn't undo his guilt. Another patient (Sharon, page 262) was a young woman who had been sexually abused by her brother, and couldn't allow herself to experience normal sexual desires. She had to make the men in her life the sexual aggressors, then feel guilty, dirty, and ashamed for letting herself be seduced again. It is a guiding principle of everyday life, but one we keep forgetting—*we feel guilt about feelings and desires without being aware of the feelings and desires themselves.*

This is one of the major reasons why people with depression are usually full of guilt and self-blame. Instead of the normal fluctuations of happiness, sadness, disappointment, joy, desire, and anger that most people cycle through many times a day, depressed people feel a kind of gray neutrality that translates into subterranean tectonic shifts in mood. But even though we aren't aware of the emotions, we still get to feel guilty about them. When the meek, depressed wife of a bullying husband doesn't consciously feel angry at his treatment, she will still feel guilty about her rage without even experiencing it, and that will just feed her depression. This is one of the great secrets of depression. The depressive is full of guilt about feelings, desires, and impulses he's not even aware he has. *If you're going to feel guilty anyway, you'd better know what it is that you feel guilty about. If you know, you can do something about it.* The first step in overcoming the guilt is to become aware of the feelings.

Learning to Feel

How do you go about recapturing the ability to experience emotions? First of all, it's necessary to understand that emotions are innate, instinctual responses that are with us from infancy on. When the baby is feeling warm, comfortable, and secure, she experiences an emotion we can call contentment or happiness. When she experiences something that pleases her, like a new puppy, she experiences joy or delight. When something startles her, she feels fear. Left alone for too long, she feels the beginnings of sadness. The capacity to experience these emotions is hard-wired into the human nervous system. If someone steps on your toe, you feel pain. If someone steps on your psychological toes—for instance, by being rude or unfair—you may feel anger, jealousy, outrage. If you don't experience these emotions, it's because you are spending psychic energy to keep them out of awareness. This psychic energy could be better spent on other things.

These emotions are hard-wired into us, just as they are in higher animals—dogs, cats, horses, monkeys. That's why we feel emotionally connected to them. Darwin pointed out how the infant's ability to express emotion even before she can talk has important survival value for the species. The baby looks scared and we feel a natural desire to comfort her; she cries from hunger, we feed her; she giggles in happiness, we play with her (and thus give her the opportunity to learn through socialization). The function of emotions is to amplify or call attention to the situation that elicits them. If the infant couldn't express these feelings, she would die, because we wouldn't know how to care for her.

Emotions give us vital information about life. They are signals to us about our values—what feels right and wrong, good and bad. When we're confronted with a moral choice, we should pay special attention to our feelings, because if we think too much, our defenses go to work. We can rationalize doing the easier thing, instead of the right thing. Our first, gut feelings are usually honest and objective. We should pay special attention to our first reactions to new people and situations. Negative impressions are quite often messages from the amygdala, the danger-sensing center of the brain, that there is something to be wary about here. We should look into those impressions carefully and mindfully. Sometimes it's a warning that this person wants something from you but isn't being honest about it—but if you don't pay careful attention, you can forget about your first impression and open yourself up to manipulation. Positive first impressions are also important; they may be nothing more meaningful than that you think you could have fun with this person, which may be a self-fulfilling prophecy that will bring more fun into your life, not a bad thing.

Emotions in themselves are absolutely value-free. They are reflexes, like salivating when hungry or withdrawing your hand from a hot iron. It's how we *express* emotions that carries such important social and individual values. We have some ability to control how we express emotions, but we get in trouble if we try to control how we experience them. If a man gets angry and beats his wife, that is both socially condemned and psychologically destructive. But if he tells her why he's angry and then tries to work things out, or if he blows off steam by exercise, or throws himself into his work, those activities are both socially approved and psychologically productive. The point is that although we have control over how we express emotions, we've developed the belief that we shouldn't even feel some feelings—an almost impossible task.

It takes a great deal of practice for the depressed person to learn how not to experience emotions, but we get very good at it. Women get especially good at not feeling anger and men get good at not feeling sadness. All of us stop experiencing much joy or happiness. It seems as if when you lose the ability to feel painful feelings you also lose the ability to feel positive ones. We go through life numbed.

The Function of Defenses

We can stop feeling our feelings because we overuse certain psychological *defense mechanisms*—denial, isolation, and repression, among others—to help keep feelings unconscious. Defenses help protect our conscious minds from awareness that underneath, we are in conflict with ourselves. We are constantly trying to find a balance between what we want, what we think we should want, and what reality will let us have. When external reality is too overwhelming—such as the death of a loved one—we can go into denial and momentarily forget what's happened. When our desires are in conflict—for instance, sexual desire for someone our conscience tells us we are not supposed to desire—we may change that desire into a wish for someone else, turn it into hate, intellectualize it, or any of a number of other possibilities. Defenses are like art, a creative synthesis. The mind unconsciously creates something that was not there before.

Defense mechanisms themselves are necessary for human existence. They are often creative, adaptive strategies for dealing with difficult situations or people. But people with depression overuse their defenses as ways to try to avoid feeling, and we run the risk of losing the ability to feel altogether.

All defenses distort reality to some extent, but some do it more than others. So-called immature defenses, like denial and projection, can stand reality on its head. In *denial,* I honestly don't see how my alcoholism hurts others, although it's plain as day to any objective observer. This is why people get so angry at alcoholics. It's very difficult to believe they really don't see things as they are. But the alcoholic lives in a different reality dominated by the bottle. In *projection,* I attribute my feelings to others. Coming home from work grouchy and angry, as many husbands do, we project that anger and interpret our wife's or child's neutral comments as hostile and provocative. Soon we've got the fight we wanted. Other, so-called mature defenses may distort reality only a little. Humor, for example, works by shifting one's perspective: what had seemed all-important and frustrating seems ludicrous, perhaps trivial, with the help of humor. Mature defenses let us keep a more accurate perspective on what is going on around us than immature defenses do. Unfortunately, depressed people use the less accurate defenses too much.[1]

Defenses, over time, distort our character as well. Besides trying not to feel your own pain, you may become someone who is unempathic and unsympathetic, someone who avoids emotional situations altogether. A cold, detached personality. Or you rationalize too much, forget the value of honesty to yourself and others, and say only what's convenient. People will stop trusting you.

Because depression won't let us feel our feelings, we develop mood changes instead. One minute we'll be feeling pretty good, then without warning we feel depressed—sad, discouraged, no energy. One of the favorite phrases of depressed people is "out of the blue"—"It just came over me, out of the blue, and I felt so awful again." We've stuffed our feelings so much that just one more drop is enough for them to break through in a wave of sadness, regret, or guilt.

The basic principle that the depressed person has to learn is that these mood changes do not come out of the blue—*mood changes are always caused by an unfelt feeling.* The feeling is usually triggered by an interpersonal event, although sometimes it is just a response to a memory, something we read about, or hear on television. Something happens that makes us angry, makes us feel hurt, sad, or scared—or even happy—but the event doesn't register on our consciousness. The feeling seems disconnected from reality; we don't understand what's going on in ourselves so we feel inadequate, out of control, frustrated—depressed again.

Accordingly, the depressive must monitor his or her own moods to help detect the feelings underneath. Trust that there is always a precipitant to a mood change, and use a Mood Journal to help analyze the connections between events and the change in mood. In this log you're simply asked to describe your mood changes and the external and internal events accompanying them, in the hope that you will begin to see the connections. It's a way of helping you to be more observant and objective.

Review the Mood Journal every day, ideally at the same time of day, when you have a few minutes and can give it your attention. See what patterns you begin to notice. After a few weeks' practice, you should begin to see the connections between your mood changes, external events, and internal processes. Once you can see that mood changes are caused by what's happening to you, you can stop pretending that they come "out of the blue."

This is an important and powerful tool. If you use it correctly and regularly, you can begin to get around your own defensive system. *This may not feel good at first.* You may find yourself worrying more, feeling perhaps a bit more edgy. You are going to become more aware of things that upset you. This awareness is what depressives try to avoid. Just remember that this avoidance sacrifices your true self and makes you depressed. You may see your defenses at work in how you use the Mood Journal. You may forget to use it (repressing a conflict between your wish to get better and your fear of change). You may get mad at it for suggesting things you don't want to hear (projecting your anger at yourself onto an external object). You may think it is boring and a waste of time (isolating your affect and intellectualizing your feelings). Try very hard to stick with it nonetheless. If you do it for a week, you're bound to learn something valuable; if you do it for a month, you'll learn a great deal, and you'll automatically start to become more observant and accepting.

The depressed person often feels there is no reason for feeling depressed (or angry, or scared), and thus feels crazy or out of control. But if we take the trouble to investigate, to get underneath our own defenses, we usually find that there are perfectly good reasons for feeling the way we do. Understanding that is the first step toward doing something about it.

Mood Journal

Date, time	Mood change	Externals (who, what, where, unusual circumstances)	Internals (thoughts, fantasies, memories)

Instructions: When you detect a shift in mood, write down the change (*e.g.,* from neutral to sad), the external circumstances (what you were doing, where, with whom), and the internal circumstances (what you were thinking about, daydreaming, or remembering).

Trying to change yourself in this way is hard work. It helps if you can laugh at yourself. I'm the kind of person who buys self-help books about getting organized, then misplaces them. When I worked at the clinic, I lost the same book on "accounting for nonprofit managers" (not my favorite subject) so often that I finally bought three copies. There *is* a perverse gremlin within us that resists change, especially the kind of change that someone else says is good for us. My strategy has now become to appreciate the gremlin's tricks on me, then try to outwit the little beast. So if you find yourself losing this book, or if you find that life always interferes with completing the Mood Journal, just assume that your gremlin is at work. Laugh ruefully at the games he's playing with you, then see what you can do to be smarter than he is.

Anger

Anger is a particular trouble spot for most depressives. We are often aware of a feeling of estrangement from the world, our noses pushed up against the glass watching real life behind the window, and a consequent bitterness, hurt, or resentment lurking in the background. At the same time we may feel it is our own fault we feel this way — after all, we imagine that we could just jump into the midst of life if we chose. So there is a lot of anger in our lives, conscious or not, which we may recognize yet feel we are not entitled to. This anger and self-blame can feed on itself in a vicious circle, so it is often nearly impossible to be sure that we are justified in feeling the depth of anger we experience in any particular situation. We second-guess ourselves constantly and often end up doing nothing but driving others crazy, Hamlet-like.[2] Some of the defenses we use against awareness of our anger, like passive-aggression, just make others angry at us, while we sit in smug superiority looking down on those who can't "control" themselves. In other circumstances, our guilt makes us self-sacrificing: we will absorb ill treatment from others as if it is our due, but eventually we will get pushed too far and explode in a tirade of anger that unloads all the steam we have built up. If we do this often, we get a reputation as a difficult person and we get avoided. If we do this rarely, we get a reputation as a crazy, unstable person who bursts out inappropriately.

It's important to remember that anger, like all other emotions, is neither good nor bad in itself; it's just an innate response we have when someone steps on our metaphorical toes. Anger can be used for many worthwhile purposes. It's the fuel that feeds our desire for justice, what makes us want to see wrongs put right. What is scary is that it feels as though it can run away with us. But I think that's largely a myth about anger, because few of us ever do really lose complete control. The wife-beater frequently says words to this effect: "I couldn't help it. She made me see red, and then I didn't know what I was doing. I'm sorry I hurt her, but I lost control." But (usually) he didn't really lose control. He didn't beat his wife until she died; he didn't strangle her or shoot her or stab her; he just beat her until he felt like he'd won the dispute. There was some judgment there, some decision to stop before an invisible line was crossed. Anger usually doesn't take absolute control of us, but its expression can be so heady and can make us feel so good that we indulge ourselves in carrying the fight forward till our opponent is humiliated. Saying that we were so angry we lost control is an excuse. We had control, but we still did something shameful.

Many depressed parents are deeply ashamed of their anger at their own children, and a great deal of child abuse results from parental depression. Children know when parents are depressed, and it scares them, because they don't know if the parent is going to be capable of caring for them. When children are scared, they naturally become more demanding and difficult; they start testing to see if they are safe. Mom gets to feel even more depressed because her children won't listen to her, but she doesn't believe it's right to be angry at them. Dad alternates between withdrawal and rage. It's an explosive combination. The same dynamics apply in elder abuse. Caregivers in this position need real help. A combination of psychotherapy and medication for the depression with concrete, practical, in-home support and guidance in effective skills—in parenting or in caregiving for the elderly—makes the difference.

Anger can't be escaped, but we can tame it, live with it, and make it safe, even use it for productive ends. Practicing assertive communication and behavior, as described in Chapter 10, can help make sure that anger is constructively expressed and doesn't hurt people important to us. And as we develop assertive skills, we find that we feel less aggrieved and isolated and thus have less to be angry about.

General William Tecumseh Sherman, remembered now as the wrathful arm of the North who burned Atlanta and much of the South, was a textbook case of a man with a characterological depression that developed into a full-blown major depressive episode early in the Civil War. He had a breakdown, and disgraced himself and the Union Army. But within a few months, events cured his depression permanently.

Sherman, like so many depressives, experienced loss early and as a young man always felt like an outsider with something to prove. Sherman's father died when he was nine, leaving his widow impoverished. The family was broken up, the children sent to live with relatives and friends. Sherman was taken in by Thomas Ewing, a powerful politician who treated Sherman fairly—but Sherman always felt in his debt. Sent to West Point, Sherman found his calling, graduating third in his class and going on to a successful early military career. But he chose Ewing's daughter Ellen as his wife, binding himself further into the Oedipal struggle to prove himself; their letters reveal Sherman's continual need to gain respect for what he felt he lacked inside.

At the outbreak of the Civil War, Sherman was already depressed because of business reversals. However, his reputation for skill and integrity won him a high position in charge of operations in Tennessee—even though he clearly expressed his desire to serve in a lesser role, under someone else. After a few months of service, he was not sleeping, not eating, imagining spies and enemy armies where none existed, demanding reinforcements for no reason that anyone could understand. The newspapers got wind of this and labeled him a coward.

He went home to his wife, who not only gave him her emotional support but also enlisted her powerful family and went directly to President Lincoln, who knew Sherman and perhaps understood a fellow sufferer. She reported back to her husband, "He said he wanted you to know... that he had the highest and most generous feelings towards you" and that "your abilities would soon merit promotion."³

Brought back into active duty gradually, Sherman developed a relationship with Ulysses S. Grant that lent him some strength and led to a lifelong bond. "He stood by me when I was crazy," said Sherman later, "and I stood by him when he was drunk: and now we stand by each other always."⁴ The taciturn Grant and the excitable Sherman made an odd couple, but they each gained from the relationship. Then, at Shiloh, Sherman's life and character changed permanently. In the first action of the battle, Sherman's party suddenly came under fire; his aide-de-camp was shot from his saddle, and Sherman was wounded. He went on to be wounded again that day, and had three horses killed beneath him. Surprised by the rebels, he spent the remainder of the two-day battle in the front lines, rallying his troops and showing great personal courage. Whether it was because he was emotionally ready for a crisis, or because he was so surprised he didn't have time to become anxious, he proved something to himself and his troops.

It is as if he never looked back from that moment. If in the past he had made his own life hell, he spent the rest of his life giving it to other people. Freud thought of depression as anger turned against the self; Sherman developed the ability to use that same anger against his enemies, much to the dismay of Georgia. He went on to apply the same fire and discipline as postwar General of the

Army, earning the respect and admiration of all. At his funeral in 1891, his most distinguished enemy, Joe Johnston, served as pall-bearer, contracting fatal pneumonia by going hatless in February New York weather. "If I were in his place," said Johnston, "and he were standing here in mine, he would not put on his hat."[5]

Joy and Pride

Anhedonia is the technical term for the depressive's inability to experience joy. In the depths of major depression, nothing touches us, not the most intensely pleasurable activities, not the most familiar comforts. We are emotionally frozen. There seem to be actual physical changes in the brain that interfere with feeling good.

Less dramatic than anhedonia but a much more pervasive problem among the depressed is a condition that doesn't even have a clinical name. It's the gradual withdrawal into isolation and indifference that creeps up on us as we live with the disease. Robertson Davies called this condition *acedia;* it's akin to the deadly sin of sloth. But it's not merely laziness, it's a gradual closing down of the world.[6] As depression makes us lose interest or pleasure in things, our range of activities constricts. We stop taking chances, we avoid stimulation, we play it safe, and we begin to cut ourselves off from anything that might shake us up—including loved ones. It's the rot that sinks into marriages and makes people vulnerable to affairs. It's the hardening of the attitudes on the job that makes for petty, passive-aggressive bureaucracies. It's the withdrawal from our own children that leaves them questioning why we bother to live.

Pride is what we're supposed to feel when we've accomplished something, but, like joy, it's not something that depressives experience very often. This is partly because of our inherent perfectionism. We rarely feel that anything we've done measures up to our own standards. As we'll see in Chapter 8, depressives consistently evaluate their own performance more harshly than do nondepressives, whereas nondepressed people tend to overrate their own performance. Thus depressives are pessimists rather than optimists, sadder but sometimes wiser.[7] Even so, there are times when we do accomplish something that is objectively worthwhile. Do we allow ourselves to feel good about it? Not usually, and not for long. Pride, like joy, is a feeling we suppress.

One reason why we don't allow ourselves to experience these pleasurable feelings is our wish to remain in control at all times. Intense feelings of any kind are destabilizing; we start to worry that we will keep on inflating with good feeling till we pop like a balloon, or float off into the stratosphere never to be seen again. Another is our fear of retribution; we've been conditioned to expect that something bad inevitably follows something good, so we'd better not let ourselves feel too good. Better to feel numb or neutral than to feel the crashing disappointment we fear will follow good feelings. Most important, perhaps, is that for the depressive, feelings like joy or pride evoke painful memories of past disappointments. We remember the father who was never satisfied, the mother who didn't seem interested. The bereaved child within us, who has never stopped grieving for those incomplete relationships, is awakened at times of celebration, and becomes the ghost at the feast. No wonder we're tempted to stay numb.

Depressives assume that everyone else is happy most of the time, and that there is something wrong with us for not feeling the same way. On the contrary, there is good reason to believe that the normal state of the human mind is one of mild anxiety.[8] Most people, when asked to think of nothing, or when put in situations in which external stimuli are limited, begin to worry.

The important implication for depressives is that happiness, instead of being a normal state of being that we don't experience because something is wrong with us, is something that must be cultivated.[9] It's true that others experience more spontaneous joy when a good thing happens than we do, but joys are inherently fleeting. We need to practice feeling good. When we feel happy, we need to express those feelings to others. When we feel proud, we need to let ourselves sustain the emotion. We will find that we don't explode or float away; on the contrary, we can trust that the mind's normal anxiety will eventually reassert itself without any effort on our part. We will have to face the painful feelings, the old disappointments that get stirred up when good things happen, but every time we do so, we accomplish a little more of our grief work: we grow stronger, and the old hurts have less power over us because they diminish in proportion to new, reparative experiences.

I worry that the symptomatic relief of depression provided by medication or brief therapy only helps the patient regain a previous level of functioning that was depressed to begin with. As we will see, there's evidence suggesting that the way antidepressants work is by making us less sensitive to all our emotions. Acedia, the absence of feeling, makes for empty lives, and it seems to be on the increase. Getting control of anger, guilt, and shame is not enough for recovery from depression; we also must take responsibility for learning to feel good. We might prefer to play it safe, to avoid or control all emotions, but we simply can't; it doesn't work; our selves and our relationships deteriorate into brittle, bitter, vulnerable shells. We may no longer be depressed but it's only because we're empty. While learning to feel may be temporarily upsetting, in the long haul it adds richness and meaning to our lives.

Learning to Express

There's a crucial distinction between feeling feelings and expressing them. The depressive effort not to feel is usually an unconscious process—we're not aware of denying or stuffing feelings. We often express our emotions with the same lack of awareness, but we need to be more mindful about this. It's not healthy, kind, safe, or wise to express all our emotions. We want to feel them and then make deliberate decisions about how to express them. Choosing not to express won't necessarily make us depressed, but trying not to feel will.

Expression of feeling serves important social functions. It

communicates our meaning to others much better than words alone can say, and they feel something in response. When we wail and cry in grief, we elicit sympathy. When we get angry, our voice gets louder, our nostrils flare, we fill our lungs with air to make ourselves seem bigger (much like dogs or cats, who can also make their hair stand on end), and the object of our anger may be intimidated. When we yawn, others yawn; when we laugh, others laugh. Emotional expression helps us feel connected to others, a part of society, a part of the group.

Expression also helps us feel our feelings. Ask anyone who has ever acted. When we act sad, we feel sad; when we act happy, we feel happy. For the experienced actor, these artificial mood changes don't last, but in everyday life, "going through the motions" often helps us feel the emotions expressed by the action. This is how role play and reenactment in group and family therapy works. Getting the patient to begin to say the words that have been held back so long opens the floodgates of emotion. Considering the relief achieved through this process, it's remarkable how much people hold back from emotional expression out of habit and fear, not out of rational choice.

If you have a spouse or trusted loved one, you are one step ahead in learning how to express yourself emotionally. You and your partner can make a deal and take turns engaging in the following exercise.

Exercise 1: Learning to Express

- Sit comfortably in a quiet place where you will be uninterrupted for a half hour.
- Speak freely and uncensoredly about what's on your mind. Don't worry about making sense, just let yourself ramble. It can just be the events of the day, a problem that's absorbing you, a memory, a fantasy. As you speak, pay attention to how your body feels. Are you feeling sad, downcast, angry, happy? Try to find ways to put those feelings into words. Or are you feeling constrained,

embarrassed, self-conscious? Try to identify what's making you feel that way and move beyond it.

- Your partner will listen sympathetically with full attention. The only comments your partner may make are those that will draw out feelings more. Your partner may not intrude his or her own thoughts, ask for clarification, voice any criticism, or change the subject. Instead, he will say things like "That must have made you mad," or "You seem pleased, but I'm not sure I understand why." In other words, the partner's comments can be addressed only to the emotions in your communication.

After a little practice, you may become aware that you are feeling more than you thought you did. This is exactly the desired effect. People with depression tend to be overly controlled in how they express emotions. As you think about how you are with your loved one, is it possible you could begin to be more expressive now in other situations as well?

I know a woman who, when her depression is coming on, loses the ability to see colors. Everything turns to shades of gray and brown. Emotions are the colors of life. Without emotions, life is just stale, tasteless, dull, and gray. Gaining strength in the ability to experience and express emotions is the first step toward recovery from depression. The emotional self is a part of the self that has largely been lost to the depressive; reestablishing contact with it may take time, but it's worth the effort. We have this unfortunate idea that we should be master of our emotions, that they are part of our animal nature that must be controlled at all costs. Instead, we should seek to live in harmony with our animal nature, to get that side of us and our intellectual and spiritual selves to live together with affection and respect.

Behavior

CHANGING OUR BEHAVIOR is at the heart of undoing depression. If we don't get up and make some changes in our lives, we're not going to learn any new skills and our brains are not going to change. Certainly we have to change our thinking and feeling habits as well, but that can only take us so far.

People with depression generally are working too hard but not getting anywhere. There is often a frantic, driven, compulsive flavor to our methods. Sometimes there is an obvious pattern to how we defeat ourselves; at other times, the pattern, if any, is very subtle. Regardless, we never seem to make as much progress as our activity level warrants. We seem to be afraid to stop, back off, take our bearings, and see if we are still headed in the right direction. In order to recover, we must change these habits. This may come as a shock for some people, who experience their depression as something outside themselves, who are proud of their hard work and stamina, and don't want to question habits that have brought them pride. I don't ask you to give up hard work, I just ask you to make sure that it gets you where you want to go. In this chapter, you will be learning to evaluate how much procrastination and other forms of self-destructive behavior interferes with productive activity, how to develop greater willpower so that you're not a prisoner of bad habits, and how to relax and have a little fun.

Overcoming Procrastination

Most people who are depressed have a hard time being productive. Work—and here I mean everything from paid employment to child-rearing and housekeeping to the kinds of "work" we assign our-selves, like reading a good book or planting a garden—is a chore to the depressed. It drains us, leaves us feeling as bad as before, physi-cally worn out and emotionally depleted, instead of proud of our-selves and invigorated. Other people with depression seem to work very hard all the time, but there is little payoff for their efforts. As with so much of depression, there is a real chicken-or-egg question: is work so difficult because we're depressed, or are we depressed in part because we can't accomplish anything? And as with so many chicken-or-egg situations, we face a false dichotomy: the truth is, poor work habits and depression reinforce each other.

Depressed people tend to be great procrastinators. Procrastination means putting off for a later time what "should" be done now. The "should" may come from without, as with the teenager who dawdles over homework, or from within, as with me planting my garden. When it comes from without, it's easy to see the rebelliousness that procrasti-nation expresses. When it comes from within, it's hard to see immedi-ately what purpose procrastination serves—but it may serve many.[1]

Procrastinators have some big false assumptions about how work works. They assume that really productive people are always in a positive, energetic frame of mind that lets them jump right into piles of paper and quickly do what needs to be done, emerging only when the task is accomplished. On the contrary, motivation follows action instead of the other way around. When we make ourselves face the task ahead of us, it usually isn't as bad as we think, and we begin to feel good about the progress we start making. *Take a step, and motivation follows.* Closely allied to this misunderstanding about motivation is the idea that things should be easy. Depressed people assume that people who are good at work skills always feel confident and easily attain their goals; because they themselves don't feel this way, they assume that they will never be successful. But again, most people who are really successful assume that there are going to be hard times, frustrations, and setbacks along the way. Knowing this in advance, they don't get thrown for a loop and descend into self-blame whenever there's a problem. If we wait until we feel completely prepared and really motivated, we'll spend a lot of our lives waiting.

Procrastination can also help protect the depressed person's precarious self-esteem. We can always tell ourselves we would have done it better if.... The paradigm is the college term paper rushed together in a furious all-nighter. The student protects himself from the risk of exposing his best work by never having the time to do it right. This allows him to protect his fantasied sense of himself as special and uniquely gifted. Procrastination is also a result of the depressed person's tendency toward perfectionism, a crippling problem. Research has shown that the more perfectionistic a depressed person is, the worse his chances of recovery.[2] Trying so hard to make every single little piece of a project perfect, we doom ourselves to disappointment and frustration.

There is a wonderful, sad vignette by Aaron Beck, the originator of cognitive therapy for depression. He had a patient who, despite his deep depression, managed to wallpaper a kitchen. Here's how the dialogue went:

THERAPIST: Why didn't you rate wallpapering the kitchen as a mastery experience?

PATIENT: Because the flowers didn't line up.

THERAPIST: You did in fact complete the job?

PATIENT: Yes.

THERAPIST: Your kitchen?

PATIENT: No, I helped a neighbor do his kitchen.

THERAPIST: Did he do most of the work?

PATIENT: No, I really did almost all of it. He hadn't wallpapered before.

THERAPIST: Did anything else go wrong? Did you spill the paste all over? Ruin a lot of wallpaper? Leave a big mess?

PATIENT: No, no, the only problem was that the flowers didn't line up.

THERAPIST: Just how far off was the alignment of the flowers?

PATIENT (*holding his fingers about an eighth of an inch apart*): About that much.

THERAPIST: On each strip of paper?

PATIENT: No...on two or three pieces.

THERAPIST: Out of how many?

PATIENT: About twenty or twenty-five.

THERAPIST: Did anyone else notice it?

PATIENT: No. In fact my neighbor thought it was great.

THERAPIST: Could you see the defect when you stood back and looked at the whole wall?

PATIENT: Well, not really.[3]

How can you be happy with anything you do when your standards are so high?

David Burns, in *The Feeling Good Handbook,*[4] has a five-step process for defeating procrastination:

1. Cost-benefit analysis. Choose a task you are procrastinating on. Make a list of the advantages of continuing to procrastinate. Now make a list of the advantages of getting started. Be very honest. You may be procrastinating on some tasks because it is not in your best interests to complete them, but you haven't recognized that yet. After listing the advantages and disadvantages, weigh them against each other on a 100-point scale. If the advantages outweigh the disadvantages, now make a similar list of advantages and disadvantages of getting started *today,* and again weigh them against each other on a 100-point scale. If the advantages of starting today outweigh the disadvantages, go on to the next step.

2. Make a plan. Write down the time today when you will start. Now make a list of any problems or obstacles you can think of that might interfere with getting started. Next, for each of those problems and obstacles, identify what you will do to overcome them. Now you have no excuses.

3. Make the job easy. Set realistic goals. Don't expect a perfect product. Don't expect to work for five hours straight. Decide in advance about what you can reasonably expect to accomplish in the reasonable amount of time you want to allocate to this project. Decide which steps must come first. If you want to paint the house, maybe getting to the store to buy the paint is enough progress for the first day.

4. Think positively. Identify any negative thoughts and feelings that are associated with the task; for instance, "Painting is boring" or "The house will look okay for another year" or "I should wait till I'm more in the mood." Now for each of those negative thoughts, think of alternative positive and realistic thoughts that will help you feel more productive and motivated; for instance "I can listen to my iPod while I paint," or "I'll be proud of the house when it's done," or "I'll feel good about getting started."

5. Give yourself credit. Review your progress when you've accomplished the first day's goals. Take time to let yourself feel good about what you've done, and about taking a step toward dealing with procrastination. Make a reward—an ice-cream cone, time with a book, a relaxing bath—contingent on accomplishing the first day's goals.

If this process seems too complex to you, there's also the Irish way of overcoming procrastination. Confronted with a wall too high to climb, the Irishman throws his hat over it. Now he *must* find a way over the wall. If I have to paint a room, I'll likely get the paint and start the first coat as soon as I can, disrupting the whole household in the process. That way I'm fully committed, and have to finish quickly.

There is another simple, useful process psychologists call *chaining,* or making one event depend on another event's being accomplished first. You can make chains that help you get a lot of work done. I want to go play Tomb Raider on my computer, but I'm going to let that be my reward for first going through my outdated magazines. As I go through the pile, I find there's one I really must renew my subscription to. Now I have to do that as well before I play Tomb Raider. Renewing that subscription reminds me that I have a stack of unpaid bills nagging at me. Maybe I can't get the bills all paid, but I can take twenty minutes to get them organized and make a commitment to myself to pay them tomorrow. Now I can go play my computer game feeling a little less overwhelmed by events and a little more deserving of some time to goof off. As you get used to this practice, your chains can get longer and longer without feeling burdensome.

Self-destructive Behavior

It's a cliché that depressed people are self-destructive. After all, suicide is the extreme end of depression. Of milder forms, we say "He keeps shooting himself in the foot," or "She's her own worst enemy." We romanticize the self-destructive tendencies of artists like Dylan Thomas or Kurt Cobain. But this is a very complex and difficult subject of which we have only a dim understanding.

What exactly does it mean to be self-destructive? There are two concrete meanings. One is to engage in behavior that is clearly dangerous or will have a bad outcome. The other is to engage in behavior that backfires on us. The behavior is not, in and of itself, dangerous or harmful, but it has unintended negative effects. Although anyone's plans can backfire, for the depressive this becomes such a pattern that we assume there is an unconscious process at work, sabotaging us.

This discussion leads us to two important defense mechanisms, *acting out* and *passive-aggression.* Remember that defenses are ways of keeping unacceptable feelings, impulses, and wishes out of consciousness. They are as much a part of being human as having fingernails, and help make life much easier for all of us. But some defenses are more adaptive than others.

Acting out means the direct expression of a wish or impulse without the feelings or thoughts that accompany it; it's almost always self-destructive simply because it's not being controlled by the wiser parts of the brain. This is the hallmark defense of adolescence. Juvenile crime is often said to be "acting out" — the child expresses his rage at abusive parents and unreliable authority figures through behaviors such as vandalism, drug abuse, or interpersonal violence, and just doesn't see the implications of his behavior. In my relatively tame adolescence, one of the favorite activities of my group of boys was "lawning" — driving our parents' cars late at night over neighbors' lawns, tearing up grass, shrubs, and small trees. Aside from the obvious attack against the symbols of suburban conformity, what makes me realize it was acting out is that we all thought it was just hilarious and thrilling. We experienced none of the hostility that now, in retrospect, it seems so clear we were expressing.

Therapists often reason that acting out is different from antisocial aggression because the acter-outer unconsciously wants to get caught. In Chapter 17, you'll meet Jason, who accidentally dropped his stash of marijuana at his mother's feet, twice. Jason was asking for limits, asking for his mother to express her love by demanding that the behavior cease. People like Michael Jackson and Elvis Presley may ultimately die because their fame surrounds them with friends and hangers-on who are unwilling to say no to them. Their star power or aura of genius may get their friends caught up in denial, so that no one sees the danger ahead.

Passive-aggression is a difficult concept to explain, though we all experience it. It involves making others feel the destructive energy that we ourselves can't directly express. In psychotherapy, the patient who threatens suicide when her therapist is about to go on vacation is seen as passive-aggressive — she does not feel her anger at the abandoning therapist, but is likely to make the therapist angry with her. In everyday life, anyone in a position of little authority may resort to passive-aggressive behavior as a means of retaining some control — adolescents who refuse to do chores despite repeated warnings, until the parent finally yells, get to feel a certain satisfaction out of being picked on. In the office, the person who insists on doing everything exactly according to the rules doesn't acknowledge his own desire to control everyone else, though they certainly feel his control. Passive-aggression is also the archetypal guilt inducer — George Vaillant refers to the dramatically self-sacrificing person who "gives away the biggest piece of cake in such a way that the recipient ends up feeling punished."[5]

Viewed in this light, procrastination is a form of passive-aggression that the depressive uses very cleverly to make himself feel miserable. The resented authority is not the abandoning therapist or the bossy parent, but the part of the self that says to the depressive, "You really should (wash the dishes, paint the living room, get a better job...)." Instead of acknowledging the conflict between this part of the self that sets standards and moralizes and the part that feels entitled to have the biggest piece of cake, the depressive will procrastinate. Instead of washing the dishes, he will go to the store to buy a new sponge, and while there be tempted by the display of canning supplies and decide now is the time to put up pickles. The next day he'll have more dirty dishes, a lot of cucumbers, and no pickles, because in the middle of the project he'll get frustrated and sit down to watch *Oprah*. He'll be temporarily distracted but his low opinion of himself and his idea that he can't meet his goals has just been reinforced. Of course he may be distracted from these feelings by taking up a whole new project from *Oprah*.

Finding more direct and healthy ways of expressing anger, developing autonomy, and acknowledging a need for intimacy is the obvious strategy to disrupt self-destructive behavior patterns. In clinical practice, many depressed patients are completely unaware of their self-destructive behavior, and many patients who come in because their behavior has gotten them into trouble are completely unaware of their depression. Getting these links established is not easy therapeutic work.

Two Faces of Depression

The self-destruction of depression can take many forms. Many of the depressed patients I've worked with have been pushing themselves too hard, working ineffectively, so driven by fear that their behavior is largely mindless, defensive — in over their heads but forgetting how to swim, struggling, drowning. There is another type of depression, though: those who literally can't get out of bed. They blame themselves for this, and feel guiltier, and feel more and more that there's no use in trying.

Can't-Get-Out-of-Bed Depression

Many people with depression are weighed down by lethargy; they feel a total absence of energy and hope. For some, it feels like an existential crisis: *Why bother? What difference will it make?* Robert, in Chapter 1, was like this. He didn't feel much of anything, and so saw no point in trying to get better. Others, however, simply don't have the energy. They feel as if it is both impossible and pointless to do the simplest things — get out of bed, brush your teeth, make a phone call. Depression can make your entire body hurt, any movement excruciating. Andrew Solomon, in *The Noonday Demon,* gives a chilling account of his months spent like this.[6] Days would drip by slowly, and he would exhaust himself just getting out of bed to go to the bathroom. He lived alone and might have starved to death had not his father moved in to help.

Most people with lethargic depression don't reach this extreme, but they find every activity a great obstacle. It's as if they go through every day with an extra sixty pounds strapped to their arms and legs.

When the day is over, they have to collapse. They have no energy for anything beyond the bare minimum. They hurt throughout their bodies. Sleep is not restorative; they wake up in the morning feeling just as exhausted as they did yesterday, and the thought of getting through another day may bring them to tears. In fact, very often their sleeping patterns become chaotic, so they are never really fully out of bed and rarely really asleep. In a state like this, your condition dominates your thinking; you ruminate endlessly, worry about what's wrong with you, get mad at yourself, and feel guilty. Of course this just makes matters worse.

Sometimes these people are not aware they are depressed; they think the despair and guilt they feel are a natural result of their helplessness. They may go to a physician and get diagnosed with chronic fatigue syndrome or fibromyalgia or chronic Lyme disease or something else. But there are no reliable treatments for these conditions, just as there is not for depression. Antidepressants or stimulants or omega-3 capsules often, but by no means always, help. The patient in this state may wear out his family and friends, lose his job, drop out of school. People can eventually get better, but baby steps are required. Set the alarm, and get up. Have a little breakfast. Read the newspaper. Then you can go back to bed if you want. String together a week like this, and try to do a little more the next week. And so on. Patience is essential. Keeping in mind that this is a very real disease, not simply feeling sorry for yourself, can help.

People in this can't-get-out-of-bed depression really can benefit from someone in their lives who can be both a nurse and a cheerleader, to help them when things are bleakest but nag or cajole them into some physical exercise when things are better. Eventually the exercise will become easier, but practice in the meantime can help shorten the episode and minimize the damage. At the same time, the person doing the nagging also needs to know when to back off and just bring soup. It's a very difficult role, but you don't have to be perfect at it—love, good intentions, and good communication count for a lot.

Spinning-Your-Wheels Depression

Other people with depression don't experience this overpowering lethargy, but instead push themselves too hard and don't get anywhere. This is the kind of depression I'm most familiar with. These are people who can't prioritize, for whom everything seems like an emergency. They're adrenaline junkies, always procrastinating, then running to be on time. They take on too much because they fear that if they stop or slow down the emptiness will catch up to them. They seem to never have time to enjoy themselves, or take a day off, or fix a healthy meal—but they are angry at themselves for this. They are extremely frustrating to loved ones, because they always have good intentions and seem to try hard, but they never really slow down to listen.

People with spinning-your-wheels depression are often caretakers or martyrs, or both. At work or in the family, they may work harder than anyone else but rarely ask directly for recognition of their efforts. They can push themselves to extraordinary limits, right on into old age, fixing meals morning and night, doing the cleaning, the shopping, and the laundry for their overly dependent adult children who still live at home. At work, they may be the boss's executive assistant, working fourteen-hour days for low wages, never taking time off, and taken for granted. In these cases, hard work itself becomes a skill of depression, something that demands so much attention that you rarely think about yourself, your own needs and feelings. If people like this are forced to take time off (usually only because they have burned themselves out), they find that they have no real interests in life, no relationships, no goals. Their overactivity has been an effective distraction from their very low self-esteem, something that usually dates right back to childhood. They usually come to therapy because they have been let down so hard by someone that they feel cheated and angry; or they've had a period of enforced idleness and started to really feel their depression for the first time.

Willpower

People with overactive depression like this are afraid to change, and people with underactive depression really believe they can't. In either case, more self-control—plain old willpower—is essential to recovery.

Remember those jugglers—the college students who practiced juggling every day for three months, allowing the scientists to see gradual growth in gray matter in certain areas of the brain? In my last book, I reviewed all the research showing that willpower is not a character trait doled out at birth, but a set of skills you can learn, like juggling, tennis, or typing. Every time you exercise willpower, you make it easier to use next time, because you're overriding the circuits in your brain that have been reinforcing your weak self-discipline. But if you want to get it written into your brain circuitry, you'll have to practice every day for a while. Here are the tips I found to make this practice easier, adapted with permission from *Happy at Last:*[7]

- *Avoid triggers and distractions.* If you're an alcoholic, stay out of bars. If you eat too much, avoid food shopping. When you have to shop, go in with a list, rush in, and rush out. If you watch too much television, don't sit in your favorite chair. In fact, move it (or the TV) to another room. If you're trying to work at your computer, turn off your Web browser and e-mail. (I sometimes have to go to the extent of unplugging my wireless connection, so I have to get up and go to another room before I can waste time on the Internet.)
- *Avoid enablers.* These are people who make it easy for you to perform your self-defeating behavior. People you go on a smoking break with. Drinking buddies. People who make excuses for you. Explain to these people that you have to put some distance between you while you overcome your bad habit. Your partner may be an enabler, if he or she encourages you to be lazy or feeds you too much food. Try to explain and enlist his or her help.

- *It's usually worse than you expect.* Remember it took three months of daily practice for the jugglers. We psych ourselves up to go on a diet, for instance, by telling ourselves we can lose five pounds the first week. When we don't, we give up. Instead, prepare yourself for the long haul.

- *But it's not as bad as you fear.* Nobody died from starvation on a diet, and most people don't really experience a lot of discomfort. Same goes for giving up any bad habit. You may have a couple of rough days, but they don't last. And pretty soon you start to get some good feelings — pride, self-respect — from sticking with your regimen.

- *Don't try unless you're ready.* All the times you've made a half-hearted attempt and given up have eroded your confidence and will-power. Don't try again unless you've really thought this through and are ready to go to the mat with your problem.

- *Ask for help.* Make a public commitment — that in itself will help keep you honest — by asking those close to you for their help. They might, for instance, avoid talking about food or wild parties while you're around. They might be especially attentive, giving you some recognition for progress, or sympathy when you're having a tough time. Or you might join a group, if there is one for your problems: AA and WeightWatchers are very effective, and the group support helps a great deal with your own motivation.

- *Stimulus control.* If you have trouble getting down to work, for instance, try this: Work only at your desk and only work at your desk. When you find yourself distracted or anxious or unable to decide what to do next, get up from your desk and give yourself a short break. Take your misery elsewhere. Don't try to work when you're not at your desk. Eventually the desk (computer terminal, kitchen, easel) becomes a less dreaded stimulus because it is only associated with productive activity.

- *Reward yourself.* You're doing something that will change your life, and you need to give yourself recognition. You might want to give yourself a special gift or take a trip when you feel you've conquered the problem. You might want to give yourself smaller daily or weekly indulgences as tokens for progress.

• *Baby steps.* Unfortunately for real therapists, Dr. Leo Marvin (*What About Bob?*) was right. You have to learn to walk before you can run. This willpower business is tough. Measure your success in inches. You'll get discouraged, and you may even slip up sometimes. Be sure to give yourself a lot of credit for every good day you have.

• *Don't obsess—distract.* Our brains are constructed so that we can't force ourselves *not* to think about something, especially a worry or a temptation. You can't make a self-destructive impulse disappear by wishing it away, but it often works to make yourself think about something else. Make a list of good memories that you can refer to when you need it; or a list of pleasant activities you can use as distractions—talking with a friend, a walk, a cup of tea, turning the music up really loud and dancing by yourself.

• *Don't let a slip kill your resolve.* Don't slip; but if you do, don't beat yourself up too much. Too many people leap to the conclusion that if you fall off your diet once, you've ruined your chances for success. That's just a rationalization for quitting. Instead, remember that you're attempting a very difficult thing. If you can't be totally perfect, it doesn't mean you're hopeless. Nor does it give you an excuse for giving up. Remember that if you slip up after a week, the effect on your brain of all that week's practice doesn't go away because you slipped. You can pick up where you left off.

• *Savor the positive results.* Pay attention to your feelings as you get out from under that burden you've been carrying around. You may feel freer, stronger, more proud of yourself. You may look better, have more time, and get more done. Let yourself savor these feelings mindfully, with focus and pleasure.

An increase in willpower is great for depression. We generally think of ourselves as weak, lacking character, victimized by life. If you've been fighting depression for a long time, you probably understand that demonstrating willpower a couple of times is not going to completely undo that distorted perception of yourself, but it will start to chip away at it. Just as important is the ability to stop some self-destructive behavior like smoking or overeating, or get better at something that's good for us, like expressing our feelings. As we successfully address more and more elements of that vicious circle, eventually we're going to feel cured.

Depression, Alcohol, and Drugs

If you have problems with alcohol or drug abuse, that's the first place to start applying your new skills of willpower.

Sean was literally driven crazy by his wife's decision to separate. In retrospect, we should have understood that Sean was in an "agitated depression," someone who complains of anxious symptoms more than depression, but is profoundly depressed and impossible to soothe.

A blue-collar worker, Sean had prided himself on being a good father, but knew he was not a terrific husband. He worked hard and made a good living, but he liked to go to the bars and drink after work. Sometimes he would have too much. He'd come home and his wife would yell at him. More than once he hit her. He was ashamed of this, but didn't stop until it was too late. Finally she moved out, taking their children with her. Sean sobered up and joined AA. He pleaded for her to give him another chance, but she wouldn't consider it.

Sean's therapist didn't know what to do with him. The only thing that mattered to him was getting his wife to reconsider, and that was outside his control. When the therapist tried to talk about ways of being a good father even if a divorce took place, Sean wouldn't hear about it. He showed up for all his sessions but didn't find any relief or comfort. He would pace the office, sweat, yell, and cry with frustration.

One night Sean was picked up by the police, asleep in his car in a park. He had a loaded rifle with him. He told them that he had planned to meet someone who was going to buy the gun, but he fell asleep. The police confiscated the weapon and called his sister, whom he was staying with. He told her the same story, and left for work.

On his way to work he stopped in a gun shop. He asked the clerk to see a shotgun. While the clerk had his back turned, Sean loaded the weapon and shot himself in the head. Without his wife, or without the opportunity to undo the pain he'd caused her, Sean couldn't live.

Sean should have been in a psychiatric hospital or a residential substance-abuse program, where he could have been protected from his own impulses. If medications had worked for him, even as an outpatient he might have been safer. But he wouldn't accept any of these alternatives. He became so depressed when he stopped drinking that it only makes sense to believe he was depressed to begin with, and had been treating the depression with alcohol.

There is a very clear link between depression and substance abuse, especially alcohol. Some people who have depression become alcoholics because drinking temporarily numbs the pain. Some alcoholics, when sobered up, find that they are terribly depressed, more so than is accounted for by the effects of their drinking alone. Others become depressed because cleaning up the mess they've made of their lives is overwhelming.

Alcohol is perhaps the most effective drug there is. It causes an immediate sense of euphoria, gives confidence, and lowers inhibitions — all of which feel very good to someone with depression. Unfortunately, these effects are only temporary, and the after-effects only reinforce depression. After the initial euphoria, alcohol causes a depressed mood. The person feels weak, guilty, and ashamed — and is often in worse trouble because of decisions made or actions taken while intoxicated.

Alcohol is in the same class of drugs as popular tranquilizers like Valium and Xanax, and the general anesthetics—it is a "sedative-hypnotic." These drugs have a depressant effect on the central nervous system. They slow down thinking; they interfere with balance, coordination, and muscular control; and in larger doses they can make us unconscious and interfere with automatic central nervous system functions like breathing. The reason why alcohol is so popular as a recreational drug is that its effect comes in stages. Its initial effect is to depress the inhibitory functions of the brain. It reduces inhibitions and takes away our anxieties; it makes us feel more smart, interesting, and capable; and it permits us to take risks that we otherwise wouldn't.

But these initial desired effects are only temporary; within a few hours, the sedative effects of alcohol take over. We feel sleepy, confused, lethargic, and irritable; we lose motor control, coordination, and balance. With regular use we develop a tolerance for alcohol—it requires larger doses to produce the desired effects—and we develop a dependence on it. We need it, we crave it, we don't feel like ourselves without it. Eventually the body adapts to alcohol use and will complain—through withdrawal symptoms like anxiety, insomnia, tremors, and hallucinations—when alcohol is stopped.

There is just nothing good to say about heavy alcohol use. Eventually, drinking becomes a life, a self. Recovering alcoholics will say "the bottle was drinking me." The overriding goal in life becomes to drink and to maintain ready access to alcohol; we go to work in order to earn money to drink; we plan our nonwork activities around alcohol consumption. And family and friends get evaluated primarily on the basis of whether they help or hinder drinking. That is why AA succeeds where nothing else does with alcoholics: it offers a new life. The concept of the "recovering alcoholic" is an identity to replace an old one based on alcohol.

For many depressives, alcohol is a constant temptation, if not a real problem. Alcohol becomes, for a while, a trusted friend who is readily available, whose effect is predictable and reliable. Lacking the ability to soothe ourselves when troubled or energize ourselves when depressed, we turn to alcohol. William Styron makes no bones about the fact that his first episode of major depression resulted from being forced to suddenly give up drinking:

> *Alcohol was an invaluable senior partner of my intellect, besides being a friend whose ministrations I sought daily—sought also, I now see, as a means to calm the anxiety and incipient dread that I had hidden away for so long in the dungeons of my spirit.... [But suddenly] I discovered that alcohol in minuscule amounts, even a mouthful of wine, caused me nausea, a desperate and unpleasant wooziness, a sinking sensation and ultimately a distinct revulsion. The comforting friend had abandoned me not gradually and reluctantly, like a true friend might do, but like a shot—and I was left high and certainly dry, and unhelmed.[8]*

Alcohol is usually a lot less faithful than Styron described. It's very common, after an evening of drinking, to wake at three or four in the morning when the effects of alcohol start to wear off, in a very anxious and confused state. You begin to obsess, either about the challenges of the next day, or all the ways you screwed up the day before, and you can't get back to sleep for hours. F. Scott Fitzgerald, a renowned drinker, wrote in his account of his breakdown that "in a true dark night of the soul, it's always 3:00 in the morning."[9] All these nighttime battles leave you exhausted and barely able to function the next day.

The chances are that if you're depressed and use alcohol at all, it's a problem for you. Those initial disinhibitory effects feel too good; it's like magic for someone who feels anxious and insecure. Most depressed people either don't use alcohol at all, or else struggle with it. Our battle with alcohol becomes one more manifestation of the depression. We get in trouble, we make resolutions to change, we discipline ourselves for a while, then the trouble starts again and we feel confirmed in our sense of ourselves as hopeless failures.

If any of this sounds like you, then my advice is simple and direct: stop drinking and get your depression treated. Consider checking in to a rehab program; your insurance will probably pay a good portion of the tab. Just removing yourself from the opportunity to drink for a few weeks may make all the difference in the world. Check out AA groups in your area; you may find a terrific support system. AA meetings used to be difficult for depressives because they weren't tolerant of feelings or medication, but more and more groups are opening up their attitudes on these issues. Regardless, you have to stop drinking, and you have to face the fact that you will be changing yourself from this point on. You have to challenge the emotional habits of depression that perpetuate its cycle, and you won't get better unless you do.

The same applies to any other drug that you might abuse, whether you get it from a doctor or from the street. Some people with depression are able to use milder drugs only occasionally, for recreation, but they're the exception. The euphoria or excitement that drug use brings is a big temptation to keep on using more. Depressed people in general are much better off living a sober lifestyle. You have to develop pride in your self-discipline, and develop the ability to feel good on your own. This may take some time, but it's worth it.

Learning to Relax

Most of us depressed people are not exactly the life of the party, but this is not entirely our fault. We would like to be looser and more relaxed, but we literally don't know how. Generally we are either engaged in frenetic activity to keep our demons at bay, or sunk into depressed lethargy, exhausted by our own busy-ness. We have to take ourselves by the hand and teach ourselves to relax. We need to make a conscious effort to learn to slow down, relax, and enjoy the small pleasures of life.

We'll see in Chapter 15 that most people are happier at work than at leisure; so everyone could benefit from learning how to make the best of leisure time. Especially for those with depression, who have a nagging sense of guilt that gets worse when we're not productive and the tendency to sink into self-hating lethargy when there's no outside stimulation, we need to deliberately find ways to add joy and satisfaction when we're not working.

One approach is to make leisure more like work: to add opportunities for deeper engagement or productive activity in our downtime. We can do this by cultivating activities or hobbies in which we can have a sense of growing mastery of a skill or knowledge base, like a golfer who continuously refines his game, or a cook who is always trying to find new things for the family to enjoy. Improving your home or garden or stamp collection always makes you feel better. Members of the choir benefit not only from pride in their growing skills as singers but also from the sense of being part of a committed group that does something requiring skill to bring joy to others. That brings us to another approach to downtime, which is to make it meaningful — like joining the local rescue squad, volunteering for a charity or a political cause, or simply making an effort to better the lives of others in small ways every day. And of course most of these activities bring us into contact with others, in shared tasks or in playful activities like singing or dancing. There has been a lot of research indicating that most people find leisure activities the biggest source of long-term satisfaction.[10]

At the same time, it would be nice if we could enjoy doing nothing in particular: just take a Sunday off and read the paper, watch TV, maybe take a little walk, without hearing the Inner Critic and becoming overwhelmed with negative thinking. You have to be pretty far out of the woods of depression in order to do this, so consider it a recovery milestone when you can. I believe that regular mindfulness practice will help develop this ability, because you'll rarely be bored. Mindfulness shows that there is always a lot going on beneath the surface, always something new to see or learn. So maybe we should think about developing skills for more passive activities—reading, playing, exercising your imagination, lying in the hammock, simply relaxing. These activities seem so antithetical to today's world that we need reinforcement and practice in order to do them right, without either feeling guilty or having the nagging sense that we ought to be doing something *productive*. These things are productive, but not as we usually define the concept. They produce good health, an active mind, and the opportunity to get in touch with our interior selves. They make us more at ease, more fun to be around, more at home in our skin, and more comfortable with the concept of rewarding ourselves with what really matters.

Of course there are other, more traditional, ways of relaxing, if we give ourselves time for them. Prayer, communing with God, is one. Walking, when it can be performed as a focus of attention in itself, can permit the passive attitude of meditation at the same time as the body is exercised. Sports that demand concentration—swimming, golf, tennis—can have the same result (of course you don't want to be caught up in a competitive spirit, but to pay attention to the movement of your body and its interaction with the forces of nature). Intimate conversation, and indeed the act of sex, can take us out of ourselves and help us relax, as can reading a good book, taking a warm bath, weeding the garden.

I want to say a special word about music. I never could play an instrument well, but I learned early what music could do to one's soul. In the darkest hours of my adolescence, I would stick my head inside our old-fashioned cabinet record player and get swept away by Borodin's Polovtsian Dances or Strauss waltzes, later by the Beatles and the Rolling Stones, Bob Dylan and Joan Baez. Music short-circuits consciousness and goes directly to the part of our brain that has to do with emotions and mood. It can reliably lift us out of depression—but to do so, it can't be played as background music. You have to stop what you're doing, pay attention to the music, and play it loud. Even sad music can stop a depressed mood. After all, depression isn't sadness, it's the absence of feeling, and sometimes a good cry is healing.

Then of course there are pets. Pets don't necessarily lift us out of depression—they can get lazy with us, and they'll love us even if we neglect them—but they certainly can help. If we live alone, they can give us play, companionship, and, best of all, that unconditional love. Having someone around who's always happy to see you can do a lot to shake you out of black moods. If we take the trouble to imagine how another species experiences the world, we become more mindful and less caught up in our own bleak perspective. People with depression are sometimes afraid of making a commitment to a pet, but you have to start somewhere with commitments.

Recreation means re-creation of the self. What all recreation does is make us stop our driven, frantic behavior to look around and listen. Losing self-consciousness temporarily in meditation or some other form of relaxation, we can come back to our problems with a different perspective. We may have spent all day butting our heads against a wall. When we step back, we may see that there is a door in the wall we didn't notice in our frenzy of activity. We need to give ourselves time to heal from the emotional bruises of the day. As we do, we may be momentarily frightened by feelings, thoughts, and images that we ordinarily try to keep out of consciousness. This is where we have to start learning that our own feelings are nothing to fear.

8

Thinking

IT'S BEEN TESTED AND PROVEN for forty years now that depressed people have certain characteristic ways of thinking that keep them stuck, unable to find new solutions. There are distinctive biases in our perception of ourselves and the world, characteristic logical errors that support the depression, and false assumptions and beliefs that never get tested against reality. These thought patterns become entrenched and automatic; it takes therapy or serious self-examination with a good self-help book for us to become aware of them, and then it takes mindful practice to replace them with more logical or healthy thinking.

Distorted Perception and Bad Logic

Aaron Beck, his colleagues, and his successors are the leading researchers on how depression affects thought processes and how the way we think affects our depression. They developed the whole field of cognitive behavior therapy, which is still the *sine qua non* for treatment of depression.[1] It's easy to teach, it can be put in a manual, and it's so consistent that it can be used for meaningful research. It was the first psychological treatment that was empirically demon-strated to be effective against depression.

The thesis is that recovery starts by identifying thought processes that reinforce depression, and teaching the patient to become more aware of and challenge those thought processes. And it seems to work at least as well as antidepressants, in fact definitely better over the long run. Beck and his group have identified a "cognitive triad": three patterns of distorted thinking, common to many people with depression. This is not theory, this is fact; depressed people reliably and demonstrably differ from others in the following ways:

1. The self. The depressed person is his own worst critic. He sees himself as defective, inadequate, or deprived. He thinks that he deserves unhappiness because of his flaws, and that because of his deficits he is unable to achieve happiness. He tends to underestimate and criticize himself, and he lacks hope because he believes he is missing the essential character traits that lead to fulfillment.

2. Present reality. The depressed person interprets interactions with the everyday world—people, events, and inanimate objects— differently from other people. He sees the demands the world makes on him as impossible to attain. He interprets his interactions with the world as representing defeat or deprivation, whereas an outside observer would see some successes in the failures, some acceptance among the rejections.

3. Future expectations. The depressed person has a negative expectation for the future. He doesn't anticipate relief from his present suffering, and when he considers trying something new, he expects to fail.

Interacting with the distorted perception of the depressive are a number of ways we consistently make errors in logic and judgment. Beck has observed and categorized a long list.[2] The most important are:

• *Overgeneralizing,* or the tendency to assume that if it's true once, it's likely to be true all the time. Just because you perform poorly on one test doesn't mean you will continue to do badly, but the depressive is likely to think so.

• *Selective abstraction* consists of focusing on a detail taken out of context, ignoring other evidence, and drawing conclusions on the basis of the detail. If I'm depressed when I give a speech, I'm likely to remember the awkward pauses and the questions I don't feel I answered adequately, rather than the 90 percent of the speech that went over well. Unless I watch myself, I am likely to judge the whole experience on the basis of a few negative details.

• *Excessive responsibility.* People who are depressed tend to assume that they are responsible for bad things that happen, while good things are caused by others, by luck, or other factors that can't be controlled. When the car skids on an icy road, the depressive thinks, "I shouldn't have been driving today," rather than, "The road is icy."

• *Self-reference.* Depression leads to a negative self-conscious-ness, a tendency to magnify one's own part in things, even to believe that you are the center of attention. The depressed child in the school play thinks that all eyes are on her, that any mistake she makes will be the talk of the town. You also assume that you're to blame when-ever anything goes wrong.

• *Catastrophizing.* Depressed people are well known for taking bad news to the extreme: "I had a flat on the way to work today. I must need new tires. They'll all go bad and I can't drive to work. I'll have to quit my job. I'll never find another job. I'll starve."

• *Dichotomous thinking* refers to the tendency to see every-thing as good or bad, black or white. The depressive puts himself in the bad category, people he admires in the good. He doesn't see faults or weaknesses in those he admires, nor does he see strengths in himself. He extends this kind of thinking to include those who seem to like him, deciding that they must be in the bad category, too — uninformed or ignorant if they are stupid enough to like him. Thus Groucho: "I wouldn't belong to a club that would have me as a member."

• *Emotional reasoning* means that whatever you feel is true; going with your guts instead of your brain. "Jane gave me a funny look just now, and it scared me. She must be out to get me."

It should be evident that these kinds of cognitive errors are self-fulfilling prophecies. If you expect to do badly on tests, your chances of doing well are diminished. The negative expectation may mean that you won't prepare, that you'll be more anxious, and that you'll have difficulty concentrating and remembering. The little girl in the school play is more likely to present herself badly because her excessive self-consciousness interferes with her skills. Expecting the worst all the time can lead to never really trying. Dichotomous thinking means never being able to evaluate oneself as highly as others.

Beck has also identified a number of *depressogenic assumptions*—false beliefs that set us up for depression:

• In order to be happy, I have to be successful in whatever I undertake.
• To be happy, I must be accepted by all people at all times.
• If I make a mistake, it means I am incompetent.
• I can't live without you.
• If somebody disagrees with me, it means he doesn't like me.
• My value as a person depends on what others think of me.

There are many others. They are so glaringly illogical that they have to be kept out of conscious awareness. It's only when we back off and take an objective look at our own behavior that we can see assumptions like these at work. We don't arrive at these beliefs through logic and experience, rather through making assumptions that fit with our own guilt, self-blame, and endless picking at ourselves. Such beliefs are pervasive and insidious in their effects on our lives. We can't possibly be accepted by everyone at all times; some people will want things from us that violate our dignity and our most basic values. Others will want exactly opposite things from us, and we must choose one or the other or run the risk of alienating both. If we feel that we can't live without another person, it means we'll do anything to avoid displeasing them, and then where's our self-worth? If we feel that everyone who disagrees with us doesn't like us, we are likely to distort our own principles and values for the sake of pleasing others, and then we won't think much of ourselves.

These depressed assumptions are supported by automatic negative thoughts — the knee-jerk reactions that have become the default mode of thinking under stress. One patient noticed how one day when she started listening to people praising her performance, other thoughts immediately began to intrude: "Oh, no, they don't know the real you, they don't know how pathetic you are, they don't know what a loser you are." It's a minor breakthrough when people realize that these thoughts have been going on in the background for a long time, and for the first time they begin to experience the voice as something alien. Many people, once they become aware of this pattern, experience a certain grim joy in recognizing how they "do it" to themselves. Some like the acronym ANTS for automatic negative thoughts, because like ants they seem to creep in from nowhere to spoil the picnic.[3] Patients can learn to counter such thoughts by simple commands to the self: *Don't go there. Don't listen to that voice. Worry about that later. That's not my problem.* You can visualize rubbing out the ANTS with the sole of your shoe. Mindfulness practice (see Chapter 9) will help dramatically to achieve this detachment.

Jon Kabat-Zinn[4] and others have suggested that we get in the habit of noticing how we endlessly judge things. Sit in a quiet place for fifteen minutes. Don't try to control your thoughts, but passively notice them as they rise to the surface. Notice how we attach values to them — this is good, that is bad, this is pleasant, that is scary. This judging is a habit, borne of stress. We are not really evaluating things objectively, we are attaching values to them based on old experiences, stereotypes, and surface impressions, which are probably not true—but they turn into self-fulfilling prophecies. If you keep a grim look on your face, people will avoid you, and your belief that people are unfriendly will just be reinforced. But if you just try smiling more, you'll get a different impression of people. The depressive usually judges things as negative, painful, difficult, or frightening, but this is a bias, a mindset we can put aside. Because most of our attention is directed at the self, we judge ourselves negatively too: helpless, weak, dependent, incompetent, and the default person to blame for everything that goes wrong. But we don't have to keep on judging; we can see that all this judging comes from our stress, from our need to quickly classify each new experience so we can be ready for the next one. Instead, we can learn to take each new experience as unique. In doing so, we may realize that hopelessness comes from our habit of judging.

Cognitive therapy consists of an organized effort guided by the therapist—but requiring the active collaboration of the patient—to change these faulty habits in thinking. Beck generally ducks the chicken-or-egg question: does faulty thinking lead to an experience of the world and the self that we call depression, or is depression something else, one manifestation of which is this kind of faulty thinking? Empirically, the question doesn't need to be answered. If changing thinking patterns leads to relief from depressive symptoms—and it often does—who cares which came first?

Pessimism and Optimism

Martin Seligman is well known now for developing the field of positive psychology and his *Authentic Happiness* book and website. But he earned his reputation in academic psychology long before this, for conducting the original studies that led to a "learned helplessness" model of depression. Seligman studied dogs under conditions in which some could escape from mild electric shocks, others not.

Exposed to new situations, those dogs who had escaped in the past continued to escape, but most of the dogs who had not been able to escape did not even try. Even when it was obvious that safety just required jumping over a small barrier, these dogs simply lay down and whimpered—they seemed to have developed the concept that they were helpless to control their fate.

These experiments sound cruel, but Seligman was certain of his purpose. He had always been fascinated with the problem of what makes some people bounce back from stresses that make others collapse. As a boy of thirteen, he had seen his father, who seemed so strong and reliable, suffer a stroke that left him paralyzed, despondent, and helpless. As a college student with ambitions to change the world, he saw helplessness in every aspect of society. He was determined to try to explain the problem. His experiments were the beginning of the end for the simple-minded behaviorism of B. F. Skinner and his followers—so influential in American psychology but finally a blind alley—who argued that we learn things simply because behavior that is rewarded is repeated, behavior that is punished becomes less frequent. According to the behaviorists, dogs should have been unable to form cognitions or expectations like helplessness—and man's cognitions were simply artifacts of reward-punishment sequences. The learned helplessness phenomenon was impossible to explain through behaviorism.

Learned helplessness is very much like depression. It can explain many self-defeating patterns of behavior—the wife who endures an abusive husband, the troubles people have with diets, smoking, drinking, the negative expectations of inner-city youth. These people have learned the concept that there is nothing they can do to escape or change. Equally important, though, is an aspect of Seligman's work that has received comparatively little attention—some dogs never learn helplessness. In later experiments with humans, in which various noxious stimuli were administered under situations of control and no control, some people never gave up. With both dogs and people, it was impossible to teach about one-third of subjects that they were helpless. What makes the difference? What accounts for this determination not to give up in the face of consistent failure?

Although Seligman is a cognitive-behavioral psychologist, he has a different view on the cognitive habits of depressives from that of Beck.[5] Seligman focuses on the concept of *explanatory style*—the different ways we have of thinking about how the world works. He notes that people who tend to give up easily have certain explanatory styles in common. They tend to see bad events as *permanent* and good events as temporary, whereas people with an optimistic explanatory style perceive events in just the opposite manner. Thus, when something bad happens to a depressed person, he might think, "I'm all washed up," when a more optimistic person might think, "I can get over this." And when something good happens, the depressive will think, "I got lucky" instead of "I deserve this."

Besides permanence, another dimension of explanatory style is *pervasiveness*. Pervasiveness refers to how much influence one event will have on the rest of our lives, how much it seems to exemplify a predictable pattern rather than a specific case. Pessimistic people see bad events as more pervasive than specific. "There's no such thing as an honest mechanic" rather than "That mechanic is dishonest." Optimistic people tend to see bad events as unique rather than pervasive: "I don't feel well today" versus "I'm always getting sick." Of course, the reverse is true for good events. Pessimistic people see them as unique, lucky breaks rather than a part of a pattern: "I got lucky on the math test today" rather than "I'm good at math."

The third aspect of explanatory style is *personalization*. When bad things happen, we can blame ourselves, or we can blame others.* When good things happen, we can assume that we were just in

---

* Of course, to blame others consistently and unrealistically is no healthier than to blame ourselves all the time. Ideally, we want to perceive the world clearly and objectively. But all of us have some tendency to generalize in predictable patterns.

the right place at the right time, or think that we had something to do with it. People who tend to blame themselves when bad things happen have low self-esteem: "I'm stupid," "I can't do anything right." People with healthy self-esteem are less likely to accept blame: "It's your fault as much as mine," "I refuse to let you make me the bad guy in this argument." Optimistic people tend to think they can cause good things to happen; pessimists think it's just luck. The culmination of permanence, pervasiveness, and personalization in depression is "Things are always rotten everywhere, and it's all my fault." The more objective and optimistic way of thinking is "Things are sometimes rotten, but not all the time, and there are many forces at work when things go bad."

Seligman is the only writer I know to give an operational definition of hope. He says that hope consists of the ability to find temporary and specific (i.e., nonpervasive) explanations for bad events. When faced with a setback, the hopeful person sees it as unique: "I didn't get that job, but the interviewer didn't seem to like me, and I didn't really prepare as well as I should. I'll do better next time." When explanations for bad events are more permanent and pervasive, no one can be hopeful: "I didn't get that job. None of the interviews go well. I always get nervous and make a fool of myself. I'll never get the job I want." Depression can almost be defined as the abandonment of hope. When we're depressed, we feel that hope has abandoned us, but this is a two-way street. Our thinking has become so prejudiced, our view of the world so constrained, that we blind ourselves to hope just because it doesn't fit our paradigm.

Identifying and Challenging Beliefs

Cognitive therapists want to arm us with the strengths of empirical science. They want us to conduct research on ourselves — to observe ourselves objectively, to draw conclusions from our observations, and to test the validity of those conclusions against wider experience. They may suggest slightly different methods, but it all comes down to:

- Identifying stressful situations
- Examining our thoughts and behavior under stress
- Determining what beliefs underlie our responses to stress
- Learning to challenge those beliefs
- Identifying alternative responses to stress
- Examining the effects of those responses, incorporating them into our belief system and behavior patterns if successful, modifying them further if not

It's vital to emphasize that we can only become aware of our self-destructive beliefs through therapy or some means of objective observation, not through introspection; it's like trying to see the back of your head. A simple form to use for recording these observations is reproduced on page 134. The depressogenic beliefs we have will get in the way of seeing ourselves clearly, so we have to do the recording. In cognitive therapy, this is part of the work the depressed patient must do to help his recovery, to begin to develop new strengths and skills to replace the old ones that reinforce depression.

If this feels to you much like the Mood Journal, don't be surprised. Both are designed to help you recognize characteristic patterns of responding to external events—the Mood Journal to recognize patterns of emotional response, the Daily Record of Dysfunctional Thoughts to recognize patterns in thinking. These dysfunctional feeling and thinking patterns are manifestations of our own psychological defenses at work. They help insulate us from facing some unpleasant truths—you *can't* always have what you want, I *am* mad at my child, I *am* attracted to my friend's wife, I *can't* please everyone. I don't want to tell you that the honest, regular use of either of these tools will be easy. What are defenses for, if not to protect us from harsh reality? But we must keep in mind that reality, though it may be harsh, is real, while the depression we create for ourselves in trying to avoid it is not only harsher yet but unnecessary.

Daily Record of Dysfunctional Thoughts[6]

Date	Situation	Emotion(s)	Automatic Thought(s)	Rational Response	Outcome
	Describe: I. Actual event leading to unpleasant emotion, or	I. Specify sad, anxious, angry, mixed, conflicted, etc.	I. Write automatic thoughts that preceded emotion(s)	I. Write rational response to automatic thought(s)	I. Rerate belief in automatic thought(s), I–100
	2. Stream of thoughts, daydream, or recollection leading to unpleasant emotion	2. Rate intensity of emotion, I–100	2. Rate belief in automatic thought(s), I–100	2. Rate belief in rational response, I–100	2. Specify and rate subsequent emotions, I–100
Jan. I	I. 2.	I. 2.	I. 2.	I. 2.	I. 2.
Jan. 2					

Instructions: When you experience an unpleasant emotion, note the situation that seemed to stimulate the emotion. Then note the automatic thought associated with the emotion. Record the degree to which you believe this thought: I = not at all, 100 = completely. In rating degree of emotion I = a trace, 100 = the most intense possible.

Cognitive therapy has become so accepted now as a standard treatment for depression that some are considering depression largely a symptom of dysfunctional thought processes. This runs the risk of encouraging the depressive's belief that he needs more control, not less. If he continues to be depressed, he is likely to feel that he has done a poor job of applying cognitive methods, which just reinforces his sense of self-blame and inadequacy. Depressives need to get out of their heads and into their hearts and their bodies. If you're using cognitive therapy you must remember that depression is a very complex condition, that changing faulty thought processes is just one of many possible ways of treating it, and that addressing these thought processes is going to have repercussions in other areas of your life: how you process feelings, how you communicate with loved ones, how you feel about yourself.

Depressive Realism

If the depressed reader is feeling a little beaten up right now about everything that's wrong with the way you think, take heart: in some ways, depressed people tend to see reality more objectively than the nondepressed. For instance, depressed people tend to be more accurate judges of themselves than "normal" people are. Asked to give an impromptu speech in front of an audience, then asked to rate their performance, people who are depressed tend to be more objective than the nondepressed; people who are not depressed tend to rate their performance more highly than objective observers do. Not that the depressed are objective; they have a negative bias and rate themselves lower than average. But the nondepressed are biased to rate themselves *much* higher than average, with a greater degree of error than the depressed.

Another example from the lab: college students are given a controller and asked to play a video game. What they don't know is that in actuality the controller doesn't work, and the video game is playing itself at random. The more depressed students are quicker to figure this out—they will turn to the experimenter and complain that the controller is broken—while nondepressed students will go on happily pushing buttons. They develop the illusion of control,[7] while depressed people stick with what's called "depressive realism." It's as if most so-called normal people see the world through rose-colored glasses—certain comforting illusions that protect them from frustration and despair—while depressed people dispense with those illusions. Sadder but wiser.

But there's a complication. Although depressed people may evaluate themselves more accurately than the nondepressed, there is still a powerful negative bias. Plus, depressed people vastly overestimate the performance of others. Those impromptu speeches? Depressed people give others scores that are far too high compared to the norm. The same pattern is found when you ask people to estimate how socially accepted they are.[8] Nondepressed people think that others like them, even if they don't; depressed people think that others don't like them, even if they do. They may view themselves a bit more accurately than nondepressed people, but they view others less accurately.[9]

Julie Norem, in a thoughtful book called *The Positive Power of Negative Thinking,*[10] points out the virtues of what she calls "defensive pessimism." Defensive pessimists expect and prepare for the worst, but are not so depressed that they can't be pleasantly surprised when things turn out well. She suggests that if you think this way, it's fruitless to try to turn yourself into an optimist; instead, control your pessimism to keep it from turning into depression and cynicism. Among other things, being prepared for the worst can help insulate you from disappointment. Defensive pessimists do things like work very hard to prepare themselves, while optimists may blithely assume they'll breeze through. In some situations, that optimism is a self-fulfilling prophecy; confident, optimistic people tend to be liked more by other people, and they benefit from a "halo effect" that results in others overrating their performance. On objective tasks, however, the defensive pessimist who has done his homework will outshine the unprepared optimist. There are other benefits to being a little cynical; for instance, defensive pessimists make good attorneys and physicians, careers in which you have to think through and prepare for everything that could go wrong.

Anyone who's been through a serious episode of depression is far too wise to develop the kinds of positive illusions that sustain others in wishful thinking and happy expectations; defensive pessimism may be the best adaptation that a depressive in recovery can hope for. But I have to point out that the virtues of depressive realism and defensive pessimism do not apply to anyone who's seriously depressed. If you're in that state, your thought processes are so distorted, so hopeless and negative, that you have to change them drastically if you want to get better. Later on, as you're on the road to recovery, knowing about the cognitive distortions of optimists and depressive realists will help you gain greater objectivity.

Stress and Depression

Exercise 2: Your Dirty Laundry

Take a piece of paper and make a list of everything that's wrong with you. All the parts of yourself that you like the least, that embarrass you or make you ashamed. Bad habits from nose picking to yelling at the dog to things that actually hurt others. Weaknesses and character flaws like being anxious or letting others walk all over you. The things that make you wince or give you a sudden sinking feeling when you think about them: social awkwardness, can't catch a fly ball, pimples, all the things you think are wrong with your body. Even things that other people have accused you of but you're not sure you're guilty of—but keep you wondering—your old girlfriend who said you were selfish; the work colleague who seems to think you don't pull your weight. Give this a good ten minutes, you want to get everything out there. Please don't read the next paragraphs until you've finished your ten minutes; we don't want to give the gimmick away.

Okay? Now think about how many years you've struggled with these issues. If you're like everyone else, most of them have probably been there since adolescence or early adulthood, when we first become socially aware enough to realize that we're different from others. Some have probably been there since childhood. In any case, a good long time.

Can you step back and simply listen to the voice that tells you all these bad things? Does it remind you of someone? Does it sound like a family member, a character on TV or in the movies, or a monster of your own making?

How many ways have you tried to change these things you dislike about yourself? Resolutions, therapy, self-help books, confessions, pledges, groups, or drugs. How often have you tried? Does the thought of trying again seem unbearable, or are you still willing to fight?

Out of all your efforts, how often have you succeeded? Obviously not very often, or these things wouldn't still be on your list. You've probably tried everything you know. Are you willing to consider the idea that maybe you don't know how to change these things? That maybe the conventional powers of the mind aren't the right tools?

What if I suggest you stop fighting? What if the fighting is actually making the problem worse, or at least keeping it alive?

The Inner Critic

If you're like most people doing that last exercise, thinking of everything that's wrong with you, you started out slow but quickly got in gear. There was a part of you that could really get in the spirit of raking yourself over the coals. That's the Inner Critic, and it's a very big aspect of depression. It's the voice that's constantly judging you and finding you wanting. It's the voice that gives you all the blame when things go wrong. It doesn't forget and it can't forgive. *What's wrong with you? Get yourself together! Why haven't you gotten to work yet? You'll never amount to anything!* If you think about it, you'll realize that this voice pops up most often when you're under stress. It's the voice of fear, looking for a simple explanation for a confusing situation, and it settles quickly on the usual suspect.

There's another part of you that tries to defend against the attacks of the Inner Critic. I call it the Timid Defender. It can't be effective because it uses the usual habits of the mind that never work: the same old defense mechanisms like denial, rationalization, dissociation. Distractions like alcohol and drugs, overspending and overeating. It has us trying to escape or forget about the Critic, but that backfires, because while we're escaping or forgetting, we're giving the Critic more ammunition. The Critic, it seems, always knows better. *You just make a fool of yourself, pretending to be something you're not. Kidding yourself. You can't fool me that easily!*

This is how misery persists. We make ourselves miserable by blaming ourselves, then we make ourselves more miserable by trying to hide or run away from our own conscience. It never works. Therapy works by changing the rules. Therapy doesn't silence the Inner Critic, nor strengthen that Defender; instead, it helps people detach from this struggle. When people are beating themselves up, I suggest they're being too hard on themselves. When they're in defensive mode, I help them face what they're afraid of.

A good friend of mine uses the phrase *compassionate curiosity* to describe the ideal therapist's attitude toward the patient. We begin therapy with a much more compassionate, kind, understanding stance toward the patient and his problems than the patient has himself. And we are curious, in a calm, unafraid way — we want to understand how things got to be so bad, and we assume that by fearlessly facing reality we will help the patient find relief from his distress.

That battle between the Inner Critic and the Timid Defender is much like the way inconsistent parents treat their children. When the Defender is in charge we indulge and spoil ourselves; we let ourselves off the moral hook; we make promises to ourselves we know we won't keep. But that Inner Critic is still there like an angry parent, waiting for our defenses to slip—as they always do—ready to condemn us, always finding that we don't measure up. We vacillate between spoiling ourselves and punishing ourselves. And, as with children who are raised that way, we end up frightened and traumatized, with no self-esteem and a lot of self-hate. Compassion replaces all that with patience, gentleness, love, grace, mercy, concern. It suggests giving up judging and replacing it with empathy, a willingness to face the truth and all your feelings about it, without fear but with confident strength.

Curiosity suggests a little cool detachment from the emotional heat, a desire to understand objectively why we feel what we feel, why we do what we do—especially when it's troublesome or self-defeating. *Why did I get angry just then? What's making me so blue today?* We look at ourselves, not to torture ourselves, not to give ammunition to the Critic, not with desperation for a quick fix, but with compassion, sincere interest, and the belief that there are answers that make sense. No matter how nonsensical our behavior, no matter how odd our feelings, there are always reasons—and knowing the truth will help set us free. We look a little deeper than usual, with more objectivity, and we don't just slap ourselves on the wrist and make an empty promise to do better next time. *Why? What's bothering me? Why am I afraid to look?* We understand that our feelings are just human; they won't destroy us or drive us crazy. Most likely, they are tapping on our shoulder, trying to tell us something important.

When we're bouncing around between the Inner Critic and the Timid Defender, who's at the controls? Who's running our lives, making our decisions? It's like we have the Three Stooges up in our heads. Moe, the brutal sadist, torturing us while the ineffectual Larry whines pathetic excuses. Curly, the id in this metaphor, full of appetites and drives, causes all the trouble in the first place. Nobody's in charge of our lives, and the plane is yawing and swooping all over the sky, never getting anywhere and always in danger of crashing. We need a wise, calm, resourceful pilot to step in and get rid of these characters. Yet we need to find him within ourselves. That's where mindfulness comes in.

As I said, we start picking on ourselves because we're afraid; we have stresses we don't know how to handle. But no one has a stress-free life. Sickness, loss, financial problems, job problems are things that all of us will have to deal with. Yet in reviewing new cases week after week at our mental health center, I was constantly struck by how often bad luck had played a major part in contributing to people's psychological problems. I often wonder if I would be coping as well as my patient if I'd had the same string of experiences. Stress is the backdrop to all our lives now; bad luck is often the tipping point. Contemporary society is so different from what our bodies and minds were designed for that we're in a state of perpetual stress, which constantly floods us with stress hormones, and constantly pushes us back over that invisible cliff into depression and anxiety. It's very difficult for anyone now, but especially anyone with depression, to make the kinds of life changes that will significantly reduce the stress load—changing careers, setting goals and following your priorities, enlivening and enriching your relationships.

Worse still, depression and stress affect our ability to remember, concentrate, and make decisions. For instance, people who are depressed have much greater difficulty remembering random information than people who are not depressed. When given new material, they have more difficulty connecting it with what they know already—the information does not get organized in ways that help it get learned or recalled. The cognitive impairment that depression inflicts is most evident on tasks that require complex processing or independent thinking.[1] Other research has revealed the neurological mechanisms that result in the depressive's hypersensitivity to errors in simple tasks.[2] It's not bad enough that depression causes us emotional pain, makes our behavior self-defeating, and drives others away from us. But because our thinking is damaged, when we try new pathways in an effort to recover, we're handicapped at the outset because we have more trouble remembering and absorbing information, and we're distracted by trivial inconsistencies and errors. Cognitive therapy perhaps heals some of this damage by focusing our attention on our thought processes and making us follow the discipline of logic. But the brain damage caused by depression and stress can be healed more directly through practicing mindfulness.

Mindfulness

Mindfulness is certainly not an original idea from me; in fact, I'm still learning to apply its principles and techniques with my patients and with myself. So let me give you a little background: about twenty-five years ago, Jon Kabat-Zinn and some colleagues began to investigate the effects of meditation on the mind and the body. They eventually developed an eight-week stress reduction and relaxation program (now generally called Mindfulness-Based Stress Reduction; MBSR). Because they were working at the University of Massachusetts Medical School, they had to design their research to meet the tough standards of academic rigor. That's why it really drew attention when they were able to demonstrate that meditation significantly helped conditions as diverse as major depression, chronic pain, anxiety and panic, bulimia, psoriasis, fibromyalgia, mixed neurosis, mood and stress symptoms in cancer patients, and stress, anxiety, and depressive symptoms in the general population.[3] Later studies showed that if "normal" people practiced MBSR, they experienced the kinds of brain changes that are associated with positive moods, and their immune systems were strengthened.[4] I would like to point out here that if a patentable drug were showing such results, the drug company owning the patent would soon become the richest in the land, and we would be seeing at least three television commercials per night touting its benefits. But because mindfulness seems so simple, yet at the same time requires self-discipline, it's not going to generate such heat. Nevertheless, it is catching on, in its own quiet way. A new psychotherapeutic approach to depression, called

Mindfulness-Based Cognitive Therapy for Depression, is showing great promise. I discuss that further in Chapter 14.

Mindful meditation practice has been shown to affect how the brain deals with emotions, especially in the prefrontal cortex (PFC), which many brain scientists consider the actual physical location of our self-awareness. Meditation practice results in an increase in activity in that prefrontal area, where the brain processes positive feelings and controls negative feelings, an effect that lasts even when we're not meditating. This area of the brain contains a set of neurons that control messages of fear and anger from the amygdala, the fear center. It seems that the more we practice this effect, the easier it gets; we learn to control disturbing emotions just as we learn to ride a bike; after a while we don't have to think about it, it just happens.

Buddhist monks, who practice meditation for hours daily, have been found to be the happiest people in the world, by some measures. Richard Davidson has been studying the relative activity of the left and right lobes of the prefrontal cortex, and has found that, among the people he's tested all over the world, more activity on the right is associated with unpleasant or depressed moods, while more activity on the left means happiness and enthusiasm. People who consistently have greater activity on the left typically have fewer troubling moods and recover rapidly when they do. When Davidson tested an advanced Buddhist monk, he found that he had the greatest difference between left and right lobe activity of anyone yet tested.[5] This observation has been repeated with other monks. While we may not wish to completely detach ourselves from the world and meditate for hours a day, we may want to get that left prefrontal cortex more activated through some regular meditation practice. Generally, it's been found that the more you meditate, the more the left lobe becomes active, while the right lobe slows down.

Mindfulness-Based Stress Reduction is an intense, but brief, program. Mindfulness, however, is a way of life. Kabat-Zinn described the mindful state as "paying attention in a particular way: on purpose, in the present moment, and nonjudgmentally."[6]

To me, mindfulness means deliberately trying to attain a new attitude toward your thoughts, feelings, and everyday experience—"an attitude of openness, compassion, and objectivity; a deliberate effort not to be guided by old habits of thinking and behaving but to see each experience in its uniqueness."[7] It means seeing yourself without illusions but with love.

If mindfulness isn't clear to you yet, consider that you're very well acquainted with its opposite, mindlessness—the hurried, hypervigilant frame of mind that has us always rushing to cross to-dos off our lists, so pressured that we're not able to listen or concentrate or really evaluate new information. Instead, we quickly put it into one of our prefab stereotypes: good, bad, boring, a new emergency, or I'll think about it later (meaning I'll forget about it until I wake up at 4 A.M. with a whole list of worries I've repressed). Mindfulness means being in the present moment, but slightly detached. It means fully absorbing your thoughts, feelings, and experiences without being swept away by them.

Mindfulness also means learning to watch your mind at work, looking at yourself with compassionate curiosity. Compassion, like a close friend, suffers with us a little but also sees the patterns that we're normally too close to see. Curiosity shows us that there's really nothing to be afraid of in our own heads, but a lot we could learn. We can then turn that same viewpoint on the world. Practice makes us more observant and deliberate; we become more thoughtful about reacting to emotions and impulses; more curious, ready to look beneath the surface, not so hasty about jumping to conclusions; kinder, more patient, more tolerant of others and ourselves. One of the key elements in mindfulness is detaching a little from thoughts, worries, and impulses; not taking immediate action but expecting that if you take a step back, think, and look inside yourself, you'll probably make a wiser decision.

Regular meditation practice is the best way to achieve a mindful state, and it's been shown to have marvelous effects on mood, stress level, and health. If this looks intriguing or possible to you,

I urge you to give it an honest try, at least five days a week for two weeks. If you can do that much, you will probably start to feel some benefits — more calmness, more objectivity, more open-mindedness. But I have to warn that mindfulness meditation probably shouldn't be attempted by the most depressed, those who are paralyzed or just exhausted getting through the day, or so overwhelmingly sad that they can't escape their feelings. For these particular people, meditation will seem like a huge burden with no immediate payoff, and may only lead you to focus on your misery. Still, *most* depressed people are likely to feel that meditation practice is too much of a burden, and I again urge you to try. If you can just make yourself sit down and do the first five minutes, you can probably do another fifteen, enough for one day. Remember that your depression is largely a response to the stress that you are under, not a weakness you're to blame for, not an illness that can only be cured with medication. Mindfulness practice is the best cure for stress.

Here's a basic routine for meditation that many have found helpful:

Exercise 3: A Simple Mindfulness Meditation

• *Find a quiet place where you will not be interrupted for a half hour or more. Turn off the phones, the TV, the stereo. If you have pets, make sure they won't distract you. I find it helpful to turn on a fan, both for the cooling effect and for the quiet noise.*

• *Try to meditate at roughly the same time every day, but don't do it when you're overtired or overstressed or have just eaten a big meal. One of the best ways to achieve lasting health and happiness is to give yourself an hour every day devoted to exercise and meditation. I very much enjoy meditation while I am cooling down from exercise.*

• *Sit in a comfortable position. If you want to sit on the floor in a yoga position, it helps to have a thin pillow under you. Tuck your feet under your knees, but don't strain. Sit upright, with your back straight. Let the weight of your head fall directly on your spinal column. If you want to sit in a chair, try to put your feet flat on the floor, hands in your lap or at your sides. Again, sit upright, with your back straight. Posture is important, because it helps to keep you from falling asleep.*

• *Close your eyes, and start to breathe slowly and deeply. Not so deeply that you strain yourself, just comfortable. As you breathe, you may find it helpful to focus on a word or phrase, timing it to your breathing. "In... Out." You can change this to suit your mood. When I'm fighting cravings, I think "Wave... Rock." The waves of desire are very powerful but the rock remains. Other times I like "I am here... I am home." You will find phrases that have meaning for you.*

• *Focus on your breathing. As other thoughts or feelings come to mind, let them pass, and return your attention to your breathing. Visualize these distracting thoughts and feelings as bubbles rising to the surface of a calm pool of water. They rise and burst, the ripples spread out and disappear. The pool remains calm. Return your attention to your breathing.*

• *Don't judge. Don't worry about doing this right, just try to do it every day. Remember that the distracting thoughts and feelings are the normal noise in your brain. It takes practice and skill to get in touch with the quietness underneath. Every time I practice, I have to spend the first few minutes clearing my head of thoughts about what I'm going to do as soon as I finish; I've been so conditioned to be "productive," to keep myself busy.*

• *When I'm preparing for meditation, and when I feel restless, I like to remember the perspective of a Buddhist nun in a workshop I attended: "If you have a fussy baby, do you shout at the baby? Do you get angry at it? Do you shake it? No—you* build a cradle *for the baby."*

That's what we have to deliberately allow ourselves to practice: to treat ourselves with care and concern. That's also what meditation does for our restless, anxious minds; it builds a structure we can feel safe in.

- *Return your attention to your breath.*

- *You will find yourself frequently distracted by intrusive thoughts—sometimes nagging thoughts about chores you have to do, sometimes memories that may be pleasant or unpleasant. You may also be distracted by emotions—primarily impatience and anxiety. Remember that these intrusive thoughts and emotions are the normal noise your brain makes because it's so used to functioning under stress. Even the most adept meditators can still get hijacked this way. It may help to visualize, for instance, putting these thoughts into a box or on a list that you can look at later. Or simply say to yourself, "No thank you." Don't get upset with yourself because you do get distracted; don't tell yourself you're not doing it right, simply return to the focus on your breath. Judging yourself is another habit, one you can put aside while you're meditating.*

- *Return your attention to your breath.*

- *If you get distracted, or get upset, try to cultivate the attitude of compassionate curiosity. Approach your frustration with an attitude of openness, of understanding, of friendly interest. "I wonder what could be going on here?" rather than "I can't do this right."*

- *When you are ready to stop, open your eyes. Stay seated for a few moments while you appreciate the calm state you are in.*

- *If you have to use an alarm, make it something quiet, not jarring. Some guided meditation CDs include a section with nothing on it but temple bells at regular intervals. Or you can program the timer on your cell phone or PDA to alert you with a gentle sound.*

People often expect meditation to lead them to brilliant insights, to higher levels of consciousness, to a state of near-perfect bliss. That's not the purpose of this kind of meditation; this is more like a training program for your brain. When I do this exercise in workshops, I routinely ask for a show of hands of how many people began to experience intrusive thoughts. *This is boring. My back hurts. I have to stop and get milk on the way home. I must not be doing this right. Meditation isn't for me.* Everyone in the workshop has thoughts like these. This is the voice of your judging mind, your Inner Critic. The voice is a product of stress, of the need we feel to classify our experiences quickly into simple categories without experiencing them too deeply. If you're depressed, that voice is usually turned on yourself. Instead of acting on these judgments, just notice how your brain is always judging. Judging is your frontal lobe, the "higher" mental center, trying desperately to hold on to control, while your focus on the breath is uncoupling it. One of the chief principles of mindfulness is to learn to suspend judging, because it leads to categorical, rigid, mindless thinking. But don't judge yourself for judging; it's a hard habit to break. Just notice it, and try to let it go. Try to be amused by it. *There I go again, like a doorman at a fancy club; you're in, you're out. My poor frontal lobe must be really scared at the idea of losing control.* You may notice that, five minutes after you have one thought, you'll have another that directly contradicts the first; yet both, at the time, feel equally true and equally urgent. So this judging is not a rational process at all, though it pretends to be.

Sometimes when I meditate, I think of the little pond in my backyard. It's a very peaceful scene, with a small fountain, water lilies and frogs, and lots of sunlight. When I start thinking about ways to improve the pond, I know I'm having trouble focusing. *Get a better filtration system, fix the stones around the edge so they stop falling in, change the plantings.* That's the problem-solving mode our minds have been trained to be in—even to the extent of creating problems when there are none. My pond is fine as it is, but my caveman mind is always striving. My insecure mind is always trying to make things better. My consumer mind is always looking for something new. Sometimes just being still is a very difficult thing.

Admittedly, learning to be mindful with or without meditation is not easy. If we were raised in a safe and secure home, this is a skill that comes naturally to us as children, but we tend to lose it as we settle into adulthood. Regaining it requires effort. First of all, you're not likely to take it seriously, because it sounds so simple that it's easy to dismiss. And in the midst of depression, feeling overwhelmed with everything in your life, who's ready to try anything that adds another half hour to the day? Remember the AA saying, "Just because it's simple doesn't mean it's easy." Try to remember that three months of daily juggling practice results in restructuring the brain. So don't give up after a week or two, feeling that you're "no good" at this. That's the depression talking. If you've given it two weeks, you've already begun to make some changes in your brain; you won't lose them if you get discouraged and skip a day or so. Just climb back on the horse.

Steven Hayes, the architect of Acceptance and Commitment Therapy, makes a fascinating point.[8] We have marvelous minds that are very good at solving problems, but many of our biggest problems can't be solved—hurt, pain, loss, disappointment, rejection, illness, fear, anger, and jealousy, to name a few. When we expect our marvelous minds to solve these problems, we make matters worse for ourselves because we get frustrated. Then we feel inadequate, blame ourselves, and question our competence.

Try a thought experiment: *Say you're feeling sad. Try not to feel that way. Try as hard as you can. Make yourself happy instead.* As soon as you hear that, you know it's nonsensical; no one can control their emotions that way. Still, chances are you try it all the time, somewhere under the level of total awareness. After all, it seems logical enough; we have such magnificent brains we ought to be able to control a simple thing like a sad mood. But it's like the "don't think of a pink elephant" command. Ironically, the more we try to suppress a thought, feeling, or image, the more it keeps popping up in our minds. So you'll be constantly reminded of your sad feelings, which will make you sadder. You'll also feel inadequate and incompetent, because you can't do a simple thing like get out of your sad mood. Instead of directly trying to control our feelings, instead of defending against them, denying, projecting, rationalizing, we have to do something different.

Depressed people, for instance, are naturally enough going to believe that thinking intensely about their problems will lead to solutions. But when thinking turns into rumination, it just perpetuates the feeling state of depression; so they feel worse, more immobilized and helpless.[9] Most of us think, at times: *What's wrong with me? Other people don't seem to worry like I do. Other people seem to be in control of their lives.* Of course, we don't see all the misery they carry with them. We're trying to solve all the problems associated with merely being human, and we can't. We expect ourselves to master a world we simply weren't designed for, a world where we're always in fight-or-flight mode, and we can't do that, either. But we feel like we can't give up.

This is the big news coming from brain research. We literally can't change ourselves by thinking our way out. It's true that we have to use our thought processes to understand our situation, and understanding can lead to new perspectives, and new solutions—but the solutions have to be put into action. Once you're sealed up in the tuna fish can with your worries and sadness and pessimism, you can't get out unless you somehow acquire a can opener. Practicing mindfulness is the can opener.

Detachment

The depressed person makes himself miserable partly by trying to control things he can't control. Indeed, some researchers feel that excessive worrying is the hallmark of depression. Depressives *ruminate* on their problems, chewing over the same issues endlessly; we find a counterargument for every possible solution to our problems, and so end up taking no action at all. This ruminative thinking style is a distinctive characteristic of depression; some feel that women are more prone to this kind of thinking, whereas men are more likely to take action, and that partially accounts for why women are more vulnerable to depression (and why so many more men are in jail).[10]

Julia is a patient who has benefited from detachment. She and her husband both come from highly dysfunctional families; they've been together twenty years, ever since college, and have built a good life for themselves and their two children. The fly in the ointment is her husband's drinking. He doesn't drink much in terms of quantity, but it seems to hit him sometimes very quickly, so that he seems dangerously drunk: confused, slurring words, losing the thread of the conversation. Julia sometimes wonders if he's been secretly drinking. But equally often, she has seen him have three drinks over the course of an evening and seem unfazed.

Julia and her husband have talked a lot about this over the years. He agrees he needs to be careful about alcohol, but doesn't want to give it up. Julia worries a lot, when he's away on business trips, or when he's had a drink with his coworkers before driving home. She knows she's a ruminator, examining every encounter from every angle, which sometimes just leaves her more confused. But she has realized that her efforts to police her husband backfire; he resents her scrutiny and sometimes will open a beer at home as if he's looking for a fight (he often doesn't finish the beer). Now he and Julia have reached a compromise: if he will just be honest with her about when he has a drink, she will not come down on him for it, unless it's clearly bad judgment. I suspect that this is not the end of the problem, but it's helping right now to maintain what in many ways is an excellent relationship.

Julia could never have done this without having practiced mindfulness and detachment. She started practicing with her pre-teen children. She has seen that her refusal to get involved in their squabbles means they blow over more quickly. She's established firm boundaries about what constitutes acceptable behavior at home, and the children largely respect that. When they don't, Julia calmly and firmly enforces the consequences. Now she's trying a version of the same thing with her husband. It won't be easy for her to give up obsessing about him, but it's within her abilities now.

Detachment is a skyhook we desperately need, the ability to rise above the noise in our heads and see the big picture. Detachment suggests a certain degree of insulation from contagious emotions—not being caught up in others' panic or anger, but making our own decisions about the emotional meaning of a situation. It means recognizing that crisis situations eventually get resolved, that even feelings like panic dissipate, and that what we can do about the situation and other peoples' feelings is limited.

Detachment implies an ascetic discipline, an Eastern value system differing greatly from a Western, consumer-oriented society in which the one who dies with the most toys wins. Now that we know for certain that materialism means greater unhappiness,[11] perhaps it's time for us all to work on changing our values. Detachment sometimes means giving up—an insulting concept for many Americans, but one that we should consider more often. A strategic retreat from an impossible task is simply wise, not shameful. We can all see the wisdom of the dying man, retiring from the daily struggles of life to spend more time with his family. But we are all dying, just some of us faster than others. We have to accept reality, to play the cards we are dealt.

It seems as if depressives have an obsessive quality that won't let us detach. We often worry constantly about things over which we have no control, or tell ourselves we won't be happy unless something we can't control happens. A woman I know has two gay children. She feels she has accepted their homosexuality, but she is terribly upset about their decision not to have children. She can't be with people her age because they talk about grandchildren so much. This is very sad, but sadder still is that she sees no way out. She feels the rest of her life will be miserable because of this.

Two questions can help gain a realistic detachment: *Will this really matter tomorrow (next week, next month)?* and *What can I realistically do about it?* If I'm in a situation that is highly charged emotionally but whose outcome is not really crucial to me, perhaps I don't have to act impulsively just to get some emotional relief. If I'm in a difficult, even an important, situation but my options are limited, I only make myself miserable by wishing for the impossible.

Learning to manage stress really means managing the anger and anxiety we feel in stressful situations. Only when these emotional byproducts of stress are under control is it possible to think about facing the situation creatively.

When I was a brand-new therapist I had a client pull a knife on himself. He was trying to get me to call his girlfriend to ask her to come back to him, to say in effect that it was my professional opinion that he couldn't get along without her. When I refused, he calmly opened a huge knife, counted down his ribs to his heart, and pressed the point against his chest. "I don't think you realize how serious I am," he said.

This was a moment of pure anxiety for me. I hadn't the vaguest idea what to do. I knew I would just be an agent of his manipulation if I called the girlfriend, but how could I let him stab himself? I remembered some advice one of my casework instructors had given our class: "When you are completely stuck, get up and go to the bathroom." I got up and left the room, saying I had to get some advice. I went down the hall and told a colleague what was going on. Then our boss walked by, and I repeated the story. My anxiety was catching, and after ten minutes or so of discussion the three of us eventually decided I would have to call the girlfriend. But when I went back to tell my client, he was gone. Of course he must have begun to feel foolish holding a knife to himself in an empty room. He called me later in the day, furious at me for walking out on him, but that was okay with me.

I got lucky. In pure panic, I remembered a mentor's advice, and it turned out to work better than I had a right to expect. I detached myself, quite literally, from the power struggle this client was trying to create. We need to learn to detach ourselves from our own interior power struggles. When we're caught up in our emotions, when we feel on the spot, pressured to come up with the vital solution that seems out of reach, our ability to think is just about absent. Our bodies are full of fight-or-flight hormones, which are good for fleeing from saber-toothed cats. But they don't help—in fact, they absolutely hinder—creative problem-solving. We can't come up with new solutions, we can only think of what is instinctual or what we've done before in similar situations. Whatever we do, it is just more of the same stuff that hasn't worked before.

Stuck in a stressful situation, you have only three choices: you can alter it, you can avoid it, or you can accept it. Each of these may be the best solution for a particular situation; none of them is inherently any better than the other. Western culture values action—we admire people who take action to alter their predicaments—and so you might assume that altering the situation is always best. Avoidance sounds shameful and acceptance sounds passive. But there are many things in life we can't alter and others that are not worth the trouble; wisdom has to do with knowing what's worth fighting about. Caught in the road with an eighteen-wheeler bearing down on you, you don't fight about the right of way, you *avoid* getting run over. We practice avoidance like this all the time but don't acknowledge it. And acceptance means just facing reality. With the stress of an illness, for example, there is no avoiding it and no one to fight about it with, though many people fire their doctors for giving them bad news. The point is to review your options and make a conscious decision; don't beat yourself up if you can't change an unalterable situation. Don't vacillate between half-hearted attempts to change it and trying to accept it. Think about it: alter, avoid, accept.

It should not come as a surprise to the reader at this point that I suggest we need to understand our thought processes from a different perspective than the one we take for granted. A more mindful approach to thinking is called for. When we observe ourselves mindfully over the course of time, we see how our thoughts are constantly changing. What seemed like a huge issue yesterday has somehow gone away today; the terrible importance that we attached to addressing this problem has become detached, and the problem assumes its proper proportions. Observing ourselves mindfully, we become used to the idea of *thoughts as mental events,* things that are happening inside our brains. We stop thinking of our thoughts as the absolute truth or as moral imperatives that we must act on immediately. We see how our thoughts are influenced by feelings, the stress of the day, the weather, the background music, how much coffee we've had, how much Zoloft is in our systems, and we trust them less. That doesn't mean that we dismiss our own thoughts, or become so laid back and detached that we don't care about anything, or that we can never make up our minds because we can always see all sides of an issue. We may trust our thoughts less, but they are still vital information to us.

We can go on and practice thinking mindfully. We can consider the evidence of our thoughts and feelings together, and make our decisions accordingly. We can recognize the impact of stress in the pressure to make quick decisions, and we can practice patience, waiting until we're as certain as we want to be. Then we can observe carefully the impact of our decisions.

Relationships

ONE OF THE bitter ironies of depression is that depressed people crave connection with others while the nature of the disease makes it impossible for us to connect. David Karp writes, in *Speaking of Sadness:* "Much of depression's pain arises out of the recognition that what might make one feel better—human connection—seems impossible in the midst of a paralyzing episode of depression."[1]

People with depression can be very difficult to live with. We need a great deal from others, but we are embarrassed and confused by our needs, so we don't articulate them well. Some of our difficulty with other people stems from our faulty emotional, behavioral, and cognitive habits, as discussed in the previous three chapters, but a great deal of it comes from our "relationship habits"—our expectation of others and our communication skills. Part of the reason why depressed people can have unrealistic expectations for others is that we rarely state our needs directly, instead keeping secret wishes locked in our hearts. If we can take the risk of being good communicators, we can say what we want of others. They may not be able to give this to us, but they are less likely to abandon us than we think. Instead, we can enter into negotiations and quid pro quos, the stuff of real relationships.

Rejection Sensitivity

People with depression can be quite sensitive to the feelings of others, but their perception is skewed in a way that perpetuates the depression. In the lab, they have trouble recognizing and responding to facial expressions of happiness, but seem oversensitive to expressions of sadness.[2] So they don't respond with joy to someone else's joy, but they do resonate with sadness. Depressed people have permeable boundaries to their selves; other people's feelings (except for the positive ones) get right to them. They also have faulty radar, difficulty "reading" people, because what they want and need from others distorts their perception. They overuse the defenses of projection (attributing one's own feelings to others) and introjection (taking in the feelings of others and making them part of the self), which means that feelings in a relationship become a confused, contagious mess.

An interesting observation about people with depression is that they seem to react more intensely to rejection, loss, or abandonment than other people do. It is as if they are thin-skinned, very aware of subtle cues of approval or disapproval from those around them, and thrown for a loop by little signs of disapproval that might be shrugged off or argued about by another person. A term used to describe this quality is *rejection sensitivity*.[3]

The researchers who developed the concept of rejection sensitivity were interested primarily in psychopharmacology, and it seems as if the effects of SSRIs bear out their ideas. Antidepressants seem to make people less easily derailed by setbacks and rejection. They are still aware of these events, but it seems as if the medication helps them gain greater objectivity. A patient who was always upset by her husband's teasing now sees it as his way of expressing affection; another patient tries for a promotion she had avoided before because she now sees the world won't fall in if she doesn't get it. As we'll see in Chapter 12, this effect can go too far; but many highly sensitive people need something to turn down the volume, at least temporarily.

This is also a subject where some of the most exciting changes in psychotherapy have been taking place. In self psychology, the focus has been on the depressed patient as "narcissistically damaged"—needing excessive reassurance from other people or from the outside world in order to feel whole, competent, alive. In intersubjective psychotherapy, the focus is on the boundary between the patient's and therapist's world, especially on what makes the patient feel rejected, depressed, or hurt. In dialectical behavior therapy, a major theme is "radical acceptance"—joining the patient's world, seeing it through her eyes, not attempting to fix her. In family therapy, the focus has been on boundary violations—the tendency to be too easily influenced by what others say, think, or feel, the tendency to confuse one's own thoughts and feelings with others'. To use myself as an example: my mother's suicide left me with grave doubts about myself. If she had truly loved me, as a mother is supposed to love a child, how could I account for her abandoning me through suicide? Didn't this mean that I was essentially unworthy of love? Would I not then look to others to help me feel better about myself, but at the same time be afraid of real engagement because of my self-doubts, leaving myself feeling essentially alone and hopeless? In my present relationships, would I not need to take special care that I communicate my wants and needs clearly, not blame others for being unable to make me happy, not seeing it as my responsibility to make everyone else happy? Do I need individual therapy with someone skilled in self psychology, or family therapy to help me straighten out the boundaries of my relationships? Or is it just that I have a low threshold of sensitivity and need medication to make myself less sensitive?

Maybe the ideal therapeutic regimen would be a little of all three, and maybe any one of the three could be of significant help to me. I think it is no accident at all when new ideas and research converge like this, even though it may make things more confusing for us for a while. We have scientists from different perspectives trying to understand what are the most important psychological issues of our time: a loss of identity, a sense of emptiness or estrangement, and desperate, self-defeating attempts to regain a feeling of being centered and whole. These are problems not just for the depressive, though we may feel it more acutely, but for our entire culture. Naturally scientists are trying, albeit from different perspectives, to understand who it is who comes seeking help. We don't have to try to explain Freud's hysterics with neurologically impossible paralysis or blindness — they have almost disappeared from Western culture because the social conditions that brought on their symptoms have disappeared. We have to try to understand people who are depressed, who put too much stock in the opinions of others, who have the sense of being outside life, who try too hard and feel they never succeed.

Depression is both caused by and a cause of poorly functioning relationships. We may be born more sensitive to rejection than the next person, but it's possible to learn how to control this sensitivity and make our relationships work better by learning how to communicate more effectively.

Metacommunication

What's wrong with these conversations?

SHE: What time is the concert?
HE: You have to be ready by seven-thirty.

SHE: How many people are coming to dinner?
HE: Don't worry, there's plenty of food.

HE: Are you just about finished?
SHE: Do you want dinner now?

Regardless of how the questioner identifies the feelings that these responses engender, the questioner now has a choice. He or she can act based on these feelings or can express them verbally. I have the impulse to pick up and throw the nearest object when I'm spoken to this way, because I feel infantilized. But I'm better off to say it verbally: "I feel like you're overprotecting me. You're assuming you know what I want, but you're wrong. Please just answer the question directly." This is a form of *metacommunication,* or talking about how we talk. The content of a conversation is what we talk about; the process is how we conduct the talking. Content is lyrics, process is music. Which is it that most directly speaks to feelings? From the point of view of feelings, process, like music, goes directly to the emotional brain, while content must be analyzed intellectually. If we feel listened to and respected, if the listener looks us in the eyes, nods, and asks questions, we can take a rebuff more easily. If we feel dismissed or patronized, if the listener doesn't look at us or seems distracted, we're likely to be dissatisfied even if we get what we want. All our communication takes place on these two levels, words and music, text and subtext, content and process. There is the communication itself—the content of the message, what the sender consciously wants the receiver to understand. Then there is the meta-communication, equally if not more important. Metacommunication provides a *frame* for the message. The frame tells us how to interpret the content. Saying *I hate you* in a loud, angry voice is very different from saying it with a big smile and a mock punch on the shoulder (after you make a bad joke) or with the invisible quotation marks that say "Don't take this seriously" (after you've won a hand at cards). Metacommunication is also about the relationship between sender and receiver. Metacommunication says things like *I care about you, I'm better than you, I defer to you, I have the right to order you.* To a great extent, metacommunication is in the "music" of speech, the tone, the facial expression, the posture.

Here's one of my favorite examples from literature, from *The Great Gatsby:*

> *"Who wants to go to town?" demanded Daisy insistently. Gatsby's eyes floated toward her. "Ah," she cried, "you look so cool."*

*Their eyes met, and they stared together at each other, alone
in space. With an effort she glanced down at the table.*

"You always look so cool," she repeated.

*She had just told him that she loved him, and Tom Buch-
anan [Daisy's husband] saw. He was astounded.*[4]

Content communication goes to the left side of the brain, the hemi-
sphere that uses logic and likes facts. Metacommunication—both
verbal and nonverbal—goes principally to the right side, the feeling
side. When communication and metacommunication convey messages that support or amplify each other, we have *congruent* communication, and we "get" the message with both mind and heart. But
when the content of the message says one thing and the metacommunication says something else, that's *incongruent* communication.
We're likely to be confused, anxious, or irritated.

Shifting the focus of the conversation from content to process can
be a very effective way of resolving communication problems. When
my wife asks what I want for dinner, pasta or chicken, and I say I
don't care, what I'm often missing is that she's asking for a little companionship, a little mutual ownership of a decision. If I say, "Chicken
sounds good," but say it with a "Don't interrupt me" attitude, I'm still
dismissing her, even though I've answered her question. She will feel
diminished (and I'll feel guilty, even if I'm not consciously aware of
it). What she can do is say, "Don't ignore me like that," or "It wouldn't
hurt you to take your nose out of your book for a minute"—shifting
from content to process, letting me know that I've been rude, letting
me know that she just needs a reasonable amount of attention. (Of
course, the burden is not on her, but on me, to be more thoughtful.)

Assertive Communication

Depressed people often fall into the trap of people-pleasing, trying
desperately to make others happy in an effort to gain attention or
love. This usually just scares others away, because they know it's

fundamentally dishonest. You're giving the impression that you're willing to say or do anything to be liked, and that you have no internal values or standards that you won't compromise. Learning how to be more assertive teaches the depressed person a whole new set of communication skills that can replace some of these self-effacing, walk-all-over-me habits that have become second nature. There are now dozens of books, tapes, and classes that you can take to help you learn how to be more assertive. Most of us, especially the depressed, suffer in silence when people are rude, threatening, or manipulative, and we end the encounter feeling diminished in self-esteem. Or occasionally we will lose our temper and descend to the level of the other person, which doesn't resolve the dispute and also leaves us feeling bad about ourselves. Acting assertively, on the other hand, strengthens self-esteem. If we treat ourselves as if we are worthy of respect, others are more likely to treat us the same way, and we also send the message: "I'm as good as anyone else."

Being assertive means knowing your rights and giving yourself the same respect you'd give another person. It does not mean being pushy, demanding, controlling, or selfish. In fact, part of assertiveness training is learning to listen carefully, to make sure that you understand clearly the other person's position and that you carefully consider his or her rights as well as your own. Being assertive means identifying what you want and asking for it in clear language that maintains respect for others.

There are many good resources for learning assertiveness, some of which are listed in the Recommended Reading section.[5] Edmund Bourne, in *The Anxiety and Phobia Workbook,* has a simple outline for developing assertive responses.

1. Objectively evaluate your rights. What's wrong with this situation? Do you have a right to expect different treatment than you're getting? We all have basic rights we tend to forget about, including the rights to change our minds, to say "I don't know," to be treated with dignity and respect, and to feel our feelings.

2. Choose a time when you want to deal with the situation. For a conflict with a loved one, a coworker, or someone you are in regular contact with, establish a mutually convenient time when you can discuss the problem. Realize that some situations need to be dealt with on the spot, before greater damage is done.

3. State the problem in terms of how it affects you. Make it clear exactly how you are hurt or inconvenienced by the other person's behavior. This may be all you need to do. Sometimes people are just not aware of their impact on you. Use calm, objective language that avoids criticism.

4. State your feelings, using congruent verbal and nonverbal language (this takes practice). This is also where "I statements" come in. "When your stereo is loud, I can't get my work done" (step 3). "I get worried that I can't meet my deadline" (step 4). The other person is not responsible for the way you feel, but has a right to know about it. If you don't state your feelings, you're assuming that the other person can read your mind.

5. Tell the other person what you want. Use simple, direct language. Keep it specific: "I want you to help with the dishes," not "I want you to show more consideration for me." Address the other person's behavior, not his personality or character, to avoid putting him on the defensive.

6. Describe the consequences. Clearly spell out what will happen if the other person does or doesn't cooperate. This should not be a threat, but a natural consequence: "If I can get my work done, we can go out later." When you're dealing with someone you know to be a refusenik, you may point out the natural consequences of his refusal: "If you don't let me get my work done, we won't have enough money to buy the things you want."

People with depression are rarely good at being assertive, and assertive people are less likely to be depressed. I don't think that assertiveness training alone can cure depression, but learning these skills can certainly have powerful consequences for self-esteem. It can teach us how to express our feelings, remind us of our inter-personal rights, help get our needs met, and resolve confusion and conflict in relationships with others. Most of all, we can't expect to have self-respect if we don't treat ourselves with respect. It's more of the depressive's magical thinking, wishing that self-respect could be given to us like an inheritance. On the contrary, self-respect, like every depression-fighting skill, has to be learned and earned.

Ambiguous Communication

It seems natural to expect that those close to us understand us per-fectly. But it is a wish that grown-ups must abandon. One of the points that marriage counselors have to make is that expecting the spouse to read one's mind is just unfair and silly. If you don't com-municate it, you can't blame your partner for not understanding it.

Many of the techniques of assertiveness will help prevent ambigu-ous communication. A common problem occurs when nonverbal and verbal messages seem to contradict each other, creating confusion. A sulking "Go ahead, leave without me, I'll see you later, I really don't mind" only mystifies the hearer; should she listen to the words (go ahead) or the music (the sulk)? A half-hearted "If it's no bother, can you bring back some ice cream?" doesn't justify a pout if the traveler forgets the ice cream. The person who apologetically asks to be treated fairly is shooting himself in the foot. He has a right to be treated fairly, and he doesn't have anything to apologize for at all.

Ambiguity doesn't come only from conflict between verbal and nonverbal communication. Often our words themselves contradict each other. Sometimes we can't put our feelings into words. Some-times we want contradictory things. Sometimes we just don't know what we want. This doesn't prevent us from getting mad at those close to us when they can't guess what would please us most. Unam-biguous communication is more work than we're used to. To be clear, we must know our own mind, and then articulate our desires specifically, paying careful attention to what we say and how we say it. We have the idea that communication, especially between loved ones, should be effortless, that people who are truly close should be able to almost read each other's minds. This is a dangerous belief. But careful, unambiguous communication can become almost second nature as we practice, and it becomes rewarded by greater levels of intimacy and satisfaction in relationships.

A depressed patient has gone to a quasi-religious retreat over the weekend. She uses the experience to tell me she's not happy with the way therapy is going.

"I've been disappointed in all my therapists. I respect you, but I wanted something more... spiritual. A spiritual guide, a leader.... Someone who really understands me, what I want and what I should do. There must be people who are so enlightened that they give guidance and ask for nothing in return. I don't like the money part of therapy, either."

I try to imagine someone who gives guidance and asks for nothing in return. Though there are saints and truly unselfish spiritual leaders, they are rare, and they do ask for discipline. Most people who give guidance expect, at least, obedience.

I tell her that, in a way, the money is a guarantee. She doesn't have to do anything else for me other than pay her bill. She doesn't have to like or respect me. She doesn't have to take my advice or live up to my expectations. When I accept her fee for a professional service, the exchange of services is open and aboveboard.

She moves on to reflect on her history of relationships with men. Her husband was an older man who had been her supervisor at work. He seemed so confident and knowledgeable. She felt he could teach her things. But after a short time, she realized he was extremely controlling. If she didn't wash the dishes his way, he would have a fit. He told her she was a child, that she was capable of nothing. Eventually she somehow found the strength to leave him.

But she still wants a guru, someone who she feels can understand her perfectly. She's not ready to give up on the childish belief that someone who loves us enough can understand us without the work of communication. She doesn't see how even a well-meaning guru can do harm because he's not used to the flattery and the power, or that she might find obedience more unpleasant than freedom.

Projection and Projective Identification

Two additional defense mechanisms misused by depressives that add mightily to problems in communication are projection and projective identification. *Projection* means that I take my feelings, disconnect them from my conscious awareness, and attribute them to you. "You really want to fight, don't you?" People who are very thin-skinned overuse projection. They can take their own bad feelings about themselves and project them onto others, seeing themselves as constantly rejected victims of discrimination, and they collect grievances everywhere. *Projective identification,* a confusing process, seems magical but really does happen. It's when, because you attribute anger to me, I really do want to fight. But it's not just anger, it's any feeling; I catch the feeling you tell me I'm having. And "telling" me is hardly ever that direct. If you for some reason want me to be angry at you, you may tiptoe around me, ask questions in a fearful tone, show the body language of cowering. Pretty soon I will indeed be angry, and neither of us is conscious of how we got that way. The projector and the recipient can get bound together in horribly complex webs of feeling from which there seems to be no escape.

A husband promises his wife he'll be home by 8:30. He arrives at 9:15, without calling. Dinner is ruined. His first words are "You're not going to spoil our evening because I'm a little late, are you?" He's telling her she has no right to be angry at him, and she swallows her anger. This is a form of "gaslighting," one spouse making the other doubt her sanity. Gaslighting is a form of unconscious manipulation that can have disastrous impact on the recipient's self-esteem.

Like all defenses, projection and projective identification are attempts to resolve a conflict between our needs, our fears (or our conscience), the expectations of others, and the strictures of reality. I need love and intimacy but I fear the risk of loss. If I let someone get close, I can be hurt. I can take that fear and project it, making anyone who comes close to me seem to be nosy, controlling, officious. Projection and projective identification can distort reality to a destructive, uncomfortable degree. And because they are so much a part of how we communicate in relationships, and because in human interactions things happen so fast that we can all easily get confused, these defenses are less subject to reflective analysis than denial, isolation, or repression. The best way of gaining control over these defenses is by working with a trusted partner in careful communication analysis.

Projection and projective identification are defenses that can be used by anyone, depressed or not. And they are especially likely to be evoked in close relationships, because intimacy, though good for us, is scary — we fear being engulfed, dominated, controlled; or that the secrets we have shared will be used against us; or that we will eventually be abandoned and rejected because of those secrets. People with depression are likely to take their own bad feelings about themselves and project the feelings onto the people who care about them. The depressed husband who has lost his job doesn't believe his wife really means her words of comfort and reassurance; he doubts his own worth but defends against this doubt by attributing it to her. After enough rejection, she stops trying to make him feel better, and he is reinforced in his belief that she doesn't care about him. A couple of weeks more of this irritability and self-pity, and she really begins to have the kinds of doubts about him that he was attributing to her all along — projective identification at work.

When I assume that you understand me, it's also a process of projection. When I get hot and bothered because I feel convinced I've made my wishes clear and you just stubbornly refuse to understand, I'm not communicating anything except my stubbornness. These irrational sensations of *knowing with perfect clarity exactly what the other person is thinking* are sure indications of projection.[6] They're fueled by emotion, not logic.

What we have to do, naturally, is check our assumptions. (As the old chestnut goes: "When you ASSUME, you make an ASS out of U and ME.") *Am I understanding you? Am I making myself clear to you?* The technique of repeating back what the other person has said ("I hear you saying that you're disappointed I wanted to leave the party early"), while it sounds so simple-minded it's subject to caricature, is the place to start. It's really an exercise in developing empathy.

Aside from our assumptions, we may learn something about our expectations. If I get upset because my wife spends too much time putting the kids to bed, and I tell her about it, she may question me. How much time is too much? What is it exactly that I need her for, that her time with the children interferes with? I may make the unpleasant discovery that I expect my wife to put my needs ahead of the kids. I may have to question whether this is a fair assumption, whether it is congruent with my feelings in other areas. Compromise is possible:

When our children were young I spent all day at work missing them. I couldn't wait to come home and play with them, just sharing in their easy delight. My wife, on the other hand, had spent all day with them. She couldn't wait for me to come home so that she could have an adult conversation—often about how the kids had driven her crazy, which was the last thing I wanted to hear.

After a few months we realized what was going on. I would come in and she would start to complain. I would be impatient and dismissive. She'd get hurt and angry, and I'd feel that the pleasant evening I'd planned was ruined. We developed a compromise: we would play with the kids together for a while, then I'd play with them by myself while she prepared dinner. After dinner, while I helped with the dishes, she'd take the time to vent. It helped that I, having spent a little time with the children, could now remember that all their behavior wasn't totally endearing and that she, having been given a break of sorts, wasn't quite as stressed out as she was at 5:30.

The tempting, easy thing to do when we're feeling misunderstood is to withdraw. This is something depressives are good at. We can be wonderfully resourceful at entertaining ourselves. The feeling of being picked on, misunderstood, and isolated is an old, comfortable feeling. There is something that feels right about it. It confirms our fantasies that we are the ugly duckling, the Cinderella who is just in the wrong place at the wrong time, who can't be happy because of all the mean people in the world. Withdrawal can feel self-righteous.

The hard thing to do is to hang in there and try to make the communication work. Don't assume it's all the other guy's fault. Listen carefully and empathically. Maybe you're missing something important. Maybe at least you can figure out why he's not understanding you. Successful relationships don't just happen, they take work.

We can't exist without other people. As depressives, we want too much from others, and we may protect ourselves from experiencing and expressing those needs by playing roles that aren't really us. But real relationships — built on trust, honesty, and caring — can give us the opportunity to heal, to build a new self. Children grow out of their childish needs for omnipotent, ever-attentive parents by a process of optimal frustration. The parents disappoint the child by making mistakes, by not always paying attention, but ideally they do it in synch with the child's ability to tolerate disappointment and frustration. The child learns to soothe himself, learns that he can feel safe and loved for a while even without the parents' attention. The child is building a self.

Honest, caring relationships give adults the opportunity to do the same thing. The depressed person can repair a damaged sense of self-esteem through developing intimacy with another person. The other person doesn't enhance self-esteem through artificial compliments or through reflected glory; rather the process of letting the other see yourself, warts and all, and finding that you are still loved and accepted does the work of repair.

11

The Body

WE DEPRESSIVES must learn to listen to and take care of our bodies. Divorced from feelings, we tend to see ourselves divorced from our bodies as well. But our "true self" is not only in our head, it is our whole being, body, mind, and spirit. Ignoring body messages like pain, fatigue, and psychophysiological symptoms just sends us off for unnecessary medical care—depressives dramatically overuse physical medicine—and makes us feel more depressed because the medical care doesn't touch the real problem.

Our clinic once cosponsored a panel discussion on "Depression and the Body," which drew a good crowd for a small town. I was amazed to look around and see not a single familiar face in the crowd—these were not people in psychotherapy, but people being treated for physical symptoms, each of whom had wondered if depression were somehow connected to their problems. The idea of a connection with depression made intellectual sense to them, but none of them (so far as I knew) had ever called a therapist to discuss it—they just kept going to their doctors, being treated for musculoskeletal pain, PMS, Lyme disease, you name it, despite the discomfort and expense involved in the treatment.

What Depression Does to the Body

Positive thinking is good for the body: people who believe in positive myths about themselves live longer, have fewer heart attacks, and require less anesthesia during surgery. Optimists' wounds heal more quickly than those of pessimists.[1] Being a pessimist can shorten your lifespan. Being depressed is even worse. New research is showing us more and more evidence that depression damages health. A whole new science, psychoneuroimmunology, has developed over the past twenty-five years to explore the sometimes mystifying connections between mind, body, and health—for instance, the finding that stressful experiences in childhood cause changes in the brain that seem to make you more vulnerable to autoimmune diseases in adulthood like lupus, to chronic pain conditions, to not-yet-understood illnesses like fibromyalgia,[2] and to heart disease, diabetes, stroke, and fractures.[3] In fact, it seems that the immune system is shaped by our earliest emotional experiences as infants learning to cope with stress.[4] Many have reached the conclusion that it's best to eliminate the distinction between mind and body. Much of the mind is *in* the body, in complex nerve centers in the heart, gut, and immune systems that function like auxiliary brains, in receptor systems in the muscles, bones, blood, and lymph that are tied intimately into the traditional brains in our heads.

For instance, people with depression usually have elevated levels of cortisol and adrenaline, the fight-or-flight hormones that wear out so many body and brain systems. These chemical messengers are very efficient at preparing the body for danger. When we first see a threat, the body suddenly releases electrical and chemical signals that increase heart rate, redirect energy to the muscular and sensory systems, shut down digestion and reproduction, send immune cells into storage depots, and deploy steroids to help us heal from wounds. We can see, hear, and smell better; we are more alert and can concentrate better; our skin tightens and our hair stands on end.

This is the fight-or-flight response; everything going on within us is designed to help us deal with danger more effectively. Once we feel safe, systems return to normal. Heart rate slows, and we once again get interested in things like food, sex, and comfort—items that were low priorities while danger loomed.* But when we feel in constant danger, as we do with depression and other stress-related diseases (and perhaps merely as a reaction to life today), we keep on pumping out stress hormones. This can lead to exhaustion, cardiac strain, kidney damage, muscle fatigue, damage to the digestive and circulatory system, loss of appetite and the ability to absorb nutrients, damage to the immune system so we become more vulnerable to infection, loss of interest in sex, and the constant subjective feeling of tension and fear. Part of the problem is that our bodies haven't changed much in 160,000 years, since the first human appeared. In those days, it was useful to constantly be on guard, and there wasn't any evolutionary pressure to reduce the long-term effects of stress, because no one lived past thirty-five anyway. Now, once we pass thirty-five, we start to experience what constant vigilance does to our bodies—and for some of us it happens much younger because we live with a new kind of stress.

In one four-year study of nursing home residents, those who were assessed as most depressed at the outset had the greatest impairment of the immune response as time went on.[5] Depression is a significant risk factor for heart attack.[6] Depression shortens the lifespan, even if the sufferer doesn't commit suicide, and increases the risk of other medical problems. Depression leads to higher death rates following heart attack, for both men and women, controlling for all other health and social variables.[7] Depression means increased risk of death for the general hospital population, no matter what the diagnosis, not

---

* Robert Sapolsky's wonderful book, *Why Zebras Don't Get Ulcers*, is my primary source for understanding the physiology of the stress response. Sapolsky is a fascinating individual who spends half the year studying baboons in Kenya and half lecturing at Stanford. His autobiography, *A Primate's Memoir*, is an engrossing, funny, and moving account of a scientist's life.

only cardiac cases.[8] Patients with depression visit their doctors more often, have more operations, and go to the ER (nonpsychiatric) more often than the general population. Depression is highly intertwined with nonspecific illness: one survey of almost 20,000 individuals found that 17 percent reported chronic pain and 4 percent reported major depression; but of those with depression, 40 percent also had chronic pain.[9] Chronic pain, digestive and gut problems, migraine headaches, menstrual pain and dysphoria, weight-control problems—all will add their own suffering to that of depression. They also compound the effects of depression, further restricting activity, nutrition, and self-care, and reinforcing the depressive's idea of himself as out of control, bad, or weak. In the end, people with depression experience that strange euphemism used by statisticians: "excess mortality." They die earlier than they should.[10]

The famous Nuns of Mankato study compared the essays written by a group of nuns in their twenties, when they were entering the order, with their health and life expectancy some sixty years later.[11] The researchers coded all the emotion-laden words in the essays and grouped them into positive, negative, and neutral. The sisters were a wonderful group to study because all of them had had basically the same experiences during their lifetimes, unlike virtually any other group where factors like marriage and divorce, motherhood, stress, alcohol abuse, wealth, or educational achievement would have been intervening variables, confounding the research so that you couldn't be certain that the only factor at work was the way they expressed feelings. In the end, the researchers found that the more positive feelings the nuns had expressed in their essays in early adulthood, the longer they were likely to live. Now science is trying to explain why this is so.

Depression also affects the brain directly. We stop producing dopamine, the chief neurotransmitter of pleasure circuitry in the brain. On our nerve endings, the receptor sites for endorphins, the happy hormones, get "pruned" like a tiny little apple orchard, so that pleasant events no longer result in pleasant feelings.[12]

One of my patients, an interior designer, tells me that when her depression is very bad, she has a lot of trouble with balance and coordination, and her ability to visualize a room or a tableau spatially is reduced: it all seems like different, unconnected parts. More urgently, she feels very dizzy on a stepladder. Her coworkers, who are supportive, can tell that she's gotten clumsy and dizzy. This is a very distinct change from her normal functioning. How much worse would this be if you had to work on something taller than a stepladder?

Somatization

The subject of somatization casts the whole field of mind-body medicine, especially depression, into confusion. Somatization, formally, is a psychological defense mechanism referring to the use of the body to convey an emotional or interpersonal message. People with some conditions that are seen by others as perhaps not really real, like fibromyalgia or chronic fatigue syndrome, get extremely defensive about the concept of somatization, especially when the dreaded word *psychosomatic* is used. "Psychosomatic" simply means having to do both with the mind and the body, but in popular use we mean someone has an imaginary illness and should know better; or they are perhaps faking the whole thing.

This is unfair both to the sufferers of such illnesses and to those who are trying to understand them. As we have seen, the mind-body connection is very close and we don't understand it very well. We realize now that it's quite naïve to think of the body as a machine to carry around the brain or to imagine that our "self" is located up in the skull behind our eyes — the mind and the body are one thing. People with stress-related diseases, including chronic pain sufferers, and those with damaged immune systems and autoimmune diseases, and such twenty-first-century diseases as fibromyalgia, chronic fatigue, and multiple allergies, often seem to have been made vulnerable by childhood experiences, particularly of sexual abuse or having parents with very inappropriate boundaries. If you have one of these conditions, I strongly urge you to consider that you might be depressed, and that treating the depression might be the shortest route to relieving the physical symptoms; but that doesn't mean your condition isn't real.

So somatization is not merely a psychological defense mechanism—use of the body to speak for the mind—because complex physical changes do occur and can take on a life of their own. Still, we rely on our bodies to communicate interpersonal messages all the time. The fact is that *any* illness, no matter how "real" it is, can be used by the patient to express himself emotionally and interpersonally. I have heard from my patients about many mothers and fathers who use their cancer, diabetes, or handicap as fuel for guilt-tripping the patient, as an excuse for emotional withdrawal, or as a means of manipulation. Then there are some illnesses that may not be quite real but are used for the same reason—for instance, a pain condition or "diabetes" or "heart condition" that never gets pinned down. The patient can never seem to get to doctor's appointments, and when he does, emerges with confusing or conflicting advice. Family members are left mystified about the reality of the illness.

But some people with depression are especially prone to somatization.

Stephanie was a survivor of childhood incest, who lived with an alcoholic and abusive husband and felt unable to escape her marriage because of the children. She was a caretaker, always putting the needs of others first, unable to stand up for her rights. Antidepressants didn't seem to do much for her. Physically, she suffered from frequent debilitating migraines and a great deal of fatigue. Her family doctor had referred her to a rheumatologist, who told her she had fibromyalgia and chronic fatigue syndrome, and perhaps chronic Lyme disease. Stephanie was intelligent but unsophisticated about depression and health. She assumed that these were all separate physical illnesses not connected to her depression. But I thought it made a lot of sense: that if I walked around for thirty years as tense as Stephanie, always afraid, always hypervigilant, unable to relax, my joints and muscles would ache too, and I would always be on the edge of exhaustion. I watched over the next few years as Stephanie became a guinea pig for medication: antidepressants, stimulants, relaxants, antibiotics, hormones, painkillers, steroids. She went through hot flashes, cold sweats, deep depression, hypomanic highs, disfiguring skin eruptions, severe weight loss and then gain, insomnia, nightmares, sleeping too much, severely impaired concentration, crippling anxiety, the fear of losing her mind, a psychiatric hospitalization—almost all of which I felt was due to the medications she was taking. (There were reasons I can't describe here why I couldn't intervene more directly with Stephanie.)

I think that Stephanie was expressing some of the rage she had repressed from her abuse experiences. She was reliving them, in a way, with the doctors as the abusers. She was also saying to her therapist: You can't help me. What good is your empathy? Where were you when I needed you?

Somatization may also be a form of introjection—we make the bad parent or the abuser part of ourselves, twisting our backs, giving us splitting headaches, pain in the heart, crippling menstrual cramps. In this way we relive traumatic experiences. Remember Jane (from Chapter I), whose son shot himself in the head, and her severe headaches?

If you spend a lot of time and money pursuing solutions to physical complaints and are not getting much relief—especially if you are an abuse victim—my advice is to find one internist, GP, or gynecologist who is enlightened about and interested in mind-body relationships (your therapist or psychiatrist should be able to help you find one), and develop a good relationship with him or her. Tell the doctor about your condition, but go into detail about your history and your current stresses. Make it clear you will be needing his or her help in getting symptomatic relief while accepting the limits of physical medicine to address mind-body problems. Exercise, go to spas, get massages. Even if your symptoms are exclusively physical, consider the idea of trying an antidepressant and getting some psychotherapy. No one is accusing you of faking an illness; rather, simply trying to get you good help for the effects of stress and trauma.

Gender Differences in Depression

Women are two to three times more likely than men to be diagnosed with depression. But this simple fact is complicated by many factors. Is there a bias in the diagnostic criteria? Do men manifest depression differently than women? And if it's true that women are more likely to experience depression, is this because their bodies are different, or is it the way society treats them? Do they have more to be depressed about than men do?

Let's address some of these questions.

Is it possible that women who are unhappy with their "traditional" lot in life are labeled sick merely because they don't meet male-defined standards of normality? This thesis has been considered by feminist thinkers since the seventies. It's an idea that will not go away, and I've seen how it works for some patients. Like it or not, psychiatry represents conventional values; it is an important means of social control and subject to abuse. If women are made to feel that there is something inherently inferior about being women, they are more likely to feel depressed. As mentioned earlier, in 2004 a third of women's doctor visits resulted in a prescription for an antidepressant.[13] How many of these women felt cared for by their doctor, and how many felt (like some of my patients have told me) that they were being told to shut up and go away?

Still, it's very hard to read the epidemiologic studies and conclude anything else than there is more than bias at work here; that women are indeed more vulnerable to depression. I can think of several possible reasons: one is that perhaps women have more to be depressed about than men do. Anyone who feels she has to please other people is at risk for depression. The more sources of gratification one has in one's life, and the more predictable and controllable those resources, the less risk for depression. If a woman is taught to define her worth in terms of keeping her husband or the men in her life happy, she is too dependent on arbitrary and capricious sources of gratification. If she's taught to believe that male approval is more important than self-satisfaction, she's not going to put her own needs first.

Another factor leading to more female depression, at least in America, has to do with the way women are made to feel about their bodies. The thin, emaciated look glamorized by popular culture is simply impossible for most women to achieve. As boys grow into puberty, their bodies become more like that of the idealized man — broader shoulders, better muscle definition — but girls' bodies go in the opposite direction, becoming softer and more curvaceous. Fashion's ideal is a prepubescent girl; so it's no wonder that when girls find their bodies taking them away from the ideal, they become dissatisfied with their bodies and themselves. Girls and boys are about equally likely to become depressed before puberty; after puberty, many more girls become depressed.

Another possibility why women are more likely to be depressed is that their moods are, to a greater extent than men, influenced by hormonal changes. Many women with depression report a predictable waxing and waning of symptoms that coincides with their menstrual cycle. Women whose depression worsens during the premenstrual period have lower levels of serotonin during that time than they do postmenstrually, and lower levels than women without PMS.[14] Besides the direct effects of hormones on moods, women may be more prone to feelings of powerlessness because their moods change due to forces they can't control.

Still another factor is women's experience of abuse and victimization. There is good reason to believe that sexual abuse of female children is much more frequent than anyone would like to admit; a study conducted by the American Psychological Association's Task Force on Women and Depression found that 37 percent of women had had a significant experience of physical or sexual abuse by the time they reached twenty-one.[15] A great many of my female patients were abused as children or teens, and I see the lingering effects of trauma like this in adulthood. Anxiety, difficulty trusting, difficulty sleeping, fears associated with sex, a sense of helplessness — these are enough to set anyone up for depression.

Finally, as one of my happily widowed clients put it, one good reason why more women are depressed is that they have to live with men.

So there is plenty of reason to believe that women are, indeed, more depressed than men, and it's easy to understand why this should be the case. But let me, the male writer, say a word about men and depression. Men are five times more likely than women to commit suicide. They are much more likely to become antisocial personalities, end up in jail, or to fall victim to substance abuse, than are women. They die, on average, five and a half years younger than women.[16] Poverty and discrimination seems to lead to depression in women, but to antisocial activity and drug abuse in men.[17] This certainly fits with common perception, but why should it be so?

Far too often, men get the idea that they are not supposed to feel, that they must at all times hide their feelings behind a supposedly tough outer shell. The number of men I know who have conversations with other men about anything meaningful is pitifully small. Instead of permitting ourselves to feel the emotional symptoms of depression, we defend against them by acting out (dangerous, self-destructive, or antisocial behavior), by somatization (rushing to the ER with chest pains that turn out to be an anxiety attack), or by trying to treat them with alcohol. Many men feel they are faking it, making it up as they go along, always one misstep away from disaster. They try to reassure themselves by swaggering around the house, but they wonder if women aren't really laughing behind their backs. From where I sit, women's depression may be a healthier alternative than any of these responses; men might actually be a whole lot better off if they could permit themselves to feel depressed.

Preventive Maintenance

There is now abundant research evidence to show that exercise is as effective an antidepressant as any SSRI. Several studies of older adults have found that brisk exercise three times a week was at least as effective as Zoloft in the short term, and that adults who continued their exercise program had a significantly greater chance of avoiding future depressive episodes.[18] A very good study in 2007 showed that exercise at home, exercise in groups, and Zoloft were all equally better than a placebo condition in treating major depression.[19] Many other studies have found much the same thing, but because meds are so intensely marketed, the good news about exercise is drowned out. Exercise and sports are an important part of the lives of most happy people.[20] Put simply, the more you exercise, the better you feel. Tal Ben-Shahar, a happiness researcher, says that not exercising is like taking a depressing drug; that our bodies were designed to work hard every day, to farm, build, and hunt.[21]

Perhaps most important, exercise appears to stimulate the growth of new neurons in the brain.[22] Depression appears to slow the development of new brain cells, and both medication and psychotherapy have been shown to reverse that effect. Exercise, of course, is much less expensive than either of those. Growing new neurons appears to be associated with the ability to learn new skills—what this book is all about.

The difficulty is, of course, getting the person with depression out the door to exercise. A leader of the Mood Disorders Support Group, a big (and very helpful) organization in New York, told me he once asked the eighteen members of a support group how many had joined a health club and never attended. All eighteen raised their hand.

For many, the only way to exercise is to do it without thinking, to get into a routine where you work out before you have your morning coffee, or go to the gym on your way home from work, or take a vigorous walk with a colleague at lunchtime. If you start thinking about whether or not you really need to do this today, you're sunk. There is also a secret to exercise that many people with depression don't know: that after the first five minutes, it gets much easier. (If it doesn't you're pushing too hard.) Your body warms up, your negative thinking quiets down, endorphins start to flow, and you may find yourself feeling that this is not so bad after all.

If you're prone to depression, you also have to watch how you eat and drink. There are so many good diet and nutrition books out there that I don't need to review them for you. But accept the facts. If you abuse or neglect your body, it's an attenuated form of a suicidal impulse. Instead of actively cutting your wrists, you passively develop heart disease by not taking care of yourself.

The bottom line is that self-destruction, even in these indirect ways, is not romantic but stupid and selfish. Instead of taking care of his diabetes, Sylvia Plath's father, an educator and scientist himself, took to his bed and adopted Christian Science, dying when Sylvia was only eight. The child Sylvia correctly perceived his death as suicide and never forgave him. Her anger and bitterness toward him pervaded her life, and her suicide was certainly an attempt to find release from the intensity of the emotions she felt. This family tragedy perhaps extended to the next generation, as Sylvia's adult son, who had gone to great pains to distance himself from his mother's world, took his own life in 2009.

Rest and relaxation is an important corrective to depression's slow self-destruction. It almost goes without saying that in today's world, especially if you're depressed, your body is likely to be tense and knotted, and you need to take time to relax. There are a number of ways of achieving relaxation, and there has to be one that's right for you. Mindfulness meditation, which I strongly urge you to practice unless you are very deeply depressed, will also help your body relax. Of course, there are other, more traditional, ways of relaxing, as we described earlier: prayer, walking, sports, journaling, love and sex, play, naps. Here's something I find especially rewarding.

Exercise 4: Mindful Walking

• *This is a way to get some exercise and practice mindfulness at the same time. Just go for a walk. Make sure you have comfortable shoes and that you're dressed appropriately for the weather. It doesn't have to be sunny and warm to be a good day for a walk; brisk and raw is fine. Plan for about a half hour to start with; if you want more strenuous exercise you can pick up your pace, but keep attending in a mindful way. Leave your cell phone, iPod, and BlackBerry behind.*

• *Attend to your body. Stand up straight and let your arms swing. Put your neck as straight up as possible and let your head balance on that point; notice the changes in your shoulders, chest, belly, chin, throat. Pay attention to your leg muscles as they warm and loosen up; you're giving them what they need. If you notice any pains, visualize sending your blood and its warmth to that particular area. Chances are the pain will diminish, but of course don't ignore any severe pain. Pay attention to your breath: breathe deeply, through your nose.*

• *Attend to your path. I walk the same path all the time, an old rail trail. I notice the animals, the plants and trees, the evidence of the seasons, the birds singing. But you can walk a different path every day, attending to the same things, or other distinctive features on your path. Notice your footing and be sure it's secure at all times. Walking is what the human body was designed for; notice how well your body functions in walking, how your balance comes naturally, how your weight shifts easily from one leg to the other, how your muscles know how to do this without any guidance from you. If you try to think about walking, you'll probably stumble.*

• *Attend to your senses. Listen carefully for sounds that are usually in the background, and focus on them. Notice how much more aware you can be. Look around you and see where the sun is shining from. Watch the shadows, including your own, that it casts. Look carefully at anything that strikes your eye, and again notice how much more aware you can be. Same with smells. Keep your nose open. Maybe all you'll notice is the fresh air, but think about it. Fresh air brings life and energy. If there are other smells, try to identify them, and see what they remind you of. Smells are deeply connected to the memory centers. When I smell fresh-cut grass, it takes me right back to childhood. Most of us keep ourselves too busy to notice smells.*

• *Attend to people. If you meet others on your path, make eye contact, smile, and say hello like you mean it. It will make for a better day for both of you. If you're in the city and there are lots of people on the path, look at faces. Make up stories about them — who's waiting for them at home, what's good in their lives?*

• *Attend to your mind. As in a mindfulness exercise, notice where your thoughts go. When you find yourself worrying, or thinking about other things, drag your mind back to your present experience. Focus on the rhythm of your walking. Let your unconscious attend to your worries, and keep focusing on where you are right now, how you feel, what you see, hear, and smell.*

• *If you have a dog to walk, all the better. Imagine what it's like to be a dog, to see the world from only a foot or so high, to have such a sophisticated nose, to run simply for the joy of it.*

The Self

DEPRESSION IS A LOSS of parts of the self. Instead of experiencing our inner selves as strong, vital, and joyful, we see ourselves as weak, damaged, or blameworthy. We wish that others could make us feel better, but we can't usually express such wishes directly; instead we use various self-defeating defense mechanisms to keep our wishes out of consciousness. And even though we try to suppress these desires, we still feel guilty and shameful; we consider ourselves needy, unworthy, repugnant. What can we do to reinvigorate the self, to help us capture or recapture a sense of ourselves as a center of initiative, a participant rather than an observer, a source rather than a victim of life?

Guilt, Shame, and Depression

Though in common speech we often hear people say, "I'm really feeling depressed today," depression is not an emotion. Sadness, disappointment, and fear are emotions. Depression is an illness. One of the manifestations of depression is a persistent complex of emotions like sadness, fear, and anger. We all experience the emotions associated with depression when we are grieving, hurt, or disappointed.

Guilt and shame, while they can be very powerful feelings,

perhaps more powerful than any others, are not primary emotions in the sense that they exist in the infant's repertoire almost from birth. They seem to find expression only after the first year or so of life, when the infant's interactions with caregivers are already complex. Though guilt was the focus of most of Freudian psychoanalytic theory and treatment, shame seems to be more of a factor in today's psychopathology, and is certainly intimately connected with depression.

We feel guilt about our actions—things we do or don't do: we take unfair advantage, we break promises, we lie. We feel shame about who we are—we experience ourselves as unworthy, uncouth, repulsive, stupid. The Catholic Church has known for centuries what to do about guilt—all it takes is sincere repentance and a firm intention to change. If we feel genuinely sorry for our actions and resolve to do better in the future, we don't have to feel guilty anymore. Freud then taught us how to address unconscious guilt: drag the guilt-inducing but forbidden impulses into the light of day, and their power over us withers away. But there is no easy resolution for shame. We can't so easily change who we are. It's hard to make ourselves believe that we are good enough.

Guilt and shame exist in what some call the "preconscious" world—we manage to forget about them most of the time, but when we go to bed at night, they pop up out of the darkness. Sometimes people with depression unconsciously look to others in their lives to undo these feelings we carry around, but it's impossible, because we don't really believe we deserve forgiveness; we believe our defects are far too deep.

Part of the reason for the popularity of the recovery movement is that it helps detoxify shame. Alcoholics have always been expected to be ashamed of themselves—they are seen by nondrinkers as weak, irresponsible, lacking backbone, degraded. But when they share their stories with others who are sworn not to judge them, who will praise them for their courage just for admitting the problem, who share the same problem and seem to be able to live with it, the shame of alcoholism is detoxified. John Bradshaw, the author of *Healing the Shame That Binds You*,[1] a recovery movement bible, taps this theme by constantly reiterating his message of freeing oneself from "toxic shame."

Shame serves a purpose for the infant.[2] When his smiles, coos, and gurgles fail to engage a preoccupied parent, he looks down sadly and seems to experience shame. It keeps him from making a bad situation worse by continuing to seek a response when none is forthcoming. Later, he learns to discriminate better: if mommy looks disgusted at a dirty diaper but praises the child for BMs on the potty, shame comes to be associated with messiness, self-esteem with cleanliness. But if mommy, because of her own depression, anger, or frustration, seems inconsistently annoyed at some times and responsive at others, the child cannot learn adequate discrimination. Shame comes to be associated with the self of the child, not the child's behavior or products.

Shame is also connected to our ability to meet our own standards. If we have a strict moral code and fail or slip up occasionally, we may feel guilty. Guilt, in moderation, is good for us and society. It keeps us on our moral toes and out of trouble. But if we consistently fail to meet our own goals — or if we feel that our goals are set too low so that we are not challenging ourselves — we feel shame. It's no longer that our behavior is sometimes substandard, but that we — our selves — are unable to produce meaningful, effective, worthwhile behavior. Reviewing our priorities, then making a deliberate effort to spend more time and energy in activities that help us achieve them, as described in Chapter 15, can gradually help alleviate this kind of self-blame.

Shame, like guilt, can be forced out of consciousness — denied, repressed, split off. The adult consumed by shame may consciously feel only some of the symptoms of depression — a sense of futility, a desperate but self-defeating desire to please, a focus on aspects of the self (as with anorexia or psychosomatic illness) as a vehicle for concerns about the whole self.

Depression is an ironic disease, the Catch-22 of mental illness. In a national survey, a significant minority of Americans were found to think of depression as inherently stigmatizing — but these were the most depressed. People who felt depression was shameful were more likely than the average person to have experienced depression themselves and more likely to report feeling "really depressed" at least once a month.[3] A pervading sense of shame is a precursor to depression; and accepting that one has an illness and needs help is also too often seen as shameful. But shame can only thrive in darkness and secret; dragging our bad feelings out into the light of day, sharing them with people we trust, can be of enormous benefit.

Another antidote for shame is a more enlightened self-awareness. Use of a log like the Daily Record of Dysfunctional Thoughts in Chapter 8 will help the reader become more aware of the kinds of irrational beliefs — often motivated by unconscious shame — that interfere with healthy functioning. Once themes and issues around shame have been identified, joining a group can be the most effective detoxifying experience. Alcoholics Anonymous, Al-Anon, Overeaters Anonymous, self-help groups for depression, psychotherapy groups — exposing our shame to others who are sympathetic can help remove its power over us.

The Importance of Boundaries

I referred earlier to our conflicted feelings about intimacy, about wanting it desperately and at the same time fearing it. One way in which family therapists think about this issue puts it in terms of fusion and autonomy. *Autonomy* implies having a well-developed self, good internal resources of self-esteem, clear boundaries. *Fusion* implies a merging with others, a dissolving of the self, an aversion to taking responsibility. It may sound as if I mean that autonomy is good, fusion is bad; but a little fusion can be good for us at times, and autonomy can be carried to the extreme of distance and isolation. Fusion makes us bond with others. Everyone who has ever been head over heels in love has experienced fusion. Our feelings for the other person have taken over our entire functioning, so that we can't concentrate, we feel giddy, and we may feel invulnerable (and in fact anesthetized). It's like that experiment many of us saw in chem lab. We keep on adding one clear liquid to another, drop by drop, until suddenly the entire solution turns deep red. We are permeated by love.

Fusion also comes in the midst of fights. Who hasn't had the experience of not being able to remember what started a fight, who said what to whom, and when? The rage, like love, takes over all our functioning. Autonomy, on the other hand, is the gradual (and constant) struggle to define a self within the context of a relationship. We must learn not to strive to please others or merely to be different from others, in fact not to define ourselves in terms of others at all, but in terms of an objective evaluation of our own strengths and weaknesses, our own wants and needs.

Having boundaries simply means knowing where I end and you begin, understanding what is my responsibility and what is yours. Boundaries can be too rigid or too loose. We want them to be semipermeable, so that we can let others in when it's appropriate, or keep them out when it's appropriate. Codependency is one example of loose boundaries. The paradigm of codependency is the wife of the alcoholic, who is seen as "enabling" his drinking by making excuses for him, by helping him keep out of trouble, by not confronting him with the effect alcohol has on the family. She puts her husband's needs ahead of her own and the children's; she blames herself for troubles in their relationship, denying the effect of the alcohol; she feels it's her job to make him happy.

What should be within the boundary of my self? Two things, primarily: awareness and responsibility.[4] I should be aware of my own thoughts, feelings, memories, beliefs, and choices; aware of my wants and needs; and aware that I have an unconscious that can distort everything. I should know that others cannot know these things unless I tell them, and that I cannot have this awareness of others unless they tell me (and they have a right to choose not to). I have to take responsibility for my own behavior, including what I communicate, and for setting direction in my life and making myself happy. I cannot make others happy, I can't make them stop drinking, I can't make my children successful—in fact, I can't make others do anything at all. If I choose to, I can conduct my behavior so that they have a better chance of achieving the goals I want for them, but their achievement is their responsibility, not mine. Establishing healthy boundaries like these is a first step toward detachment.

But boundaries can be too rigid as well as too loose. Not everyone is codependent; some are cold, isolated, and lonely. Codependent wives are depressed (often without knowing it, because they're so busy taking care of others), but depression is also caused by distance and alienation. We want to have the capacity to let down our guard, to let others in, to share their feelings and let them share ours. We need to remember that close relationships allow us the opportunity to explore our own identity in an atmosphere of safety. We can express our feelings, and talk about our hopes, dreams, and disappointments without fear of judgment or rejection. A truly intimate relationship can tolerate this without leading to fusion, because each partner keeps in mind that he is not responsible for the other's feelings.

Boundaries are also a helpful concept in thinking about families. For a family to function, there have to be strong but permeable boundaries around relationships. There needs to be a boundary between the parents and children—parents' bad feelings or worries about each other are not to be shared with them. Parents' sex lives, financial worries, and the secrets they tell each other when they're feeling depressed are not the children's business. When a parent tells a child or adolescent a secret about the marriage, that's colluding. It may make the child feel special, more grown-up, but it's actually using the child for some selfish purpose—to gain an ally, to gain sympathy, to fight loneliness—which is ultimately damaging to the child's self-esteem. No one likes being used. Of course these boundaries change as children get older. Mothers and daughters may have their own secrets, fathers and sons theirs. These grow out of respect for the adolescent's needs for privacy and special support. The children have a boundary around their relationship with each other, which can also be quite healthy. Being able to talk to a trusted sibling is a transitional step from depending on the parents to complete autonomy — and often that trust and openness will continue into adulthood, in a special feeling of closeness that is like no other relationship. Note that divorce does not change the need for these boundaries. Divorced parents still need to make many decisions together without involving the children, need to continue to show support for the other's parenting styles, rules, and expectations for the children. Children can live through divorce much better if they still have the sense that there is a parental team caring for them, that parents may not live together but still make decisions together.

We know that people with depression tend to be over-responsible, to care too much about how others feel and not enough for themselves. We accept blame for things that are not our fault, and we can feel horribly guilty about trivial events. But I think if we carefully examine what is our responsibility and what is not, we can free ourselves from much of this depressive guilt. Unfortunately, we also have to be willing to accept real guilt, because we do all slip up. But this is the only way I know to develop self-respect.

Here's my bottom line on boundaries. We are only responsible for our actions, and our inactions. We are not responsible for how we look (within limits), our family connections, how smart we are. We're not responsible for the way others feel, except insofar as our actions engendered those feelings. We're not responsible for making others happy. We have to be responsible for making ourselves happy. We're allowed to be selfish, to put ourselves first at times; if we practice continual self-sacrifice, we're not being responsible for ourselves. If we don't do it, who will?

We must also expect responsibility from others. If we are hurt by another person's behavior, we need to let them know how they have hurt us; to do less diminishes our self-respect. We can, and should, be forgiving; but there is a line between forgiveness and being taken advantage of. We should expect the hurt not to be repeated, and we should be prepared to take action if it is.

Play

People who know my stodgy current self would hardly guess that I became a complete fool when my children were young. I would come home every night and play silly games: dragging them around the polished floor on sheets or in laundry baskets, playing train; hiding under an old mattress while they crawled on top, playing earthquake; or doing simple gymnastics, playing "funny tricks." As the kids grew up, some of these games evolved into more familiar sports like catch or Frisbee or games of Scattergories.

When my daughter left for college and my son grew into ado-lescence, I got depressed again. Consciously, I knew I was missing them. I cried when my daughter moved out; I felt lonely as I went for walks without my son. My wife and I became television addicts. As always seems to happen, it took me a while to recognize depression for what it was.

Something reminded me one night of how we had played together. I literally had to sit down on the stairs to catch my breath, the memory was so powerful and painful. This was not recapture of a repressed memory—I had never forgotten these moments—but a sudden appreciation of the impact of the loss. The opportunity to regress, to be a child again, to play with my own children in safety, had been a healing experience for me. My own childhood had been rather cold and scary; there wasn't enough tickling and hugging. My children had given me the opportunity to make up for some of what I had missed, to parent myself.

Play is essential to nurturing the self. The depressive, trying to hide from his own punitive superego like Adam from a wrathful Jehovah, feels that he'd better never let his guard down, always be busy, always be productive. But it's a joyless existence if all we care about is getting the work done. Something as simple as playing catch with the dog for a few minutes after work connects us with a part of ourselves we can lose only too easily — the child who can laugh, who can enjoy silliness, mindless physical activity.

Play changes moods. Play can lift depression. Sad children, coaxed into play, can smile and laugh and forget their sadness. Many of us have wheedled a grumpy twelve-year-old into playing Monopoly on a summer night. After a while, the grumping is gone. It may come back, but in the meantime parent and child have shared an enjoyable experience that wouldn't have happened if anyone had tried to analyze or solve the child's problem. We adults can be no different from the grumpy twelve-year-old. Our moods are subject to change. Sometimes we resist the invitation to play because if we played we might feel better, and then wouldn't we feel foolish for feeling as grumpy as we did? But we can't depend on others to keep calling us out to play. We have to make our own opportunities.

Play is not work. You can't make play out of an activity whose purpose is to accomplish something, but it's fine if you accomplish something while you're playing.

Play is usually physical. Our bodies are engaged. We move, we use our large muscles, we can sweat.

Play often involves a conscious abandonment of dignity, sometimes by putting us into roles or positions that are outside our usual behavior.

Play usually involves others. Solitary play is okay if there is no one available, but it's more fun with other people.

Play involves being spontaneous, doing what our impulses tell us. This may require planning. Games have rules to keep our spontaneity in safe limits. Spontaneity helps us lose self-consciousness, which seems to be a major point of play.

There are horrible-sounding psychoanalytic concepts like "regression in the service of the ego," and "humor as a mature defense," which are the gray analysts' way of trying to acknowledge that joy is essential but hard to analyze. I think the fact that animals play should tell us that play is part of nature, that we need to play to live.

As Carol Tavris writes in *Anger: The Misunderstood Emotion:* "For some of the large indignities of life, the best remedy is direct action. For the small indignities, the best remedy is a Charlie Chaplin movie. The hard part is knowing the difference."[6]

Taking Care of the Self

Depressives must learn to practice self-care. We can fix our leaky oil pans ourselves. What this means is a deliberate effort to practice the skills we've been talking about—changing our emotional, behavioral, and thought patterns; changing how we are in relationships; assessing our priorities and trying to live in accordance with our values—and then *letting ourselves feel proud of our accomplishments.* This may be the hardest single thing for most depressives. We have been conditioned never to feel proud. We expect that it's asking for trouble, that the Old Testament God will reach down and smite us like Job. But Job was chosen at random, and our chances of misfortune are exactly the same, whether we feel good or bad about ourselves.

If you're following the principles of this book, you're changing every day, but you must allow yourself time to integrate those strengths and successes. It will gradually build a strong, nurturing self that you can rely on in times of stress. We have to do this by allowing some time to reflect and take stock. We can do this in many of the ways described in previous chapters—through intimate conversation, through meditation, through play—but if we don't take time to do it, any recovery we make from depression will be only temporary.

This applies equally to people who have recovered from depression with the help of antidepressants. There is a fear that the pill has only temporarily cured you and that when you go off the medication you will be subject to depression again. But on a deeper level, most of these people recognize that the medication has just allowed another part of their selves to come out. Peter Kramer in *Listening to Prozac* relates how his patient Tess, depressed for twenty years, miraculously recovers on Prozac—she becomes almost a different person: assertive, witty, attractive. When she stops taking the medication, she goes back to her old ways—depressed, passive, lonely—but says, "I'm not myself."[7] She has returned to the self she was for twenty years, but she feels that the Prozac self is the real self. Antidepressants sometimes help people be who they think they are, help them act on their abilities, have the courage of their convictions, live up to their own self-image. But the effect is only temporary if we don't allow ourselves to integrate the experience.

I think that depression is best understood as a chronic condition. But we can stay almost symptom-free if we just take proper care of ourselves. I suggest that part of good care requires that we put some time aside each week to reflect on our experience. Writing in regular mindfulness practice can help you understand the recurring issues that are causing you distress, and also help you learn what gives you pleasure and helps you feel good. It is necessary to consider again our priorities and assess the day in terms of how close we came to living in accordance with them, to figure out what we can do differently next time but also to reflect on and integrate what we've done well. It can be done in church, in therapy, in a group, in an intimate conversation, in journaling or meditation, but it needs to be done.

Sometimes I give my patients a printout of the following guidelines. People who appreciate it most are usually the ones who didn't have nurturing parents and lack supportive relationships in the present. Some have posted the list in a prominent place, on the refrigerator or next to the bathroom mirror. These are very simple ideas, but taken together they develop a certain force. When you have a weak or damaged self, it can help to be reminded that it's important to take care of yourself—and by doing so regularly you begin to strengthen and heal.

Basics of Good Self-Care

- Exercise moderately but regularly
- Eat healthy but delicious meals
- Regularize your sleep cycle
- Practice good personal hygiene
- Don't drink to excess or abuse drugs
- Spend some time every day in play
- Develop recreational outlets that encourage creativity
- Avoid unstructured time
- Limit exposure to mass media
- Distance yourself from destructive situations or people
- Practice mindfulness meditation, or a walk, or an intimate talk, every day
- Cultivate your sense of humor
- Allow yourself to feel pride in your accomplishments
- Listen to compliments and expressions of affection
- Avoid depressed self-absorption
- Build and use a support system
- Pay more attention to small pleasures and sensations
- Challenge yourself

13

Treating Depression Medically

I **HAVE HAD SOME** difficulty writing this chapter because I do very much want to encourage anyone with severe depression to try medication. It can be a real help: sometimes it creates a dramatic change; sometimes it can save your life. I have seen this happen many times with my patients, and I routinely refer people with severe depression or depression compounded by anxiety to a psychiatrist. People with depression often resist medication treatment for years and years, self-destructively, because they are afraid of change. I feel, and people around me confirm, that medication has helped me greatly when I have been at my lowest. It's very frustrating for me when my patients won't try it out of fear and ignorance. I don't want to add any ammunition to this resistance.

But—and it's a very big but—medication, especially over the last fifteen years, has been vastly oversold, overpromised, and over-prescribed. Scientific research has been compromised and distorted. Greedy researchers, secretly in the pay of Big Pharma, have created epidemics like childhood bipolar disorder by playing on parents' fears and confusion. The side effects of medication have been swept under the rug. The way the drugs achieve their effect, as we will describe, carries with it a lot of unintended negative consequences, but few know about this. All this news management has paid off well: in 2005, antidepressant use had doubled from ten years before, to 10.12 percent of the population from only 5.84. The researchers expressed concern that the number of people receiving psychother- apy had declined at the same time, and that most patients were being medicated by GPs, and some of those patients were on esoteric drug cocktails.[1]

All that must be balanced against the fact that unremitting depression is also damaging, usually much more so than medica- tion treatment. Most dramatically, depression can cause brain dam- age. But it can also destroy your confidence and self-esteem so that you miss out on the opportunities of life. It can destroy relationships and make you unemployable. The longer it lasts, the more damage it causes. Adequate, prompt treatment for a first episode reduces the odds that you'll get depressed again. Up against all that, the prob- lems with medication seem pretty small. In fact, there's evidence that medication treatment reverses some of the brain damage done by depression.[2]

The drawbacks of medication are not small at all, though, if you're merely looking to be happier. Antidepressants are immensely over- prescribed to the "worried well"—people who are facing a minor or temporary life upset and hope for a pill as a cure, when they really need to take action. If you rely on medication, you don't grow in skills or self-esteem as you would if you toughed it out or solved the problem yourself (or with a therapist). Adolescents and children whose behavior is worrying or upsetting for parents and teachers need to learn new skills, not be medicated so they will be more com- pliant. Seniors—almost all of them—in group-living situations are prescribed antidepressants to enable them to put up with dehuman- izing conditions.

You see how I bounce back and forth in the last four paragraphs: one minute an advocate for meds, the next minute an alarm bell. I regret that this must be confusing for the reader, but I think confused is the appropriate way to feel about medications for depression at this time.

What's Good about Medication

Let's start by reviewing the current medications in common use. I am not a physician; I can't say anything about dosing instructions, and I can only give general guidelines about what kinds of meds are appropriate for what kinds of conditions. I have little to say about how they work, because no one really knows much about that; the original explanation, that SSRIs work by stabilizing serotonin levels in the brain, seems doubtful now, but no one has come up with another explanation.

There are always new medications in the pipeline and new research findings about current medications, so it's difficult to keep current. In what follows, I'm relying heavily on two websites that try to keep up to date: John Grohol's Psych Central and John McManamy's McMan's Depression and Bipolar Web. McManamy, a bipolar survivor, deserves special credit for keeping his site running on donations and subscriptions, and avoiding Big Pharma advertising. Another reliable resource is Gorman's *Essential Guide to Psychiatric Drugs.*[3]

Medications for depression fall into several major groups: MAO inhibitors, tricyclics, SSRIs and SNRIs, and a small group that are hard to classify. There are also the mood stabilizers that are used for bipolar disorder, ADHD drugs, stimulants like amphetamines, and antianxiety medications.

MAOIs

This term refers to drugs that inhibit monoamine oxidase, a naturally occurring chemical in the brain. In the United States, the usual drugs in this class are Marplan, Parnate, and Nardil. In Europe, these were (pre-SSRI) usually considered the first line of treatment, preferred over tricyclics, while in the United States they are often resorted to only when everything else has failed. They have some unpleasant side effects, but their main disadvantage is that they may cause a fatal stroke or dramatic increase in blood pressure if certain foods containing the compound tyramine are consumed (cheese, red wine, and pickles, among others). However, they are so effective with a small group of people that the relief they provide far outweighs the disadvantages. They are frequently cited as the best treatment available for atypical depression (see Chapter 3). In my limited experience, when MAOIs work they seem to make people a little hyper and obsessional—people will get an idea and follow it far beyond where others would have given up—but they are energized and do feel much better.

Tricyclics (TCAs)

Until the advent of SSRIs, tricyclics were the standard treatment for depression. These medications include imipramine (Tofranil), amitriptiline (Elavil), nortriptyline (Vivactil, Pamelor), desipramine (Norpramin), and doxepin (Sinequan). These are all related to anti-histamines, and in fact if you take Benadryl with one of these you may really dry up. They were derived from the serendipitous finding that tubercular patients treated with antihistaminic compounds sometimes became unexplainably cheerful. New research has shown that they have about the same success rate as SSRIs,[4] with 40 to 60 percent of patients showing signs of improvement within the first three months. Since they all are available generically, their cost can be minimal. But although they can be quite effective medications, there are several drawbacks to their use. They usually take several weeks of faithful administration to be effective, which is difficult to tolerate when patients are feeling in real distress. Side effects include urinary retention, sun sensitivity, dry mouth, weight gain, and constipation. Most important, it is relatively easy to take a fatal overdose—a few weeks' supply—so psychiatrists are in a difficult position with acutely depressed patients who may benefit from tricyclics long-term but may be given a means to self-destruction in the short term. Because tricyclics require a certain level in the bloodstream to be effective, it doesn't do any good to take one when feeling blue. Some tricyclics are rather sedating, which is a disadvantage for most people, but they can be used at bedtime for patients with difficulty sleeping. They are not addictive and you don't get a buzz with them, so they're not a drug of abuse. They must be used with care with patients who have cardiovascular disease.

SSRIs and SNRIs

Considering how vastly more popular they are, it's amazing that SSRIs actually have so many of the drawbacks I just listed for TCAs, plus more. You need to take them for several weeks to feel an effect, and you have to take them faithfully; generally, you won't feel any better just by popping one or two (but some people feel something is happening right away). Some SSRIs are sedating for some people, while others find them energizing; in fact, people have a lot of idiosyncratic reactions to them. You may get terribly anxious, not be able to sleep, and have acute digestive problems from one SSRI, but be perfectly fine with a closely related drug.

SSRIs are not particularly lethal if you overdose on them; that alone may account for why so many physicians prefer prescribing SSRIs. They are generally touted to have fewer side effects and to be more easily tolerated than tricyclics, but that impression is a holdover from the early years when we didn't know about the very common weight gain and loss of sexual interest and performance associated with their use. Almost every man I've known taking an SSRI has had to turn to Viagra or something like it; but that doesn't do anything for the subtle loss of interest in sex that affects both men and women. For many patients, these side effects alone are deal breakers. As for SSRIs being more easily tolerated, in most studies, whether it's a TCA or an SSRI, the majority of patients stop treatment within three months. The conclusion is that SSRIs are generally no more effective or tolerable than TCAs,[5] and now we know that withdrawal from them can be very difficult.

How did the SSRIs become such big news? Partly because we're in an epidemic of depression, partly because of marketing. Their development coincided with the decision to allow direct-to-consumer advertising of prescription drugs. The United States is the only country that permits this, and one wonders how much Big Pharma money went to Congress to influence this decision. *Time* and other magazines now regularly have a twenty-page news-magazine-style section called "Health on Track," which has little articles about health-related topics like prostate cancer, migraine, allergies, how having pets may keep you healthy, and so on. In small type on some pages you see printed "Special Advertising Section." And you see advertisements for prescription medications for prostatitis, migraine, hay fever, depression, bipolar disorder, ADHD, cancer, and even your dog. Almost all the commercials on the evening news have to do with drugs. Advertising is clearly saying to people: *if you have a symptom that bothers you, go to your doctor and ask for this medication by name.** This is an expansion of the idea of illness, and gives the message that if there is something that causes you discomfort or you don't like about yourself—like hair loss—don't just accept it as part of life or part of growing older. It's an illness; it can and should be treated. Your bad mood may be depression, and you should see your doctor right away.

Nevertheless, these are often effective drugs for the truly depressed, and probably what your doctor will first prescribe. The theory behind them is that there are two chemicals, serotonin and norepinephrine, that have to do with the transmission of impulses between nerve cells in the brain and seem to be associated with depression. It seems as if depressed people burn up these chemicals more quickly than other people. SSRIs were thought to help to maintain serotonin at more stable levels in the synapses, apparently

---

* You might want to check out the website Havidol.com (avafynetyme HCL), a parody of direct-to-consumer advertising. It's a fictitious drug for the fictitious disease of Dysphoric Social Attention Consumption Deficit Anxiety Disorder. Many people have not understood the joke and inquired how to get the drug.

leading to feelings of reduced anxiety, more security, and increased self-worth, assertiveness, and resilience. SNRIs are supposed to do the same for serotonin but also affect norepinephrine. Unfortunately, no one has been able to confirm that this is actually the way these drugs work.[6]

SSRIs (selective serotonin reuptake inhibitors) include:

- Prozac (fluoxetine)
- Zoloft (sertraline)
- Paxil (paroxetine)
- Lexapro (escitalopram)
- Celexa (citalopram)

Then there are SNRIs (serotonin-norepinephrine reuptake inhibitors):

- Cymbalta (duloxetine)
- Effexor (venlafaxine)
- Pristiq (desvenlafaxine)
- Strattera (atomoxetine), marketed primarily for ADHD

Some of these drugs have their own reputations in the field, some of it based on science, some not. Cymbalta is supposed to help with the physical pain that accompanies depression. Prozac is thought to be more energizing, Paxil more calming. Paxil is reputed to be the most likely to cause difficult withdrawal problems, and is known to trigger manic episodes among undiagnosed bipolar patients. Lexapro is supposed to be easily tolerated. Pristiq is just extending Effexor's patent.[7]

These drugs, in my opinion, should never be used by children, except under the most extreme circumstances. When children are in emotional distress, it's usually got something to do with what's going on at home, and there are family therapists out there who are good at helping you fix whatever the problem is. We also have no idea about the long-term effect of SSRIs on the developing brain. We have become far too quick to medicate children, putting them in chemical handcuffs when they don't behave.

They also must be used with extreme caution with adolescents. It now seems likely that they do make some teens more prone to commit suicide, but the same caution applies: we don't know what SSRIs can do to a developing mind. Most of the teens I've worked with, and the adults whose depressions began in their teens, have fairly straightforward reasons for being depressed; they don't feel loved at home, they don't fit in at school, they're being abused, bullied, or discriminated against, home is chaotic and they feel responsible. Giving kids like this an SSRI with no attempt at counseling is an insult; it's telling them to shut up and go away. It is true that there are a few teens who develop depression (or a related condition like anorexia or school phobia) seemingly out of the blue, and again we don't want to let depression rob them of years when they need to be learning how to do things, so sometimes antidepressants can be helpful. There are also young people whose depression may have started in response to their life situation, but the depression has taken on a life of its own and the symptoms are so debilitating that meds should be considered. It's important that the teen buy into this treatment, as part of a plan that includes psychotherapy, coming from loving parents who don't want him to suffer unnecessarily.

Other Drugs for Depression

• Trazodone (Desyrel) is marginally effective as an antidepressant, but it is usually quite effective for the insomnia associated with depression. Unlike sleeping medications, it can't make you high, and it doesn't lose its effectiveness over time. For many people, it's a safe and reliable aid to sleep. If you're taking an SSRI but still having trouble sleeping, I strongly recommend you ask your doctor about Trazodone.

• Wellbutrin (buproprion) is a generally well-tolerated drug, except that it carries a slight risk of seizures. Most people feel a little energized by it. Unlike almost all the other antidepressants, it does not cause weight gain or sexual side effects, which makes it very attractive, but it is not usually considered as potent as an SSRI. It is often used as a secondary drug to complement an SSRI. It may be a drug to switch to as your recovery continues and you need a maintenance medication.

• Remeron (mirtazipine) is so sedating for most people that I can't recommend its use. Unlike Trazodone, the sedation effect lingers for some time. I know some MDs prescribe it in combination with SSRIs, and report that it's helpful in that role.

Medications for Bipolar Disorders

Though officially bipolar disorder is quite rare (less than one percent of the population), there are many people with major depression or dysthymia who sometimes have *hypomanic* episodes, when they feel very good, have a lot of energy, may be very creative, may be more reckless than usual. Sometimes when these people are medicated with the newer antidepressants, they will experience a full-blown manic attack (known as "manic switching," a good reason to be careful about prescribing these things). There's controversy among the researchers about whether this actually occurs or not,[8] but I'm a believer. I knew a man in his fifties whose daughter was in the hospital for an acute bipolar episode. We gave him Paxil to help with his depression. When he next attended a meeting at the hospital for family members of patients, he took over the meeting, telling the psychiatrists exactly what was wrong with their program! He was later very embarrassed and we discontinued Paxil right away. The episode made me realize that he often lived in a somewhat grandiose fantasy world, something that took on new meaning in light of this incident — yet I knew him well, and there was no history at all of previous manic episodes.

As this incident suggests, we still have a lot to learn about the chemistry of bipolar disorder. It's being diagnosed much more frequently now (partly because the drug companies are promoting use of their new mood stabilizers and "atypical" antipsychotics, especially in young people). There is reason to believe that bipolar is linked, or can be confused, with ADHD. If you have bipolar disorder, you need to work with a good psychiatrist who is interested in the condition and keeps up with the latest research, but is not being wooed by the drug companies. Lifestyle changes are also important. Psychotherapy is essential to making these changes as well as coming to grips with the fact that you have a chronic disease that means you can't trust yourself, and facing all the hurt you may have caused yourself and others with past manic behavior.

Mood Stabilizers[9]

Lithium is as close as psychiatry has come to a magic bullet, a specific cure for a specific disease. It was until recently the treatment of choice for bipolar disorder, and many MDs still prescribe it first, despite the blandishments of the newer, more expensive drugs. Lithium in the correct dose reduces the chances of another manic episode within a year by about 50 percent. Mood swings become fewer, shorter, and less severe. It's also helpful for the depressed phase of bipolar disorder. The success rate for lithium treatment approaches 70 percent, and 20 percent of patients become symptom-free. It is generally seen as a maintenance drug—once on, the patient continues it for life—and its long-term effectiveness is proven.[10] Compliance is an issue for many patients, partly because some miss the manic highs that come with the disease. Side effects, including weight gain and skin rashes, also make it difficult for some patients to follow their prescription. The most important drawback is that lithium can be toxic to the liver and must be used carefully, especially with alcohol. It should be dispensed only by a psychiatrist who is familiar with its use, not by a general practitioner. Because it can gradually build up to toxic levels, patients must have the amount of lithium in their blood checked monthly. These factors make it difficult to use lithium effectively with patients who are disorganized or impulsive, a frequent problem with bipolar disorder.

Other mood stabilizers include:

• Depakote (divalproex sodium), a drug originally developed as an anticonvulsant, was found coincidentally to help with mood swings. Though, like lithium, it takes time to build up in your system, unlike lithium, Depakote can help rather quickly with acute manic states. It is especially useful with rapid-cycling bipolar disorder, and also with people who have a long history of mood swings, where lithium often fails. It is not especially helpful for the depressed side of bipolar disorder. It can have some serious side effects and, like lithium, requires regular blood tests. It's notorious for causing weight gain.

• Tegretol (and Trileptal, a closely related drug). Research shows that Tegretol is effective against mania about 70 percent of the time, and also that it can help with the depressive episodes of bipolar disorder. It's definitely a drug to consider, but it carries with it a lot of risks, black-box warnings, and drug-drug interactions. If your doctor hasn't taken the time to explain all this to you in detail, find another doctor.

• Lamictal — an anticonvulsant only slightly effective for bipolar disorder. Despite this, and despite some potentially fatal side effects, it remains frequently prescribed, probably because GlaxoSmithKline doesn't give up on promoting its drugs. If you're taking this and begin to develop a rash, discontinue it immediately and call your doctor.

• Neurontin — an anticonvulsant marginally effective for epilepsy and some kinds of nerve pain, Neurontin has been heavily promoted by its manufacturer (Pfizer) for all kinds of off-label uses. It hasn't shown any effectiveness in treating bipolar disorder.

• Topamax — not very effective by itself, it may have some use as an adjunct drug to boost the performance of lithium or

Depakote. Because it often dulls thinking, it's sometimes referred to as "Dopamax."

Atypicals

These drugs are called "atypical antipsychotics" to distinguish them from the first generation of antipsychotic drugs like Thorazine and Haldol. They are often prescribed in the early stages of a manic state to help the patient calm down and get control, and can be very effective. They are also prescribed in very small doses when the patient needs continued relief from anxiety or impulse control problems. These drugs include: Clozaril, Risperdal, Zyprexa, Seroquel, Geodon, and Abilify.* Though you will hear arguments favoring one drug over the others, these distinctions are weak. All these drugs are horse tranquilizers, to quote John McManamy; they are powerful sedating agents that will put you to sleep, and when you're not sleeping you'll be dopey, drowsy, and distant.

Just as with the first-generation antipsychotics, there is a risk of immediate side effects that can include tremors, restlessness, and muscle stiffness. Over the long haul, especially at high doses, there is the risk of tardive dyskinesia: uncontrollable eye movements, chewing, tongue protruding, grimacing, and lip-smacking—an ugly condition that may be irreversible. If you start to experience symptoms like these as a result of an atypical, you should get in touch with your doctor right away, and perhaps lower your dose until you can see him. There are medications you can take to help with the side effects, but most people with depression who are taking these drugs should get off them as soon as possible, because they are not really treating the depression, they are just sedating you.

Patients who've been hospitalized for a major depressive episode

* "Abilify" is a great example of drug industry marketing. Doesn't it sound like it's going to make you want to get up and dance? Sounds like *enable, amplify, ability.* But it's just going to have the opposite effect, to wrap you in a blanket and make you want to go to bed.

are often discharged with an atypical. They may not realize that they are feeling so awful after the hospital at least in part because of the medication. Don't get me wrong — many patients, especially the anxious, can use a chemical bandage like this while they heal. But see my comments in the next section about antianxiety medications.

The bottom line is this: for depression, these drugs are only appropriate as *short-term* treatment, to sedate you while you're recovering from a major meltdown.

Depression and Anxiety

A huge research project aimed at finding the comorbidity (two or more separate conditions occurring at the same time, like flu and pneumonia) of mental disorders found that in 62 percent of all cases, another disorder had led to major depression.[11] Among those who had suffered a major depressive episode within the past year, 51 percent had also suffered an anxiety disorder during the same time, 4 percent had experienced dysthymia, and 18.5 percent had also suffered a substance abuse disorder. When either anxiety or substance abuse accompanied major depression, the patient's chances of recovery nosedived. A World Health Organization study found a remarkably similar (68 percent) comorbidity between depression and anxiety worldwide.[12]

Anxiolytic drugs (tranquilizers) usually provide quick relief from anxiety, yet GPs and psychiatrists are reluctant to prescribe them because they can be abused. In the study of trends in outpatient treatment of depression from 1987 to 1997, only 13 percent of patients were being treated with a tranquilizer.[13] In my opinion, many more depressed patients could benefit from a brief stint on an anxiolytic than is standard practice. Many patients, especially those facing their first episode of major depression, are in a state of acute anxiety. Unlike antidepressants, anxiolytics can give almost immediate relief, giving a sense of a burden lifted, the heart rate, sweating, worrying, and agitation all slowed down. Almost immediately the patient begins to feel safer and more in control. Often, the patient can get the first good night's sleep in months. We've already discussed the connection between panic attacks, phobias, and first episodes of depression; these are situations where anxiolytics can help prevent the development of lifelong crippling symptoms.

It's true that benzodiazepines, such as Valium (diazepam), Klonopin (clonazepam), and Ativan (lorazepam) have some real risks. It's easy to become dependent on them, they lose their efficacy over time (so you need more and more), and withdrawal can be very difficult. These are all real disadvantages, and you need to consider them. But I think it's appropriate to use one of these drugs like a sling for a broken arm, to support and protect you while you heal. After a month or two, when the worst is over, you and your doctor need to talk about reducing your dose or switching to occasional use. Because of the dependency risk, some doctors prefer instead to give small doses of an atypical antipsychotic, which feel so bad no one will want to be addicted. They have such a sedating effect that even in small doses the patient feels like a zombie.

An antianxiety medication can be very helpful for someone who's a suicide risk. Many suicides take place because the patient is in a terribly agitated, panicked state that he thinks is just going to get worse. The drug not only gives relief, but also hope. Unfortunately, an overdose of benzodiazepines is very lethal. Your doctor should dispense just a few pills at a time, and be sure you are taking them as prescribed—this greatly reduces the risk.

Of all these drugs, Klonopin seems to carry the least risk of dependence, because it works more slowly and leaves your body more slowly, so you don't get an immediate high or feeling of withdrawal, the kinds of experiences that lead people to take more and more.

Stimulants

Some psychiatrists, interested in getting lethargic patients moving, are prescribing stimulant drugs (amphetamines like Dexedrine, or amphetamines that are marketed for ADHD like Adderal and Vyvanse). Now we have Strattera, a SNRI marketed as treatment for ADHD. As I've stated, I think we're soon going to learn much more about connections between depression, bipolar disorder, and ADHD, so it makes sense to me to try these drugs out. Of course, they have their own risks and side effects, and probably shouldn't be used with patients who are prone to anxiety, but if you're really stuck, or are suffering from fatigue or procrastination, you might want to give a stimulant a try.

Who Prescribes What?

Most prescriptions for SSRIs are written by general practitioners and other nonpsychiatric MDs, and indeed that's how the drugs have been marketed, both to consumers and to the medical community. Many doctors were glad to have something to give their stressed-out patients who really had no physical complaints. But I strongly recommend to most patients that they consult a psychiatrist for depression. (An APRN, Advanced Practice Registered Nurse, who has training in psychiatry may be an alternative to a psychiatrist, since there are so few of them in parts of the country.) Prescribing for depression is as much an art as it is a science, and good psychiatrists or APRNs often have an educated guess about which medication will be most effective for you. It can save you months of frustration, trying one pill after another. Psychiatrists and APRNs know much more about appropriate dosing and auxiliary medications. They specialize in this stuff, and they can see things that you can't and your GP doesn't have the training for, including the ability to track you over time to get a better idea about what's working and what isn't. I know that psychiatrists are in short supply, and there are some bad ones out there. If you're working with a therapist who is pretty up-to-date about meds, he or she may be able to collaborate with your GP to find something that works for you right off the bat, but if that first try doesn't work, please find a psychiatrist.

Another reason I make this recommendation is that if your first try at meds doesn't work, your depression—and the idea that there is no help for you—is reinforced. Remember that most patients don't complete the first three months of a medication trial, and even fewer will go back for a second; so try to get it right the first time.

If you're seriously depressed and you don't respond to the first antidepressant you try, you should definitely try another. Each medication helps about 50 to 60 percent of the people who try it, but it's a different group for each drug. If A doesn't work for you, there's still a better-than-average chance that B will.

If you don't reach an optimal response (close to cured) within six months or so on a medication that is working somewhat, it's likely that your psychiatrist will want to add something as a secondary medication. Maybe not another SSRI, but perhaps Wellbutrin, or a mood stabilizer, or something to help you relax, or energize you. Even a tricyclic could be added. Although this is increasingly common practice and makes intuitive sense, your psychiatrist is experimenting with you. I actually endorse this if a medication has helped only so much, but you should be aware. Because drug companies sponsor almost all research in the United States now, and because the cost of research is so high, research on the effects of two medications at the same time is still relatively rare. The drug companies don't want to know; finding a pattern might give a lead to their competition.

As for "polypharmacy," your doctor trying you out on multiple different drugs, it depends. If your doctor is connected to a big research hospital and is really up on the latest developments, you might want to give her more rope than someone in a private practice who rarely takes the trouble to educate himself. If you feel that your doctor has stopped caring and is essentially throwing darts at you, find another doctor.

Some doctors may not want to tell you that medications are doing all they can for you; they may follow your lead if you want to keep trying the latest drug or drug combo. But you may reach the point where you don't want to experiment any more, and that can be a wise decision. You may decide that your current medication regime is doing a reasonable job, and that you have to stop hoping for a magic bullet and start trying to change the way you live.

You may need to be on a medication a long time. With major depression, the more episodes you have, the more likely you are to have more; the sooner you stop your medication, the more likely you are to relapse. The general guideline is to stay on your medication at least six months after you feel symptom-free. Some people who have had many episodes should consider staying on a maintenance dose even longer than that, even for the indefinite future, if the side effects aren't too troublesome. I say this despite my warning in the next section that SSRIs may be artificially insulating you from life; it all depends on the severity of your illness. In the studies that follow people beyond an initial three-month treatment period, most patients relapse.[14] But the chances of relapse go down if you don't quit your meds too soon. That's why treatment has to go beyond the standard paradigm, be longer, more intensive, use medications as long as necessary, and include a strong component of education, self-help, and aftercare. In one study that followed people over five years, only half of patients with dysthymia reached full recovery, and of those, half relapsed. Many developed major depression.[15] It's now generally recognized that if you have one episode of major depression, your odds of having another are 50 percent; if you have three episodes, your odds of having more are 90 percent.[16] But if you stay in psychotherapy, take a maintenance dose of medication, and really work on your own recovery, you can beat these odds.

The Dark Side of Medication

As I've intimated, drug industry research on the newer antidepressants has been manipulated to maximize positive results and minimize the downside. (There's much more on this subject on my blog, richardoconnor.blogspot.com.) Here's one example: the original research that got FDA approval and set off the craze for these drugs had very low standards, which were not revealed to the public. They were generally two- or three-month trials, a very short time over the lifetime course of depression, and the definition of cure was simply no longer meeting all the criteria for major depression. You might still be feeling suicidal and wracked with guilt, but if your sleeping had improved, as far as the FDA was concerned, the drug had demonstrated its effectiveness. Then there was the fact that in all these trials the drugs proved only slightly better than a placebo—in most cases, about 40 percent of people got better with a sugar pill, and about 50 to 60 percent improved with an SSRI.[17] Added to that is the fact that many of these studies stacked the deck by excluding people who were most responsive to placebos.[18]

Subsequent studies, with larger groups over longer periods of time, have shown about the same disappointing results. The STAR*D study, with a large sample of real-world patients, without excluding placebo responders, found that about 50 percent of patients had a significant response to medication, but only about 30 percent met the researchers' definition of remission.[19] During follow-up, a significant number of these patients relapsed. Overall, the recovery rate was only slightly better than chance alone. STAR*D was sponsored by the National Institute of Mental Health and should be considered relatively free of drug company influence.

The withdrawal problems with SSRIs have also been minimized. There can be significant withdrawal effects when you stop taking SSRIs—SSRI Withdrawal Syndrome—including extreme anxiety, skin crawling, confusion, GI distress, insomnia, and agitation. For some individuals, these symptoms are excruciating. I had a patient who went through weeks of pure hell—fever, nausea, chills, extreme depression, and the certainty she was losing her mind—going off a pill I had encouraged her to take. The best advice is to discontinue any of these medications by tapering off slowly and under a physician's care.

Last but not least, there are worries that antidepressants interfere with emotional vitality. One study of nondepressed volunteers found that taking an SSRI for only a week interfered with their ability to read facial expressions, especially of anger and fear.[20] Another study of normal volunteers found that four weeks of Paxil significantly reduced their ability to feel sad or angry when appropriate.[21] A group of patients who were experiencing sexual side effects also developed significantly less ability to cry or care about others' feelings. They also lost erotic dreaming, surprise, creativity, anger, and ability to express their feelings.[22]

Therapists who take SSRIs themselves were very disturbed by these findings, wondering if it meant they were losing their ability to be empathic; many of us have stopped medications as a result. I know a musician who tried Lexapro for his social anxiety and asthma. He noticed that he no longer got chills and goose bumps when he was really moved by music. When he stopped Lexapro, he was able to get goose bumps again. He felt that he had also lost some of his ability to immerse himself in the music. Another male patient, who was prone to picking up women for one-night stands, reported that with Paxil he stopped feeling guilty. At least he recognized this was a problem.

It seems quite possible that SSRIs (and other antidepressants, for all I know) get some of their effect from an overall emotional blunting, especially of negative feelings. Their use may make us temporarily a little shallow or insensitive. As far back as *Listening to Prozac* in 1993,[23] Peter Kramer was advancing the theory that people with depression may be especially sensitive to signs of rejection, and that SSRIs helped them cope better. This is one of the reasons why I'm so against the use of antidepressants by people without severe depression who simply want to feel better. They may worry less, but it can damage their relationships, reduce their enthusiasm, make them shallower and unrealistically complacent. This may be why, in this age of stress, so many people are using antidepressants — the drugs can help people put up with things they should not put up with.

Bottom line on SSRIs? Depression is a serious illness, and these are serious medications. No one should ever take them lightly. They definitely can do harm, but the harm depression can do can be much worse. If you have a severe depression, you owe it to yourself to give medication a genuine try. But it needs to be part of a balanced plan that includes good psychotherapy and a lot of self-care. One thing medication can do is let you have the energy or hope to follow through.

ECT and Other Brain-based Interventions

Electroconvulsive therapy (ECT, or "shock therapy") is still used. It went out of fashion in the 1970s because it was overprescribed (also because of its image in the media, as in *One Flew over the Cuckoo's Nest*), but it does seem to be safe and effective with some patients who are seriously or dangerously depressed, especially those who are agitated and confused. It can dramatically stop an episode of intense, suicidal depression, and there's no doubt that it saves lives this way. It's also effective sometimes with unremitting, hopeless depression that just won't respond to anything else. Some people who have found it effective and are not troubled by the side effects will benefit from a periodic "tune-up" round every year or so. The major side effect is some amnesia and confusion, usually only for the few days when ECT is administered. But still, there are far too many anecdotal reports of more serious damage to ever undergo ECT lightly.

I have some concerns about some of the recent literature on depression that comes out of NIMH and the medical establishment where ECT is discussed sometimes as a third alternative to psychotherapy and medication. I know one purpose is to remove the stigma and fear, to make ECT more acceptable to patients who really need it. But I also can't help thinking that this is an effort to market what should be a procedure of last resort as something that the public should accept without question. I'm afraid that the effort will backfire, that people will avoid treatment for depression if they think that

ECT is a common alternative. No one should be considering ECT for you until other treatments have failed or unless you're suicidally out of control.

As for vagus nerve stimulation, transcranial magnetic stimulation, and psychosurgery for depression, as far as I'm concerned these are all experimental treatments of inherently high risk. They should be avoided, unless ECT hasn't worked, and you've spent a couple of years with a good therapist and a good psychopharmacologist, and they agree with your course of action.

Nonmedical Treatments

Omega-3 (Fish Oil)

A review published in 2007 by members of the American Psychiatric Association's Omega-3 study committee concluded that there is evidence that regular use of fish oil supplements or other sources of Omega-3 essential fatty acids does indeed lead to improvement in mood disorders. They found virtually no risks or side effects, and indeed some positive health benefits in addition to protecting against depression.[24] Fish oil apparently has some prevention value in Alzheimer's, and improves cardiac health. But there's some question as to the right dosage. One well-designed research study found an improvement with one gram a day after twelve weeks, but no improvement at all with higher doses, a confusing result. In my experience, one very active patient swears by his eighteen grams per day, while another very sensitive patient couldn't sleep for two days after taking one pill. Most over-the-counter fish oil capsules are 1000 or 1200 milligrams (1 or 1.2 grams), apparently a moderate dose. Don't take fish oil if you're taking Coumadin or any other blood thinner, but otherwise there seem to be no dangerous interactions. I'm no nutritional expert; I know there are people who will argue intensely about the purity, exact composition, and source of both OTC and prescribed fish oils, but I can't know if there's really anything of substance to those debates. I suggest that you try it at the rate of one pill a day; there seems to be a very good chance it will help your depression and your heart, and it may help prevent Alzheimer's. Put more fish in your diet, too; at least twice a week eat it as your main protein source. If you're taking a prescription antidepressant, don't quit it suddenly in favor of fish oil. Take them together for a while and then consult with your doctor.

St. John's Wort (Hypericum)

This is an herbal supplement that has some empirical support as an effective treatment for depression. It seems to work like an SSRI, and therefore should not be taken in combination with one. It's very popular in Germany, where quality is monitored by the health authorities. Unfortunately, in the United States, nobody regulates herbal supplements, so essentially you have no idea what's in the bottle, and you don't know if all the capsules in the bottle are the same dose, no matter how many testimonials the manufacturer claims. In my practice, I haven't yet seen anyone who reports they found St. John's wort effective. Being "natural" doesn't confer any special benefit to it; if you have severe depression, take an SSRI instead of St. John's wort — at least you will get a reliable daily dose. If you have a milder depression, be aware that St. John's wort can cause the same side effects as SSRIs.

SAMe

SAMe is the popular acronym for an amino acid derivative that is naturally produced by our bodies. There have been several clinical trials vouching for its effectiveness as an antidepressant. No one knows for sure how it might work, but that's true for SSRIs as well. There are apparently no side effects. It also seems to be about as effective as Ibuprofen for arthritis. It can be costly, and seems to degrade quickly in the bottle, so you need to keep a fresh supply from a reliable manufacturer. Most studies have used 1600 milli-grams four times a day, and the capsules typically contain 200 or 400 milligrams. So if you can afford it and can swallow all those pills, it might be worth a try.

To sum up: if you're really depressed—if you meet the criteria for major depression or bipolar disorder described in Chapter 2, you can't get out of bed or can't manage the normal tasks of everyday life, you have suicidal thoughts, you can't stop crying or control your anger, you're in great pain from guilt or shame, your negative thought processes keep running away with you—you should give medication a serious try. Make an appointment with a good psychia-trist. But you should be in therapy as well, with someone you trust and respect, and your therapist should agree with the decision to try meds. At the same time, do everything you can to exercise regularly, meditate mindfully, and add fish oil to your diet. If you're not so seriously depressed but are unhappy, grieving, stuck, low on energy, and rarely feel good—find a therapist first. Of course, you should also try the advice in this book that fits you: seek a more mindful attitude toward your life, address life's problems more effectively, and become more aware of opportunities for happiness.

Psychotherapy, Self-Help, and Other Means to Recovery

SOME BRAIN SCIENTISTS are now investigating what happens to the brain during psychotherapy. One study had patients with social phobia read a speech from within the PET scanning machine to a group of strangers; without treatment, there was a significant increase in activity in the amygdala, the brain's fear center. With either Celexa or psychotherapy, that excessive activity was reduced. Interestingly, the patients' anxiety levels a year later were predictable by how much change in amygdala activity was achieved at the time of treatment.[1] Other studies of depression, obsessive-compulsive disorder, and anxiety disorders have shown that psychotherapy results in brain changes very much like those associated with medication—with some interesting differences.[2] We know that depression is often associated with a decrease in activity in a small area of the brain called the dorsolateral prefrontal cortex. Now we know that ECT, antidepressants, and psychotherapy all stimulate more normal activity in that area.

These are truly exciting developments. The news that psychotherapy and medication achieve their results by similar, though slightly different, effects within the brain means that science can, by investigating those differences, discover much more about how depression works. We know that life experience changes the brain; now we're beginning to see how this special experience called therapy has its impact.

There are many ways of conducting psychotherapy, but all depend on an open, trusting relationship. For some patients, the opportunity to disclose to the therapist all the guilt and shame accompanying depression without being judged is enough to start recovery. For others, the therapist will need to provide guidance in such areas as assertiveness, communication skills, setting realistic goals, relaxation, and stress management—all problems that commonly interfere with recovery from depression.

When I was in graduate school, I had classes taught by Freudians, behaviorists, and family therapists. Freudians wore suits and ties, behaviorists wore lab coats, and family therapists wore sportswear. The Freudians and behaviorists could barely disguise their contempt for each other—it was interesting to watch them when they had to pretend to be colleagues, for example, at faculty cocktail parties. The family therapists were polite but condescending to each camp, trying to apply their point of view to campus politics, while the Freudians and the behaviorists largely ignored them. From the viewpoint of the advancement of science, it was extremely unfortunate. The different camps didn't even talk to each other, let alone read each other's literature. You would find interesting and potentially helpful articles and books on subjects like depression or empathy that didn't even agree on definitions. There was no way for one point of view to inform another.

You still find that kind of competition and closed-mindedness today, though the players have changed. Fortunately, most of it is confined to academia. Effective therapists out in the world today will use an amalgam of methods that have their roots in different theories, but their combination makes for effective, humane psychotherapy, often short-term in nature. We don't assume that the patient is in ignorance about the true nature of his problems, but instead that the patient's expressed pain and needs are the natural focus of treatment. The therapist does not have to be a silent presence behind the couch or a rat-runner in a lab coat, but instead can be a human person with some special expertise whose understanding and advice are freely given. Patients are much better off for the change.

*   *   *

Good psychotherapy can be provided by a psychiatrist (an MD specializing in mental disorders), a psychologist (PhD), a clinical social worker (MSW), a psychiatric nurse, a pastoral counselor, or a substance abuse counselor. But the fact is that someone with no qualifications at all can hang out a shingle calling himself a "therapist" or "counselor"—these are terms that are not legally defined or regulated. When you call a therapist or see someone for the first time, ask directly about the individual's professional background and training. Ask if he or she is recognized as reimbursable by health insurance—if not, you should find someone else. (Your therapist might not accept insurance, but that's a different matter.) Finding someone you trust and can feel comfortable with is most important—you should feel free to shop around. You should ask about the therapist's background, training, and experience with depression. And if after a few sessions you have any doubts or don't feel you're getting anywhere, tell your therapist about it and get a consultation with someone else. Current research reemphasizes the old observation that the emotional connection between patient and therapist may be the most important variable in effective treatment.[3] Because medications can be helpful in serious cases, their use should be strongly considered along with psychotherapy. Nowadays a good therapist should be associated with a psychiatrist or APRN who can prescribe needed medications. If you find a therapist who won't support the use of medication, go find someone else.

If I were depressed and seeking a therapist, I would consider the following factors:

1. My gut reactions: Is this someone whom I can like and trust? Do I feel at ease? Do I have any reservations? Psychotherapy is the one chance we get in modern life to tell the absolute truth about ourselves. Is this person someone I feel can bear that responsibility?

2. References. Talk to friends, your minister, your doctor. A casual professional relationship isn't a good reference. You want to talk to someone who knows the therapist well—former patients are best.

3. The therapist's experience with depressed patients, including but not limited to familiarity with cognitive, interpersonal, and mindfulness techniques.

4. The therapist's openness to medication as part of treatment.

5. The therapist's willingness to be active and directive when it's called for, not to assume that listening is curative in itself, or that the patient's needs for advice or reassurance are infantile and should be ignored.

These last three factors are things you should definitely ask directly of the therapist. We are not gods, though a few of us think so, and we will not be offended by direct questions. If you find a therapist who is offended, go find another therapist. As a matter of fact, it's best if you can see two or three people for an initial consultation and then choose the one you feel can be most helpful. This is a much more important decision than buying a new car, and we should put at least as much energy and time into selecting a therapist as we do which make and model car we want. Feel free to take a few therapists for a test drive.

Patients who request literature on depression from NIMH or other sources will often find cognitive or interpersonal therapy cited as the treatment of choice for depression. Cognitive behavior therapy (CBT)[4] identifies a person's distorted thinking habits and recasts them in a more accurate light, as described in Chapter 8. Interpersonal therapy (IPT), developed by Gerald Klerman and Myrna Weissman,[5] focuses on communication skills: learning to interpret accurately what others are saying to you (instead of assuming you know), and learning to voice your feelings, desires, and needs effectively. Many experienced therapists will use techniques from cognitive and interpersonal therapies as needed by the individual. These approaches have achieved their level of scientific respect because they have been demonstrated, in experiments with all proper controls, to be effective, at least as effective as medication, over a three-month trial period. But that just means they have met the same low standard as drugs: after three months of treatment, the majority of patients no longer meet all the diagnostic criteria for major depression. However, they can remain miserable and can relapse in another month.

The reason why CBT and IPT can be proven effective like this is because they are designed to reach a certain level of success in a three-month treatment campaign, and because they have been elaborated to such a concrete level that one therapist's cognitive therapy is much like another therapist's cognitive therapy. This is not the case in most kinds of psychotherapy, where the personality of the therapist is such an important factor. This puts cognitive and interpersonal therapy at a distinct advantage in the research, just because there is so little variability; you are evaluating the effectiveness of a set of techniques, not an art. Experienced therapists sometimes denigrate these approaches as "cookbook" methods because they leave little room for creativity. But with a cookbook, if you set out to make a cake, you get a pretty good cake every time. And all of us in the field owe the developers of these methods a great debt of gratitude, because until they were developed, it had been embarrassingly impossible to demonstrate that any psychotherapeutic method had any effect at all. There was a distinct danger of psychotherapy becoming ineligible for reimbursement by health insurance or Medicare, which would have made it available only for the wealthy.

But new research is showing that longer term psychodynamic therapy is more effective than these short-term treatments. In a large review of many studies recently published in the *Journal of the American Medical Association*, the more treatment sessions, the better the patient did.[6] These were not ten-year psychoanalyses, but the patient simply kept coming until he felt like he didn't need to anymore. The average treatment period was about a year, and the patient usually saw the therapist twice a week, sometimes more. These were patients with chronic or complex disorders, living in the real world, instead of single-symptom patients carefully screened to maximize the effectiveness of a particular treatment method. Psychodynamic therapy refers to the way of thinking that you find in this book; a belief in unconscious motivations and reactions; in our use of defense mechanisms to deny pain, and their unintended negative consequences; in the importance of childhood experience in shaping the mind and brain; in a basic conflict within all of us between intimacy and independence; in depression as a way of avoiding difficult emotional states. But I wouldn't argue that long-term treatment for depression has to be psychodynamic in nature to be more effective. Most patients in CBT or IPT continue working with their therapists well past three months, as they should as long as it's effective.

Now that we know that psychotherapy affects the brain, it shouldn't be overly surprising to find that the more therapy, the better. As I argue throughout this book, it is practice and repetition that changes the brain, not insight or changes in thinking. There is, of course, no argument that a year of psychotherapy twice a week costs more than medication (though maybe not for long if the drug companies have their way). But you also have to consider that the human cost of chronic depression and complex personality disorders—to the patient and the people around him, and to his lifetime earning power—is much greater than the cost of psychotherapy. One positive development since the first edition of this book is that most insurance companies are not as restrictive about paying for psychotherapy as they used to be, which means you may only have to pay your therapist your usual co-pay. However, you still need to be assertive and savvy about your insurance to get the benefits you're entitled to.

When I wrote the previous edition, medication still promised great things for depression, and I felt a little like an underdog advocating for psychotherapy. No more. Although the field, and popular stereotypes, continues to be fascinated by meds, thoughtful scientists and clinicians now recognize that, in many ways, psychotherapy is the better alternative. Two independent reviews of all the literature comparing the effectiveness of psychotherapy and medication for treatment of depression were published in 2008.[7] There were about thirty such studies in all, and the reviews concluded that both medication and psychotherapy were about equally effective in treating depression. Both reviews found, and emphasized, that meds were more effective for dysthymia—an ironic result, because the meds weren't designed to help dysthymia, and their success was possibly only the result of the emotional blunting described in the last chapter. Both studies found a significantly lower dropout rate for psychotherapy. Only one review looked at results at follow-up (average length of fifteen months), and found a significant advantage for psychotherapy, an advantage that grew the longer the follow-up period.[8] We don't know if that's because patients went off meds, or if meds gradually lost their effectiveness, or because psychotherapy gives patients something they can build on, but I suspect all three factors play a role.

People with depression have *symptoms* (moodiness, lack of energy, self-defeating thinking patterns, anxiety) and they have *problems* (marital conflict, poor work performance, bad decision-making, procrastination). The hope has been that medication would lift the symptoms and the patient would be able to tackle the problems more effectively alone. When meds work right, this is possible. But far more often, good psychotherapy helps the patient with his problems, and the symptoms begin to diminish. (Of course, it's really a two-way street.) Or therapy helps with symptom management more than medication can (challenging depressed thinking, using mindfulness to detach from rumination, learning good sleeping habits, communicating more effectively). Once again, it's the *practice* of new skills, in both problem-solving and symptom management, that leads to lasting change. The therapist is there, like a coach, to help when the practice isn't going well, or when there are unexpected obstacles. Depression is highly likely to recur, unless the patient has learned new methods of dealing with life's obstacles and his own feelings.

Mindfulness-Based Therapy for Depression

A new approach to treatment of depression based on mindfulness techniques has been proving itself effective, especially at preventing relapse. Mindfulness-Based Cognitive Therapy for Depression (MBCT)[9] is based on the observation that people with repeated episodes of depression begin to develop associations between sad thoughts and depressive feelings that most people don't experience. Thus, for example, most people, hearing a song that reminds them of an old love on the radio, might feel a little sad and wistful, but also feel some pleasure at the memories evoked. Depressed people, however, experience a train of spiraling negative thoughts: *Boy, she was great. How could I have let her go? Just chickened out, I guess, that's what I always do. I'll never have a love like that again, and it's all my fault. I'm worthless.* Pretty soon they're in the pits again; with depression, there is a direct link between sad feelings and the spiraling negative thoughts. As we noted above, for most people the trigger for the first and second episodes of depression is easy to identify, but it seems to only require milder and milder events to trigger future episodes, so mild that the patient is often unaware of them — a fleeting memory, a song on the radio, a tiny snub.

MBCT teaches the patient mindfulness skills to address directly that link between sad feelings and the runaway train of negative rumination. The patient learns to step back and observe his thoughts, not to automatically get caught up in them. He can say directly to himself, *I'm feeling sad, but that's only temporary; I'm not forced to let my negative thoughts run away with me. I can detach or distract myself.* The discipline of meditation training, returning thoughts again and again to the breath or some neutral object, becomes a skill the patient can apply to this self-destructive connection. The developers of MBCT have published a very useful self-help book, *The Mindful Way Through Depression*, which includes a CD of guided meditations.[10] Repeated clinical trials with MBCT have demonstrated that it can reduce the risk of relapse from 100 percent (in those with four or more episodes) to 38 percent. But all the trials have also shown that MBCT is less effective with people who have had only one or two episodes of major depression; they seemed less likely to have had traumatic childhoods and more likely to have experienced their first episode later in life.[11] My interpretation is that these people have suffered less of the brain damage that goes with trauma and repeated episodes of depression, and therefore don't require the healing experience that mindfulness provides. They just need to learn to handle their depression, and interpersonal or cognitive-behavioral therapy can help.

Self-help

Sadly, it remains true with the second edition of this book that there is no national or international effort to organize self-help groups for depression. Some national organizations, like the National Foundation for Depressive Illness and the National Alliance for the Mentally Ill, sponsor local groups, but there are not a great many. Recovery Inc. and Emotions Anonymous appeal to some, but the emphasis on controlling emotions is not what I think depressed people need. There are good resources in many communities, like the Mood Disorders Support Group in New York, but they are not linked nationally nor do they follow a common philosophy. Many mental health centers and hospitals either have professionally led depression groups or lend space to self-help groups. Without a self-help program designed for depression, many depressed people find tremendous help in groups that are not specifically about depression, such as AA, Al-Anon, sexual abuse groups, or gender issues groups. It is a shame that there is no specific self-help program, because I believe group support can be extremely helpful for depression, especially for beginners. Some "old hands" have developed informal groups of their own, but they don't encourage newcomers.

Unfortunately, the very nature of depression gets in the way of forming self-help groups. I assume that the problem has to do with the lingering stigma of depression, which patients buy into, in the form of guilt and self-blame. Depressed people naturally assume there is no help to come from other depressed people, and besides who wants to get together to talk about how bad they feel? But the fact that more and more people are just getting minimal psychotherapy, or medication prescribed by their general practitioner, only strengthens the need for such groups.

There have been encouraging developments. Daniel Lukasik, a Buffalo attorney, has almost single-handedly developed Lawyers with Depression, which has been received very well all across New York State. Lawyers as a profession are at especially high risk for depression, and Lukasik by his example has encouraged many other successful attorneys and judges to come out of the closet about their experiences. The American Foundation for Suicide Prevention is organizing community overnight walks to raise funds and awareness of suicide, and they seem to be attracting more attention every year. Programs like these will do much to reduce the stigma of depression. And the Internet has allowed long-distance groups to flourish. Many socializing sites have within them special discussion groups or bulletin boards about depression. A patient of mine has been greatly supported by a group for children of narcissistic mothers.

But lacking a support group, you have to help yourself. That's what this book is all about, and there are many other good books out there. See the Recommended Reading section for some suggestions. The belief that there's nothing you can do to help yourself is a symptom of your disease, and you have to fight it every day. Every day, do a little more reading, find something to do that stretches you, meditate and exercise, reach out to others. Review my tips about building willpower, and practice meditation. The last chapter of this book is called "A Program for Recovery," and I guarantee that if you follow that program faithfully, you will feel better soon.

Family Support

Living with someone who's depressed can be one of the most frustrating experiences there is.[12] We want to help the sufferer, but we don't know how; often it seems that whatever we do only makes things worse. Sometimes we get angry at the depressed person, but feel guilty afterward.

Depressed people have an intense need for love and acceptance, but they usually can't reciprocate, so they seem needy and ungrateful. Their tone of desperation or self-sacrifice may turn people off. The hopelessness and defeatism are very frustrating for loved ones.

The depressed person often has little energy left over to think about others, so may appear overly self-absorbed, often with a host of minor physical complaints. Their problems don't respond to good advice or common sense, so friends give up on them. Then they may feel guilty about their self-absorption, and try too hard to compensate, or relentlessly seek reassurance or forgiveness.

Anger seems to accompany depressed people like a dark cloud overhead. Sometimes they feel it themselves: they may feel that life isn't fair, they may feel bitterly that they've been deprived of something they deserve. Or they make others around them angry with their self-pity and pouting. Family members are usually afraid to express their anger out of fear of hurting the victim.

Clearly, people like this can be very difficult to live with. Something that can be of immense help to a friend or loved one is *to get an accurate diagnosis.* It's much easier to put up with difficult behavior from someone we love if we understand that he or she is in the grip of a major illness and not provoking us deliberately. Depression is an illness; it can develop very gradually or very quickly; it can come in response to life events or as a result of changes in body chemistry; it can strike anyone regardless of age or sex, wealth or poverty; but it is an illness, not a choice.

It's important to remember that depression is not an emotion, but a defense against emotions. The depressed person is keeping a lot of feelings bottled up inside. He generally expects that no one will understand him. It helps lift the depression to express the feelings, although those feelings may be unpleasant for loved ones and family members to hear. He may be angry at us for no good reason that we can see, or he may be consumed by guilt over seemingly trivial incidents. He may be very fearful or very self-centered. On the other hand, he may be telling us important truths about our relationship, perhaps ways we have taken advantage of his depression. Of course it's difficult to hear these things, but it is important that the depressed person learn that honest emotions don't drive people away.

The depressed person needs understanding, patience, and acceptance from those close to him. As friends or relatives, we may feel uncomfortable around the sufferer; we want to tell them to snap out of it, we want to give them good advice, we want to tell them how we handled similar situations. This just makes the depressive feel worse and reinforces the depressive's feeling of inadequacy. We need to listen to our friend with care and concern. A self-help group I was involved with put together a fine list of how their loved ones can help:

1. Try to be considerate, thoughtful, and empathic. If your partner had a broken leg, you would expect that their abilities and energy would be restricted, that they would be in pain at times, and that they couldn't heal themselves more quickly just because you want them to. Think about depression the same way.

2. Don't be provocative. Every relationship has the little hot buttons that can start a fight at any time. Dirty socks on the floor, the remote control misplaced, the car low on gas. You know what your partner's buttons are. Don't push them while he or she is in a depressed state.

3. Small acts of kindness are appreciated and do help, even if the recipient doesn't reciprocate. When I retreat to bed, my wife makes a point of breaking in to kiss me good night. Even though I often don't act very glad to see her, I would feel worse, lonely and unloved, without her attention.

4. Easing your partner's burden in small ways can help a great deal. Offer to do the shopping, empty the garbage, do the laundry, take the kids out for pizza. It communicates more than words the feeling that you understand how difficult these mundane chores can seem at times.

5. "Advance directives" can be a contract loved ones arrange while the sufferer is not depressed, describing what to do when depression sets in. It can be in stages: stage 1, leave me alone; stage 2, be kind, patient, and attentive; stage 3, insist I call my therapist;

stage 4, take me to the hospital. One patient loses her ability to see color when depression sets in. From experience, she has learned to tell her husband right away when this happens, because she won't let him know when it gets worse.

6. Take the trouble to educate yourself. Learn all you can about depression. Be willing to talk to your loved one's therapist. It's amazing how seeing it in print or hearing it from an authority can change your perspective. Even if you believe you understand that depression is a disease, that the patient doesn't choose to be depressed, and so forth, you need all the education you can get. These are facts we don't want to believe. Learning the facts helps you help your loved one, and also shows that you care enough to take some trouble.

I have to say that I don't believe members of my own profession have been very helpful to family members. Though occasionally there are family meetings when a patient is hospitalized, there is a long tradition against involving family members in outpatient treatment. Typically, this is seen as a protection for the patient's privacy: the patient is a competent adult who chose to consult me on his own; if I were to talk directly to family members about his condition or treatment, that would be infantilizing him, and undermine his competence. But of course the patient can voluntarily give up his right to privacy; therapists rarely ask, "It seems like your parent/spouse/child is having a lot of trouble understanding what you are going through. Do you think it would help if he or she came to one of your sessions? Perhaps I could explain something about the nature of depression, and we could work together on communication between you." Nothing goes on behind the patient's back, no one is undermined. By assuming that the family member is willing to help but just doesn't understand, we model for our client the principles of effective treatment and recovery we espouse: that we are responsible for making ourselves understood, that there are communication skills that can increase understanding, that we shouldn't assume we know how others feel.

Part 3

Putting the Skills to Work

Work and a Sense of Purpose

THE NEXT FEW CHAPTERS have a slightly different focus. Here, we assume that you are out of the deepest depths of depression and are ready to take some further steps. By emphasizing the positive and the possible here, I don't want to add to anyone's depression. These chapters are for those who are looking for ways to make sure that they don't return to old bad habits in the future. People who are really depressed can't use this kind of advice yet. They need time to recover; they need understanding, medication, support, psychotherapy—whatever it takes to get themselves out of the pits. If you're not ready yet, don't blame yourself: it's my timing that's off. Just skip ahead to Chapter 18.

Sometimes when I have spoken to business organizations, I have surprised them by advocating for hiring the depressed; but aside from taking more sick days than others, depressed people can be the best employees. We're good at being responsible. We are good soldiers, honest and industrious. We have high standards and want to do any job well. We have too much guilt to pad our hours or take home office supplies. Treat us decently, and we'll be grateful and loyal. Unfortunately for the depressed individual, however, we discount these virtues and have a difficult time enjoying the world of work.

The people who make a professional study of happiness break it down into two parts: *joy,* the immediate sensation of positive feelings, and *satisfaction,* the more quiet and sustained state when you get what you want or when you've achieved something meaningful to you. Even more subtle is a sense of *meaning* or purpose, a feeling that your life adds up to more than just getting through a long series of days. Depressed people are sadly deficient in all, of course, but satisfaction and meaning can seem especially far out of reach when we feel that our life has been damaged by years of depression, self-destructive behavior, and the wrong choices. However, it's quite possible to gain more of a sense of satisfaction and of purpose—even when it feels like life has been pretty empty up till now. One of the things you have to do is take the risk of setting some goals for yourself.

Depressed people, pessimistic and lacking confidence, tend to avoid setting goals as a way to protect themselves from disappointment. They don't realize that the absence of goals leads to a completely different, and frequently worse, set of problems. Even if you miss your target, you grow and benefit from the practice of productive activity. A famous study that compared lottery winners to disabled accident victims a year later showed that both groups had pretty much returned to baseline, as far as individual happiness was concerned.[1] If you were unhappy before you got rich, now you're unhappy with money. If you were sunny and perky before you became disabled, now you're a sunny and perky person with a handicap. But depressed people, who don't trust their ability to adapt to bad news and hence avoid setting conscious goals, find lives that lack direction. Your goal becomes just getting through another day. In the depths of depression, that may be all you can manage, but it doesn't take you anywhere. One thing about being employed is that it more or less forces you to add some goals to your day, starting with getting out of bed.

Research tells us that the simple act of setting realistic and concrete goals seems to improve both our experience and our performance.[2] If you want to write a book, for example, you'll be more productive and feel better if you set yourself goals of X pages per day or Y chapters per month, rather than just vaguely writing when you feel like it. Making a commitment like this focuses our attention on where we want to go and helps us focus our thinking on getting there. People feel happier as they progress toward their goals; they have a sense of involvement, they feel productive and useful, and give themselves ego strokes for being good and industrious. Because we're so adaptable, however, those good feelings don't necessarily last once we've got to where we're going. We have to make a deliberate effort to savor and appreciate our achievement.

As Tal Ben-Shahar, a leading happiness researcher, writes, "the proper role of goals is to liberate us, so that we can enjoy the here and now."[3] If we leave the house without purpose or direction, every fork in the road becomes another decision to make, another point where we can become paralyzed by our own ambivalence. *Will the scenery be better this way, or that way? Have we gone too far? What if there are no motel rooms? Should we stop at this battlefield, or that old cavern, or the antique center?* But if we know where we're going, our minds are saved all this hassle and we can enjoy the journey.

Making Work Rewarding

Mihaly Csikszentmihalyi has spent a lifetime studying what gives us pleasure and meaning. Using a method where subjects carrying beepers are paged at random times during the day and asked to rate their enjoyment level and describe their activities, Csikszentmihalyi has had some surprising findings.[4]

When people were paged during times when they felt challenged and felt that they were using their skills, they were described as being in *flow*. Not surprisingly, the more time a person spent in flow, the better he felt about his experience. People in flow described themselves as feeling strong, active, creative, concentrated, and motivated.

The biggest surprise to come from this research was that flow experiences happened much more frequently at work than at leisure.

When people were paged at work, they reported themselves in flow 54 percent of the time. At leisure, only 18 percent of responses were in flow. Most leisure responses fell into the range the researchers call apathy. People in an apathetic state were more likely to describe themselves as passive, weak, dull, and dissatisfied. Some jobs were clearly more stimulating than others, with people who have more autonomy more likely to be in flow than clerical or assembly-line workers; but clerical and assembly-line workers still reported feeling in flow more than twice as often at work as at leisure.

People in the state of flow, either at work or at leisure, reported it as a much more positive experience than not being in flow. These differences were very significant statistically and did not change very much across different kinds of work. However, when people were at work, they were much more likely to report wishing they were somewhere else, even if they were in a state of flow, than if they were at leisure. "Thus we have the paradoxical situation: On the job people feel skillful and challenged, and therefore feel more happy, strong, creative, and satisfied. In their free time people feel that there is generally not much to do and their skills are not being used, and therefore they tend to feel more sad, weak, dull, and dissatisfied. Yet they would like to work less and spend more time in leisure."[5]

The reason for this paradox has to do with how we define our world. Most of us have been conditioned to think of work as an imposition. Even if we are feeling challenged and stimulated, we feel it is for someone else's benefit, not our own, and we tend to see the time spent at work as subtracted somehow from the time we have available to enjoy our lives. How much better off we would be if we could change our perceptions of work, so that we felt that our time spent there was an opportunity for happiness, for attainment of goals that were meaningful to ourselves, not merely time subtracted from our life span.

Csikszentmihalyi describes the state of flow as lying between anxiety and boredom. When we feel that we can't meet the tasks that need to be done, we feel anxious; when we feel that what we

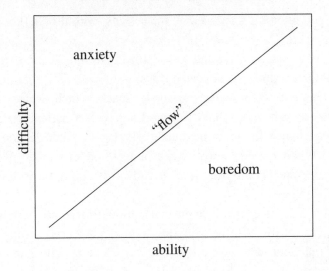

Figure 1. The state of "flow" as a balance between the difficulty of a task and the ability of the individual.

have to do is not challenging, not stimulating, we feel bored. When we feel that the task is a mild stretch for us — that it makes use of our skills, makes us concentrate, makes us grow — we feel in flow. As our skills grow and become habitual, we need different challenges to make us feel in flow.

Csikszentmihalyi and his researchers have also attempted to determine what it is that makes some activities enjoyable, others aversive. They have found that enjoyable activities have the following factors in common:

1. Enjoyable activities — work, leisure, physical, or intellectual — are goal-directed and have rules. They challenge us to use our skills. Good video games are designed so that they gradually require more and more skill from us; that's why they're so engrossing. Watching television doesn't require any skill at all. Unhappy people watch 20 percent more television than people who describe themselves as very happy.[6]

2. Our attention is focused on the activity, with little left over for other stimuli.

3. The goals are clear and well-defined. Nothing is more demoralizing than vague or changeable rules.

4. The activity provides prompt feedback, which enables us to correct our behavior. When I'm working with a patient, his level of engagement tells me immediately whether I'm doing a good job or not. When I used to work with budgets or long-range plans, I got no feedback until we were already fully committed to their implementation.

5. There is a deep involvement that helps one forget all the unpleasant aspects of life. All the troubling thoughts that pass through our minds unbidden when we are left to ourselves are prevented from bothering us. (Sounds like mindfulness.)

6. These activities give us the sense of being in control in difficult situations. This is why so many enjoyable activities involve a risk, whether it is rock climbing or performing; although there is a risk, there is the opportunity to learn very specific skills that minimize risk, and thus gain a feeling of mastery and pride.

7. We lose self-consciousness; the Inner Critic disappears. We forget about ourselves temporarily, but we finish the task feeling better about ourselves.

8. Our sense of time changes. Time may pass very quickly, as while watching an enthralling film or play, or very slowly, as some performers report who are focused on the minute details of their skills. Ted Williams, it was said, could see the stitches on the ball pitched at him. The sense of freedom from ordinary clock time seems to help us feel empowered and renewed.

Whether our work involves running a drill press, managing people, or caring for children, we all have some control over how enjoyable the activity is. For instance, in many jobs—raising children comes to mind—there is little immediate positive feedback. Children and spouse don't tell you often enough what a good job you're doing, but you can expect to be told whenever anything goes wrong, even if it's completely outside your control. We have to increase positive feedback by structuring in opportunities for it and by raising our own sensitivity to it.

For example, the routine cup of coffee with a neighbor or telephone call with a grandparent that so many parents build into their day is an opportunity to be reminded, perhaps in indirect but important ways, that the job of child-rearing is significant and meaningful and that you're doing a pretty good job at it. Spouses may need reminding directly that parents stuck at home with small children all day need confirmation and validation. Though in marriage counseling we often hear, "If I have to ask for his attention, it doesn't mean anything when he gives it," in fact it is still meaningful and it's possible to structure reminders—like a fixed time together after dinner to discuss the day—that reduce the necessity of having to ask.

Examining our definition of what is an accomplishment is another strategy for adding to our own self-worth. A few minutes of quiet reading time with a fractious child is a major accomplishment, not only because it's difficult to achieve, but also because it may be the one good thing that's happened in the child's life that day, and it may add significantly to his ability to control his own moods in the future.

As we move into a more service-oriented society, more occupations exact emotional stress instead of the physical stress that comes with labor. All positions that require managing people—from salesman to bill collector to waiter to daycare worker—require us to manage ourselves, to play a role. No one cares if the factory worker has a cranky day, but the daycare worker can't afford to be cranky. We have to put on a front and control the expression of our true feelings. This kind of control must come from a conscious, thoughtful desire to do a good job, not from the assumption that our feelings themselves are unacceptable. Sometimes you have a perfect right to be cranky, but you have to control how you express it; it's part of being a professional, something to be proud of.

Whether you love your job or not, it's important to keep in mind that work brings many rewards we often take for granted. For one thing, it brings in money. But just as important, getting up and getting in on time, sticking with it till the day is done, sometimes having to do some difficult or ugly things—these are a great source of pride and self-respect, something we might not realize until we're laid off. Here's a story about the importance of work:

Adam was fifteen, referred to me after he failed ninth grade. He didn't do any schoolwork, and was known as the class clown. Adam's father had had no contact with him since Adam was four. He had two older siblings, both of whom had been through a stormy adolescence, full of conflict with mother. Mother was a charming, soft-spoken, intelligent woman, and a closet alcoholic. She brought Adam in not because he was failing school or friendless or depressed—all of which were true—but because he started talking back to her.

Adam was about five foot three, 105 pounds, with Coke-bottle glasses. He had the large head, small frame, and vision difficulties that go with fetal alcohol syndrome. He affected a tough image, doing his best to attain a greaser look. He knew his mother expected me to fix him, and he had no interest in being fixed, but he was too compliant to refuse to come in.

As we talked and I didn't challenge or correct him, Adam opened up somewhat. He started telling me about the world as he saw it. There were always fights—in school, after school, in the mall, in the bowling alley—usually begun by several bigger, older guys who were ambushing Adam for no reason that he was aware of. Fortunately, Adam was an expert in martial arts and always managed to fight his way out of these situations. As time went on, the numbers and sizes of kids Adam was beating up kept increasing, their wounds got more and more serious, till I finally caught on that what I was hearing wasn't really happening at all. But why did he need to tell me these stories?

My consultant said I was being given the privilege of participating in Adam's reparative fantasies—the daydreams that helped him feel better about himself—and that if I was patient and didn't push him, solutions would emerge. Adam's fantasies were about all he had going for him. Clearly, he felt that he had little real protection in a dangerous world. His daily experiences in school just reinforced his sense of powerlessness. I did as I was told, and as the summer went on, Adam stopped complaining about keeping his appointments and even started bringing me fish he'd caught.

That fall Adam was in trouble in school again. He was now a year behind, taking all the same classes for the second time, with many of the same teachers, who were not thrilled to see him back. As he started to tell me little bits about how his teachers treated him, I could imagine what kind of provocative behavior on his part had elicited those furious responses. I went to school and sat in on a staff conference on Adam, and I'll never forget the gym teacher: "This kid just needs taking down a few pegs." I felt I instantly understood the problem between Adam and the school: what Adam needed was taking up *many pegs; he needed experiences where he could feel competent and successful. But he was so scared, so mistrustful, that he wouldn't let anyone see that. Instead he acted cocky, uncaring, obnoxious, clowning, all those things that drive teachers crazy. For him, accepting a directive from an authority figure would literally tear apart the fragile false self he had built, the karate expert who cut a swath through hordes of enemies every night.*

Adam found an interesting solution; he dropped out of school and got a job as a plumber's helper. He had to start work at five every morning, carry heavy equipment all day in all kinds of weather, and do most of the dirty work involved in plumbing. From all reports, he did this cheerfully and energetically. I was surprised at his attitude change, but Adam patiently explained it to me: because the plumber was paying him (treating him like an adult), the plumber earned the right to tell Adam what to do. Taking orders for money was okay; taking orders just because adults are bigger and in authority wasn't.

Though he never returned to school, I felt that Adam had turned a corner. He was able to find a way to take pride in actual accomplishment, not live in his fantasy world all the time. Through the medium of money, he was beginning to find a way to interact with adults that enabled both parties to treat each other with consistency and respect. He was able to drop his cocky facade and relate to his boss like one adult to another. I hoped that these new skills would form the basis for an adaptation to adult life.

When Work Isn't Pleasant at All

Many people are stuck in jobs they just don't enjoy (and given the economic crisis, more and more will be) but have to be thankful to have any job at all. If this is the case, there are always a few things you can do to make work more pleasant.

• Try to make the most of your job. Work is one arena where we're given the opportunity to make a contribution, and that can be a major source of happiness. To create something new or unique, to solve a difficult problem, or to influence the future can add meaning to our lives. It may take a long period of learning or apprenticeship before you become expert enough to do something truly meaningful, but if you keep track of your own growing skill level, you will feel good in the meantime. If you have a dull or routine job, keep looking for something better; don't get stuck if you don't have to be.

• If you have a job that really has no meaning for you other than a way to put food on the table, try to keep a mindful attitude about it. Don't take it too seriously. Try to show up prepared to be friendly, to find something to enjoy every day. Try to add play to your work. Meanwhile, add meaning to your life in your leisure time—develop a skill, become an expert at something, learn to sing or paint or tie flies. Volunteer your time for community service.

• Try adopting a mindful attitude toward your coworkers, your customers, whomever you come in contact with. If you can make their day a little better, chances are good they'll return the favor when they have the chance. The whole work environment can become more pleasant just because you try to make a difference.

- Handle your money wisely.* If you're only in it for the money, then use it well. Don't waste it on mindless consumerism. Save it for things that are really meaningful to you and your interests. In the long run, money can buy you only two good things: security and freedom. So try to have enough in the bank that you can walk away if you have to.

- If conditions are really miserable—if there's a bad boss or too much friction in the office—work on getting out before you become miserable too. I've seen far too many depressed people stay stuck in terrible working conditions through fear of change; often that is the single greatest source of their unhappiness. Keep your résumé handy and send it off every chance you get. Watch the want ads and the Internet. Think about relocating. Build up alternative skills, the so-called portable skills that are in demand everywhere: spreadsheets, databases, word processing, customer service.

- If possible, take advantage of the new economy. It's easier now to work from home, to work nontraditional hours, to schedule weeks off from work. Though there's a potential downside to each of these benefits, you can be your own boss and have more time for family and leisure activities. Little things can add greatly to your overall happiness. For me, a perennial insomniac, the freedom to finally sleep till 9:00 A.M. is something I appreciate very much. Although it means working till 7:00 P.M., that schedule seems to suit my rhythm.

- Retired people, in general, are happier than those still working.[7] But retired people miss the social interaction, the work itself, and the feeling of being useful. So while you're still working, pay more attention to those things. Make the social interactions more fun and supportive. Let yourself be mindful of your skills, and be as useful as you can be. Be a positive influence for others.

* I join with others recommending *Your Money or Your Life* (Robin, Dominguez, and Tilford; see the Recommended Reading list), a very sensible book that will teach you the value of money as well as show you how to manage it wisely.

Goals and Purpose

Work, for most of us, has always been the simplest and most effective way to bring structure and meaning to our lives. You hang in there until retirement age, climb the ladder slowly and carefully, collect your pension, and retire to Florida. It's a template, an easy plan to follow—but the world of work has been changing so rapidly that that kind of career is hard to find. More and more people are working at one or more part-time jobs, working off the books, making some money through the cash economy. Even those who have salaried jobs don't expect to stay with one employer for long, let alone until retirement age. While these developments may add some freedom to your life—you may be more able to set your own hours, for instance—they also mean a loss of security. This means it's more important than ever to understand your own values and set your own goals.

Most of us have probably never deliberately asked ourselves what our goals are. A few people think they know exactly what principles are important to them and what their objectives are in life. Others are mystified by this subject, believing that they never think about their values and goals. Both can be equally deluded; we tend to believe what we want to believe about ourselves, and never look at ourselves systematically and objectively. We do live our lives by certain values and principles, and we do have a sense of what we would like to accomplish for ourselves, but these are often largely unconscious. To make these conscious, we have to examine ourselves deliberately. Then we can think about whether what we do is taking us where we want to go.

For example, most of us would say that the most important thing in our lives is our family; but if you take a hard look at how you spend your time, you see little real family time. Why is this? The reasons probably have to do with the conflicting commitments you've assigned yourself, and your difficulty experiencing emotions. One of the most common ways we have of avoiding emotions is that we let ourselves become overwhelmed by busy-ness. *"Things* are in the saddle, and ride mankind," said Emerson. This is much more the case now than in his time; so if we want to do what's truly important to us, we have to make a conscious and deliberate effort to prioritize.

Here's a place to start:

Exercise 5. Identifying Your Key Values

• *Take a few minutes of quiet time and put yourself into a mindful state. When you feel ready, write down a list of ten or more things that make life worth living for you. Don't worry about making the list perfect or complete, because you'll be doing this several times. Try not to think about what you feel are the "right" values, just write what comes to your mind, without judging. If being saintly doesn't make your list but eating at good restaurants does, don't worry about it. Don't be afraid to be individualistic or selfish; if playing mah-jongg makes you happier than playing with the grandchildren, that's okay. This list is just for you; no one will ever see it but you, and you deserve to give yourself the most honest information you can. You can be general (nature) or specific (sunsets over the lake); it doesn't matter at this point.*

• *Put your list away for a few days, and do the exercise again. Don't look at your old list, start fresh. We assume that you've missed some obvious things the first time around, just because they're so obvious you take them for granted, or for any of a hundred other reasons. Then do this again, for a third time, after a few more days have passed.*

• *Now combine the three lists. If you have duplicate items, enter them only once but put a check mark beside them for each additional time they come up. If you see that some items are just similar examples of a bigger concept (like dancing and going to concerts might be considered part of appreciating music), treat them as you would duplicates.*

• *Now I want you to try and rank these items in order of their importance to you. These are going to be hard choices, but you're not locked into them. Doing the exercise itself may change some of your choices. Don't worry too much if you can't decide if sex is more important than eating well, or vice versa; but you should be able to put the items into a rough order to see, for instance, that both sex and eating well are more important to you than playing golf. Or not. It may help to imagine you're being forced to give up some of these activities. Which would you give up first?*

• *Here's the painful part of the exercise: for the next few days, keep a little diary of your daily activities. Keep tabs on how much time you actually spend in activities or states of mind when you are actively involved with your highest priorities. If you're like most people, you'll be dismayed when you see how much time is taken up with activities that are not on your list at all.*

• *You will probably see that some of your low-value activities are necessary, for the present at least: working and commuting come to mind. Schlepping the kids. But you may see that you're spending time in unnecessary low-value activities. Surfing the Net or obsessively cleaning. The classic example, watching television, takes up a lot of time for most people though they don't rank it very high. But do allow yourself some emotional downtime; we might wear ourselves out pretty quickly if we're constantly engaged in high-value activities.*

• *Nevertheless, look mindfully at how you're spending your time, and try to add more value. Plan your evenings and weekends in advance. Plan vacations around some of your highest values. Get together with friends and family more than you're doing now. Exercise more so that you have more energy. Cut back on television and Web-surfing.*

• *Finally, you can work on escaping or adding value to those necessary low-value activities. Develop a plan to change jobs if it's really demoralizing, so you will enjoy your new job more or have less of a commute. Listen to recorded books when you're commuting. Sing with the kids while you're driving them around town (they'll fuss mightily at first, but they'll get used to it).*

You'll notice that it's not so easy to change your old habits, even though it seems obvious that you can and should. Don't just give up, but look mindfully, without judging, at what's getting in the way. Are you afraid of change? Do you think if you extend yourself, you'll only get hurt? Are you just too tired? Talk about it with a trusted friend, or a therapist. We have a thousand ways of convincing ourselves we're too busy to do what we love and value. Challenging that is hard. Taking a chance is risky. But you only get one sweet and precious life—how will you spend it? If you keep the lessons of this exercise in mind, you can gradually, over the years, move your life in the direction you want it to go.

While this advice is still helpful if you're unemployed, being between jobs makes life much harder and can make depression ten times worse. We depressives can really depend on our jobs to get from one day to the next, and without that structure and value we can feel unmoored. My advice: make sure you do at least one thing every day to find a new job—or research a new field, or some further education—no matter how bad you're feeling. It can be as little as one phone call, but the discipline will keep you from going down the tubes. Of course, we hope there are days when you do much more and spend some time pursuing your long-range goals.

Organizing Yourself

Now that you know what's most important to you, here are the steps that will take you there:

1. *Specify your goals.* Goals are statements of how we want things to be. I want to have a happy marriage, I want to be financially

249

secure, I want to be healthy, I want to enjoy my work. These are all nice ideas, but they are too broad to have any real impact on how I conduct my life. To be helpful, goals should be specific, concrete, and measurable. What's in the way of me enjoying my garden, one of my greatest sources of joy? Mostly, it's the time crunch I feel. What can I do about this? One strategy might be to reduce my commute time. Another might be to work more efficiently, to put some limits on my evening hours so I have more time at home. Another might be just to reduce my work hours and live on less. If these are the things that I know are really necessary in order for me to have more leisure time this year, this is where I have to put my energy. It might mean I make less money, but I have to remember that time affluence is more rewarding than monetary affluence.

2. *Synchronize.* Are we in synch with ourselves? Do some of our goals conflict with others? If my most important goal is to work at a leisurely pace and have time to enjoy the present, but I also want to have a big house and lots of consumer goods, I'm setting myself up for depression. In the long run, we doom ourselves if our goals are in conflict. We are grown-ups and have to face the fact that we can't have it all, even when it means giving up on some things that seem important.

3. *Take action.* Start making action plans about the goals you really do want to accomplish. What are your professional goals for this year? Where would you like to be in five years? At retirement? Do your goals for this year take you closer to your long-range goals? If they don't, they should. Maybe you have to focus a lot for the present on simple survival strategies — how to get through the day, week, year. But you will feel better if you can add to your daily activities something that will help you get to your long-term goals. It can be as simple as saving a few dollars out of every paycheck, or taking an adult education class. When we feel that our everyday activities take us a step further toward who and where we want to be, we can justly feel a little satisfaction. We add to our self-esteem; we have a bit more evidence that we can have an impact on our fate; we change our neural pathways; we quiet the Inner Critic.

Make your action plans realistic and concrete. They should require some effort, but shouldn't be impossible. Prepare for some unexpected stress as you change. This is important work that is going to shake up your depression. Just as using the Mood Journal challenges your defense mechanisms, thinking about and working toward what's truly meaningful in your life can be upsetting and difficult. Don't expect it to go smoothly. Accept that your emotions will be in some turmoil. At times, you'll feel terrific; at other times, you'll wonder why you started. Just don't give up.

4. *Review.* Finally, review your goals, and your progress toward them, regularly. Make sure that you have given yourself permission to change your goals. Don't get stuck in feeling bad because circumstances and your priorities have changed. For goals that remain important, look at your action plans. Are there things you should be doing differently? Build some time into your routine when you can review your progress — at New Year's, on your annual vacation, when you pay your monthly bills, on a regular date with your partner. Give yourself credit for doing what you've done, make new plans for doing what could be done better, and *let the rest go.*[8]

At this point, I can hear some depressed patients: "This is all easy for you to say. But when you're down, it's impossible to look at life as a series of opportunities for growth and challenge. When you're down, life just seems like a whole series of tests that you're doomed to fail. It's just about impossible to get up the energy to even try." Please consider that if you're that far down, this chapter isn't for you, yet. Just concentrate on your recovery, and come back here when you're ready.

It's also true that there are many people stuck in jobs that are simply too demoralizing to bear, or would require a superhuman effort to improve. There are far too many people who will never have the opportunity to engage in meaningful work — because of discrimination, because of the failure of our educational system, because we have changed from a producer society to a consumer society, because of individual bad luck. Those of us who have the chance to do anything with ourselves that is at all meaningful and stimulating should thank our lucky stars. But if you're stuck, you must take some steps to improve other aspects of your life — your relationships, your faith, your interests.

The hard truth is, we either grow or die, challenge ourselves or stagnate. Growth and change are hard work. Depressed people — all of us — want an amulet, Prince Charming in a pill, some charm or trick or secret that means we will never be unhappy again. One of the great truths is that life is difficult, says Scott Peck.[9] Accepting that it *is* difficult, that this is the normal state of affairs, and that it never will be otherwise, allows us to transcend its difficulty. Giving up the wish for the magic charm means giving up the resentment, anger, and bitterness that go with wishing for what we will never have.

Living, Together and Apart

THE WORLD OF RELATIONSHIPS has changed so much since the first edition of this book that on re-reading it I was dismayed to find a kind of pro-marriage bias on my part. I had been assuming (along with many others of my generation) that marriage, a single, deeply intimate bond with another person, and the opportunity to be productive and generative in raising a family, was the royal road to mental health, the obvious way out of depression. While these conventional assumptions still have merit for many people, it's also true that marriage and family life can be incredibly destructive and depression-inducing. And there are many more people, never married, widowed, divorced, who are finding that they prefer the single life, that it has its own unique joys.

Depressed people tend to be overly dependent on external factors—continual feedback from others and a relentless quest for accomplishment—to feel good about the self. Because there is really little we can do in life to influence the behavior of others or to change events, the depressive's self-esteem is always in danger. Most people depend on relationships to sustain a sense of doing well and deserving love. Parents and partners can supply this for us, but so can our children, friends, coworkers, neighbors, and other people we interact with regularly. Relationships with our work, recreation, and daily routines also help sustain us. Everyone needs these relationships throughout life; they are like water to a fish. We swim in a sea of relationships that invisibly hold us up and provide us with nutrients. But the depressive's need for relationships is more desperate, and sometimes more distorted or disguised. Because he's depressed, he blocks the good things that come with connections, or avoids them altogether. It is as if the depressive has never learned how to swim effectively or float effortlessly. Instead, all he can manage is an exhausting, desperate flailing and gasping. The sea of relationships that provides others with nurture and support doesn't give the depressive any buoyancy.

Communication

Relationships are minefields for the depressed, desperately desiring yet afraid to connect. Understanding better how communication works, especially between the sexes, can be a very helpful skill.

Deborah Tannen is probably the wisest and most articulate observer of communication patterns of this generation. In her book *You Just Don't Understand,*[1] she explores the thesis that men and women speak different languages, or at least use language in entirely different ways for different purposes. This confusion in language, she asserts, accounts for a great deal of the conflict that goes on in male-female relationships, not only in marriage, but in the professional world, the playground, in all areas where males and females interact. Although this line of thinking can be carried to extremes (*Men Are From Mars,* etc.), Tannen has a perspective that is highly useful in understanding how men and women deal with depression.

Tannen says, in essence, that men and women in the United States today grow up in different cultures, which reinforce their use of language for different purposes. Women use talk for interaction, men for information. Men see the world in terms of hierarchies, and hear all communication in terms of "Who's in charge here?" Women, on the other hand, see the world as a vast network of connections, and all communication serving the purpose of establishing connections. For men, then, communication is work; it always has something to say about status, and men are constantly on guard against being put into a lower status position. But for women, communication is like breathing; it's necessary to keep oneself connected, to be part of the world.

Men may carry a genetic load for power and dominance, women for cooperation, dating back to caveman days. Raising children, farming, harvesting, cooking—women's roles in Stone Age culture— all require cooperation. But men are programmed to make sure above all else that their genes survive, so there is an inherent competition to be the one who gives the orders, which meant access to more women.

Consider, for instance, the stereotyped play of children: boys tend to play highly organized games in large groups, in which there are elaborate rules. There is always at least one leader, whose function is to make and enforce the rules, and a whole hierarchy of status positions under the leader. One of the functions of play, for boys, is to compete for higher status. Girls, on the other hand, tend to play games that emphasize cooperation, not competition; there are no winners and losers and all must take turns fairly. If a girl tries to push herself forward, she will get criticized for being bossy. Tannen makes some broad generalizations, and I'm greatly oversimplifying, but there is some truth in what she says. *Lord of the Flies* would have been a very different book if it was about a group of girls isolated on an island with no adults; they would have split up into cliques instead of killing each other.

Tannen gives the example of a friend of hers who is recovering from a lumpectomy. In talking with her sister and with a friend, she says how upsetting it was to have been cut into, and how distressing it is now to see the stitches and see how the contour of her breast has changed. The women say words to the effect of *I know, I have felt the same way.* Tannen's friend feels supported and comforted. But when she tells her husband about the same feelings, he says, "You can have plastic surgery." Whereas her friends' comments were heard as supportive, she hears her husband's comment as just the opposite. He's telling her to have more surgery just when she's telling him how miserable she feels about *this* surgery.

So she protests, and she also assumes that he is speaking for himself; that he wants her to undergo further surgery because he doesn't like the way she looks now. But her assumptions lead to more trouble. He protests: "It doesn't bother me at all." "Then why are you telling me to have the surgery?" she asks. "Because you were saying *you* were upset about the way it looks," he says. "I was just trying to help." And she knows, based on their history together, that this is the truth. So why does she feel so bad? Tannen says that she wanted the gift of understanding, but he gave her the gift of advice.

Now I've heard this same scene played out many times over in my office between husbands and wives (also between parents and adolescents). The poor schmuck is "only trying to help," but it's not the kind of help she needs. When a man's wife or child is in pain or in trouble, he wants to fix it and make it go away. He sees this as his responsibility; he feels guilty or inadequate if he can't protect his loved ones. But often it's best for the wife or child to work things out on their own, and very often they know this. They're not asking him to fix it, they're asking for empathy, understanding, commiseration.

It gets us all into a great many difficulties. Men tend to resent commiseration; they hear it as taking away from the uniqueness of their own experience, whereas women tend to hear it as caring. Men also hear it as condescension, again because they view the world in competitive terms. Men tend to be able to offer sympathy to each other only indirectly, through joking, and are still uncomfortable with it. Smart men are slow to offer advice to other men, unless the other guy asks directly. But men feel it's just fine to offer advice to women.

Women tend to resent when men offer solutions; men don't understand why women complain and don't take action. For women, talking about troubles is intended to strengthen relationships: "We're the same; you're not alone." What they hear from men is "We're not the same; you have the troubles, I have the solutions." Women show concern by probing, asking for more information. Men change the subject. Women see this as a failure of intimacy on the man's part. Men may see it as respecting independence. Why do men hide behind the newspaper when their wives are asking for contact or recognition? This is much more than a cartoon or TV comedy situation. Even Freud was moved to ask, "What do women want?" Men are scared of women's emotional needs, and they hide. Women feel hurt and rejected. It's what leads to trouble in many marriages. According to Tannen, for many men the comfort of home means freedom from having to compete and impress through verbal display (remember, communication is work for men). They see the marital relationship as one where talk is not required. "I bring home a good paycheck, I don't cheat, I play with the kids, I work around the house. Doesn't all that prove that I love her? What more does she want?" But for women, home is the place where they feel the greatest need for talk with those whom they are closest to. The comfort of home means freedom to do so without worrying about how they will be judged. Tactful wives might want to understand that the phrase *we have to talk* will scare their husbands to death, and that it's best to lead men gently into talking, as you would calm a skittish horse.

If spouses are unable discuss these differences, depression may be the result. If I continually feel that my attempts to comfort and support my wife are rejected, I feel diminished. If she feels that I'm unsympathetic and just want her to shape up, she feels diminished. We have been the most important people in the world to each other, but we each get hurt and frustrated and start to withdraw. If we feel that we can't help or understand each other, that's depressing indeed.

Tannen's observations apply to friends and casual discourse as well as intimate relationships. Some people didn't learn the basic rules of communication (see Chapter 10) in childhood or adolescence, and have grown up feeling lonely and alienated. Depressed adults, overly focused on themselves, are apt to forget about these rules. Depressed women can fail to reciprocate in the accepted, ritualized way, and friends may cut them off. Depressed men are likely to resent the gamesmanship in male-male conversation, and withdraw. It's a mistake to view these little unspoken conventions as games, however; they are important social lubricants, maximizing reciprocity and minimizing conflict.

The Single Life

It remains true that being single means you're more vulnerable to depression. But we have to look much deeper than that generalization to get an accurate picture of the risks of depression for any individual single person. I have met many patients of both sexes in their twenties and thirties, especially in my New York office, who are enjoying being single and aren't depressed because of that. I've also met many older patients of both sexes, especially in my Connecticut office, who wouldn't dream of marrying again. And of course I've run into many marriages that have caused real psychological damage for both parties. It turns out that my little slice of life, with an urban and a rural practice, is a microcosm of some greater trends. If you're young and single, country life can be much more depressing than city life. If you're older and single, living in the city is more of a challenge, and living in a rural area where you have roots and a network of connections can be easier. Of course, there are exceptions to those generalizations; many older single people are quite happy in urban areas, especially if they have a tight network of friends and family and appreciate the cultural opportunities of the city. Some older people relocate to a retirement community geared for singles, where I understand life can be an opportunity to make up for some of the good times you missed out on if your marriage had grown stale.

There are two other variables that are important to the single life: money and education.[2] Having money in your pockets allows you to go out and enjoy the nightlife, the good restaurants, vacation opportunities, and the cultural scene, all of which make life less lonely and more fun. People with a college education are often more able to appreciate the diversity of urban life and tend to have more social connections. But being poor, single, and isolated is a sure-fire route to depression for most people.

There's another thing: some people just don't want the intimacy that a committed long-term relationship demands, and that doesn't mean they're sick or weird. My generation just assumed everyone should be married, and disapproved of any alternatives. I think there's a new kind of intimacy on the scene, one that's built on multiple connections, that may be much more satisfying for people who feel constrained by a single relationship. We all have to make choices between intimacy and autonomy. Both are meaningful and important, but both have their downsides. More and more people seem to be valuing their autonomy more.

We have to keep in mind that there was indeed a sexual revolution a few decades ago, and it changed life dramatically for singles. I hear from my younger clients in the city (and from my children) that there's a complex social world out there for single people, with its own set of rules and expectations. More young people are part of a mixed-sex crowd of friends that has very clear unwritten rules about dating, friendship, casual sex, meaningful sex, and friends with benefits. Statistically, when young people are in college or first move to the city they are much more likely to engage in "casual" sex; then after a few years they drift into a pattern more like serial monogamy. This pattern of experimentation is new, but not inherently harmful. Sex is among the greatest pleasures of life; if people can figure out how to experiment without getting hurt, and then move on into more committed relationships, should we condemn them?* Meanwhile, same-sex friendships can be deeper and more committed than we

* But I don't want people who experience the hypersexuality of bipolar disprder, or the self-destructive sexual acting out of major depression, to take this section as permission to do whatever they want. Healthy sexuality requires mutual respect and positive motivation.

expected them to be in the past, and can bring people some of that new intimacy I refer to.

And I'm only talking so far about the heterosexual world. In urban areas, at least, the gay scene has a similar kind of culture, with its own rules about commitment and casual relationships, often leading to deep bonds that far outlast the sexual element. Being gay used to be a surefire path to stigma, self-hate, and depression. I'm not aware of any formal studies, but I have no doubt that being homosexual — in tolerant communities — is much less likely to lead to depression now than a generation ago.

One more stereotype to lay to rest: while some of us feared that Internet use would lead to further disconnection between people, it's turned out that the Web is a great tool for getting people together. Social sites like Facebook and chat programs reconnect childhood and high school friends; can keep families in closer communication; help us connect with other people who share our concerns or causes; and of course facilitate dating. Meetup.com has as its purpose bringing people face-to-face to share similar interests; today I see the Pasadena-area New England Patriots fan club is meeting. How in the world would people like that find one another without the Web? Lotsahelpinghands.com organizes volunteers to help individuals and families cope with serious illness or similar needs, totally free of charge. Laughteryoga.org brings people together just to laugh with each other. I mentioned earlier that one patient of mine has found a site for children of narcissistic mothers; recently she poured out her heart, posting part of her very private journal. Very soon she was feeling enveloped by support and understanding, a completely new experience for her. I have no expertise at all about this; these are just a few groups I've run across, but there must be thousands of similar opportunities available on the Web to form support networks that can truly bring meaning and connection into people's lives. Being single doesn't have to make you more vulnerable to depression the way it used to.

However, if you have depression to start with, being single can make it harder. The hopelessness and lack of energy will make it very tempting to shut yourself in and avoid contact, and that will just turn all your negativity on to yourself. If you are single and depressed, you *must* make a sustained effort to get out of the house and be with others. We need other people to keep us sane, give us perspective, and keep our thoughts slightly more in line with reality. Go back to my tips about developing willpower, set some concrete goals about connecting (find an old friend on the Web; call someone), and put yourself to work.

Love, Marriage, and Depression

As the mental health professions work more with families, parents, and children, we learn fascinating things about what leads one family to divorce, another to a successful and stable marriage. Considering what leads to "falling in love" may be unromantic but quite useful in understanding how to make marriages work better.[3]

There are powerful unconscious factors in falling in love, in why two particular people decide to marry each other out of all the people in the world, that can have repercussions later on in various stages in the family life cycle in terms of marital conflict, children with emotional problems, adolescents in rebellion, and the adult identity of the children. I choose to marry you so that I can take care of you, so that I can rescue you, so that you can rescue me, and so on ad infinitum, all totally unconscious. Falling in love, by definition, is a crazy process, deeply influenced by unconscious motivations and perceptions. Who I fall in love with, no matter how normal or well functioning I am, is determined by my particular psychological needs at the time I'm ready to enter a relationship. Those needs have to get addressed somehow in the relationship, or it will never work.

What we see in practice is that families in trouble often present themselves to clinics with an "identified patient"—the depressed mom, the alcoholic dad, the symptomatic child, or the acting-out adolescent—whom the rest of them want fixed. But the assigning of that role to someone in the family has its roots in the unconscious needs of the couple at the time they got together and the reasons why they chose each other. Some parents obsess about the needs of their symptomatic child partly in an effort to preserve their marriage by uniting for a common purpose. Some acting-out adolescents get in trouble for the same reason, to preserve the marriage; though it's totally unconscious, teens are often testing to see if they can get their parents to function like parents again. Other adolescents are expressing the secret rage of one or both parents, for instance, by being the depressed mom's champion, or provoking dad to see if he will care. Divorce is often the result of a power struggle between the parents to define who is sick, bad, or to blame. These are all scenarios in which the marital pair has either been unable to come to terms with the needs that attracted them to each other in the first place, or else those needs have changed over time, perhaps in one partner more than another, and the relationship hasn't kept up.

One useful point of view postulates — with good clinical reason — that an area of attraction between future partners is that each sees the other as a way of solving his or her own self-esteem issues. The idea is that unconsciously we think, "I have this problem about myself — I feel unworthy of love, and this person loves everyone; I can't stand to make decisions, and this person will do it for me; I've been ignored and neglected, and this person will supervise me." But the catch is that too often the partner shares the same problem and just has a different, *only superficially better*, way of dealing with it. As in a distorting mirror, we see our partner's defensive system as the ideal solution to our problem; but our partner, inside that suit of armor, is only too aware of its chinks and weaknesses and sees our fragile armor as what he or she needs.

Sharon was an attractive woman in her thirties stuck in her third unhappy marriage. Her second husband had shot her, then killed himself, in the presence of their children, because she wanted to leave him. She recovered from her wounds but seemed remarkably uncurious about why she would have had this effect on a man.

Sharon was enormously conflicted about sexuality and needed continual reassurance that she was desirable, but she was not a flirt or a tease. She seemed like a wholesome, mature woman whose primary concern was her children. Her third husband was about ten years older, very attractive in a hyper-masculine way (given to leather jackets, cowboy boots, and big belt buckles), apparently very self-confident about the issues that she was so conflicted about.

I worked with Sharon for about a year, and we couldn't seem to get anywhere. She wanted to leave her husband: he didn't like her children or treat them well, he continually tried to force her to choose him over them, making her feel like a prize in a contest. But she didn't leave; he kept charming her, seducing her, and she would come in for our session feeling guilty and ashamed. Then one day she appeared after having had a couple of drinks, and said, "This couldn't possibly have anything to do with anything, but you ought to know..." and revealed incest by her brother when she was thirteen. We went from there into deeper memories of her childhood—her feelings about her mother being uninterested in her, Sharon's attention to minor defects in her physical appearance, her current wish for plastic surgery—as expressions of the feeling of being damaged, shameful, and unlovable from childhood.

Finally, after she'd worked through some of the guilt about the incest and the anger at her mother, and started to feel better about herself, she started to see her husband objectively. She began to wonder: If he's so confident, why does he get jealous when I give my children attention? If he's so self-assured, why does he need to flirt with every woman in sight? Why does he need this kind of reassurance? *This man, who had seemed a kind of magical, mystical Svengali, became suddenly in her eyes pathetic, vain, needy. She realized, "Every man I've ever married, I thought was strong. It's always turned out that I've been the stronger one."*

A good marriage can be a mental health factory, a system for ensuring the emotional well-being of the partners and the children, when it finds a way to accommodate each parent's secret emotional needs. People who are not married don't live as long as those who are. A good marriage helps us deal with and absorb and respond to the stresses of everyday life in a much healthier way than isolated individuals can. But a bad marriage can be a crazy-making machine.

It's reasonable to understand one's life as a whole series of complicated maneuvers around the issue of intimacy. The feeling of trusting, opening up, being close to someone, being understood, is something that we all very much want. If we are isolated we go to great lengths to avoid feeling alone — we go to bars, we go to meetings, we go on blind dates, we go to work. At the same time, we fear intimacy as well — and when we are close to someone, we find ourselves putting barriers in the way. We drink, we watch TV, we read the paper; most of all we just don't listen or we listen in particular ways that lead to misunderstandings. This ambivalence — to be afraid of intimacy as well as to need it — seems to be a normal part of being human. What a marriage supplies is the opportunity for intimacy, and, through a whole series of shared developmental tasks that the partners are forced to take on together, the opportunity to grow in the ability to trust, to be honest, to care and share. Those things are all good for us emotionally; they lead to positive mental health.

But besides the opportunity for intimacy, marriage also can supply someone for us to blame for our unhappiness. Though each partner brings his or her own characteristic defenses to the relationship, marriage offers a special opportunity for projection to operate. In projection, we take unacceptable parts of ourselves and attribute them to others. "*You're* awfully grouchy this morning." Projection can become institutionalized in the marriage so that the couple play roles they've assigned to each other that are more or less mutually acceptable; the weak one, the strong one, the one who can't make decisions, the detail person. It can also be the fuel for divorce: "It's not my fault, it's your fault, that I'm unhappy, unsuccessful..." (fill in the blank).

Every marriage faces a crisis of disappointment, when one or both partners realize that the spouse is not able to cure one's own neurotic problems. Sharon's second husband tried to kill her when she attempted to disengage from him. In her third marriage, she finally realized that her search for a strong yet seductive man represented a problem she had to solve for herself. In stable marriages, these crises reoccur throughout the life cycle of the family, as people deal with different developmental issues, but let's focus on the initial crisis.

Say I'm mildly depressed. I'm ill at ease in social situations, I have poor self-esteem, I'm socially restricted because I worry constantly about whether people approve of me. I marry someone who looks as if she has all the self-confidence in the world. A few years later, I realize that she looks this way because she's really rigid, compulsive, and afraid of people—or perhaps I don't see this, but she gets sick, becomes weak and needy, and I can't stand it. What attracted us to each other was a defense—a different defense from mine, but against the same conflict. Likewise she realizes that, though she saw me as the strong, silent type, my silence comes from anxiety rather than strength. *What once were virtues now are defects.* It's as if we have a new set of eyes, and the things that once attracted us to our mate, we now see as weak, needy, controlling, interfering. Instead of loving those qualities, we hate them. We de-idealize each other; that initial stage of being "in love" is gone. Gradual de-idealization is a healthy aspect of a mature relationship; but when it turns into hate or blame, we're heading for divorce.

This is when relationships become work. That may be disillusioning, but we have to accept the fact that no good relationship survives without conscious effort from both parties concerned; and it is the "work" of relationships that leads to our most meaningful opportunities for self-exploration and self-expression. In doing this work, we strengthen our selves so that we become less vulnerable to depression.

At the same time, there is no doubt in my mind that the most stable relationships still have a foundation in the "head over heels in love" state of idealization that began the relationship. Even after fifty years, these relationships are based on affection and caring, fundamentally irrational processes that make us tend to see our partner's best qualities and tactfully gloss over the worst. There is more than a vestige of the unconditional acceptance of parental love. Knowing that we are loved in spite of everything we hate about ourselves can be powerful medicine.

Relationships Under Stress

Stress can affect our ability to function cognitively, emotionally, and physically. Under stress, our judgment is impaired; we have more difficulty assimilating information and correctly sizing up a situation. We can feel depressed, anxious, scared, demoralized. We can get physically ill. Any area of low resistance in one's body will react in characteristic ways — back, intestines, respiration, circulatory system. People with depression, under stress, become more depressed. And stress is the precipitant to almost all depressive episodes.

A good, trusting relationship can be the best vaccine against stress. The couple has the advantage of their unique relationship, which gives them the chance to express their feelings honestly and completely in a way that is close to impossible in other relationships. A crisis can, of course, bring up problems that have previously been dormant, or open up fault lines that had been patched over. Peaceful times can permit a couple to become lazy like this. But when an outside problem erupts, they will find their resources undermined by unresolved difficulties. A tendency to blame others instead of taking responsibility, for instance, may be tolerable when times are smooth, but it may destroy a relationship under stress.

A crisis can be used for positive ends.[4] A couple can use the experience to learn how to work together, to build up credit in trust and reliance, to develop an appreciation of each other's strengths, to realize sincerely how much they need each other, to have the experience of providing support. One thing that helps is simply to acknowledge the existence of the stress and that you are in the midst of a stress response. Stress brings chaos and disorganization. When a couple keeps this in mind, they can accept that their strong feelings and dramatic reactions are normal responses. They don't have to be so afraid of losing control. They can say to themselves and each other, "Something terrible is happening to us, and we are having a normal reaction. Under the circumstances, it is the natural way to feel." It's also important to recognize that stress is relative, not objective. What upsets you—financial worries, for instance—may be relatively unloaded for me; but for you to deal with my job problems might be much more demanding.

It may seem self-evident, but it needs to be stated that both partners are always involved when either is under stress, especially if one is depressed. If I'm overwhelmed with problems at work, my wife's reactions are very important to me. When my wife is ill, how I am with her—attentive and caring, or withdrawn and aloof because I'm scared—is a major factor in her ability to recover. The partner should have an important role in times of stress, but some, because they believe there is nothing they can do to help, don't offer constructive ideas, don't offer constructive criticism, and don't offer emotional support to confront the problem. When one partner is depressed, the other needs to get deliberately involved. Not involved in offering advice and solutions, unless there is a clear signal that that's what's wanted, but involved in:

- Listening, drawing out, and accepting feelings
- Exploring alternatives, brainstorming, playing out different scenarios
- Offering hope and encouragement, conveying the sense that you are not alone

A crisis in our marriage came when my wife developed a thyroid tumor. I was preoccupied with finishing my dissertation at this time. I heard what the doctors said to her—that these things are almost always benign—and accepted it at face value. I dismissed my wife's anxiety as groundless and got angry that she needed more reassurance.

Worse yet, the fact that she had to have surgery meant she had to stop nursing our son, then a little over a year old. I told myself and her that it was close to time to wean him anyway, not recognizing that for her the nursing experience was very important bonding time with our children and that she didn't want to stop until she was ready. In all, I treated my wife as if she were a needy pest, when she actually did have a lot to be fearful and angry about.

My analyst at the time was kind enough to point out that my behavior was so bad that the pressure of schoolwork wasn't a sufficient explanation. He reminded me of my reactions to my mother's dependency and depression before her death—denying, dismissing, intellectualizing. Of course I was doing the same thing again. I also was scared of the thyroid tumor. I didn't want to lose Robin. But I didn't let myself think about that. Instead of telling her that I cared what happened to her, I told her not to worry and got angry when she worried anyway.

When one partner doesn't try to help with the other's crisis, it can poison the relationship. Sometimes the one who is not directly affected by a crisis withdraws, sulks, or develops problems of his or her own. In such a case, you can speculate that they have been overly dependent on the partner who is now preoccupied with the crisis. They feel angry and betrayed because the other isn't emotionally available. They may be aware of these angry feelings but embarrassed about the selfishness that they imply—after all, when my wife has a problem, I should feel helpful, not angry, toward her—and thus close down communication. Or they may be unconscious of their anger but still avoid communication because of it. In any case, the crisis is just made worse, because the partner who is directly affected by the stress will feel resentful and betrayed. In families with traditional roles, this often happens when a child becomes ill. The mother becomes involved with the illness, and the father, feeling helpless, withdraws. Or the father might have work problems that he doesn't share with his spouse, and she, feeling hurt and left out, doesn't pursue him. You set in motion a vicious circle in which withdrawal by one leads to hurt feelings in the other, leading to more withdrawal and more hurt feelings until you have either a blowup or a distant, uninvolved relationship.

So what guidelines are there for dealing with stress in a relationship?

1. When you feel threatened by an important problem, discuss your fears with each other. Take turns listening, exploring, and accepting. Be nonjudgmental. Try to sort out which fears are real and which are just anxiety running away with itself. What's the worst that can happen? If your worst fears come true, would you be completely helpless about coping with the situation?

2. When you are actually suffering from the emotional effects of a crisis, don't make it worse by assuming something's wrong with you. Notice these self-blaming thoughts and detach from them or rub them out like ants at a picnic. Be aware that feeling depressed or scared is a normal reaction to the situation. Share your feelings with your partner. Cry, bitch, whine, moan—whatever it takes, knowing that your partner is committed to you and understands that you are under stress. Do this as often as you feel necessary.

3. In the process of pouring out your feelings, start to accept that there is a problem and that only you can do anything about it. Start thinking about ways in which you can get some relief, perhaps even some enjoyment. Even though it may sound impossible, you don't have to let your whole life be overwhelmed with the crisis. Schedule some time for enjoyable activities. Try to compartmentalize your life so that you have some time set aside for dealing with the problem, and other time for doing things that will make you feel good.

4. When you do take the time for the problem, try to use it constructively. With your partner, explore solutions or adaptations. Maybe all you can do is make the best of a painful situation. If there are different solutions open, don't make a hurried choice just to relieve the anxiety. Purposefully delay action until you're sure you have anticipated all the consequences, but don't use this as an excuse to procrastinate.

5. Give yourself time to heal. We don't bounce back from stress without wounds. We may remain sensitive, hurt, and angry. Try not

to take it out on people close to you, but don't deny the feelings. Continue to use your relationship for support.

Divorce

The divorce rate is currently about 49 percent of all first marriages. Of children today, about 45 percent will go through a parental divorce. More than twice as many children of divorce compared to those from intact families will see a mental health professional during their lifetimes. In a national sample, men and women who were sixteen or younger when their parents divorced reported significantly higher divorce rates, more work-related problems, and higher levels of emotional distress than those who grew up in intact families.[5]

One of the chief risks of divorce, of course, is that the child will blame himself. The child imagines that his angry feelings or his bad behavior are the real reason daddy left. Children hear parents argue about the kids, and think that they have caused the problem. It's the healthy child who can talk about these fears and get reassurance. The child who is more vulnerable will keep it inside, may keep it from consciousness, may internalize it into a feeling of badness that doesn't go away — thus you get some adolescents whose whole identity is tied up with being bad. More mildly, this may get played out in the relationship with father. Feeling guilty because he's really closer to mom, the child may be tense, silent, withdrawn when he's with dad. The father may interpret this to mean that the child doesn't care about him, and feel rejected. Father's visits may become less and less frequent, and the child may feel, "I was right all along, Dad doesn't love me" — a classic example of a self-fulfilling prophecy.

Perhaps the most common problem children have with divorce is that of divided allegiances. When the child still loves and idealizes mother but father no longer shares those feelings, the child is confused; what had seemed like the bedrock of his experience — that of having his perceptions confirmed by the most important people in his life — is now seen to be unstable. When parents actively try to get children to take sides, of course, that makes matters worse, because they are being asked to believe that their own feelings and experience are wrong. Children in this position often grow up with a severely damaged sense of self, a lack of confidence and trust in their view of reality. These children may become good at manipulating, having learned that they can be rewarded for telling people what they want to hear.

It's not only the children, but often also the spouses, who can suffer as a result of a divorce. While I've seen many couples whose mutual hatred and blaming can only be resolved by splitting up, I do think our society has blundered by making divorce seem like too simple and attractive a solution for very complex problems. We have the idea that marriage should be based on romantic love and that once married, we should live happily ever after. This belief is somewhat of a social and cultural anomaly. Through most of history and in most cultures, it's been understood that the purpose of marriage is to raise a family, not to make each other happy. Now too many spouses think that the first sign of trouble means that the marriage isn't working and that divorce is the answer. Often cut off from older family members who could put problems in perspective, the spouses don't realize what's normal.

A respected long-term study of the effects of divorce on families, reported in Judith Wallerstein's *Second Chances*[6] and in subsequent books, came to some chilling conclusions.

One observation was that children's experience of divorce is very different from that of adults. It is simply not true to rationalize that because an unhappy adult is probably not an effective parent, whatever makes the adult happy is necessarily good for the children—the "trickle down" theory of family functioning. An exciting love affair or a stimulating job change may make an adult very happy and at the same time make him or her less available as a parent. Parents are often forced to choose between their own happiness and that of the children, and that is simply a fact of life. Children need unconditional love, which often means that parents sacrifice their own happiness for the child's sake, and the child will be hurt by or resent anything they perceive as the parent's betrayal. And the love and affection between spouses in a second marriage does not necessarily extend to the children. Before the divorce, children can be quite content even when their parents are miserable. Only one in ten children in the study experienced relief when their parents divorced. Children need the functions of a parent and the structure of the family, aside from their love for the parents as individuals. They feel that their childhood is lost forever, that divorce is a price they pay for their parents' failures.

Perhaps the most disturbing news in this study was what Wallerstein called "the sleeper effect." At the ten-year follow-up, children who had initially appeared to be relatively unruffled by the divorce, whose parents did everything the right way, began in their early twenties to show rather serious problems that they themselves linked to the divorce. These problems included depression, anorexia, self-destructive behavior, risk taking, difficulty getting close to others, and difficulty trusting. These young adults talked of doubts about the permanence of relationships, doubts about one's judgment of others, and anxiety about and expectation of betrayal. The sleeper effect was generally a phenomenon of young women, because boys are more predictable; if they're going to have trouble, they show it early on. But issues from the childhood experience of divorce get reawakened in each child as he or she enters adulthood—some merely think about it, others act it out.

Over a third of the young adults in Wallerstein's study seemed remarkably depressed ten years after the divorce. They were drifting through life without goals, they had limited their education, and reported a feeling of hopelessness. Some stayed home well into their twenties, others just drifted. Many dropped out after a year or two of college and were in unskilled jobs. They were clearly underachieving. The authors made a clear link between this pattern and a feeling of abandonment by the father. They felt that girls in early adolescence and boys in later adolescence went through a period when father's love and good opinion became needed much more intensely. If the father did not respond, they would internalize his lack of caring: *if*

I were a better person, he would pay more attention to me. Another surprise was how many fathers were able to rationalize not helping to pay for college, or never increasing child support.

And of course, divorce often brought out the worst in parents. In most divorces, there was a clear winner and a clear loser (aside from the children). Jockeying for these positions became an important part of the identity of the divorcing parents, and negotiating the details of the divorce agreement became loaded because it seemed so important to win. The divorce became just a continuation of the same battle that fueled the divorce, the crisis of disappointment. Winning the divorce war was a way to prove to the world and the self: "Look how well I can do without him/her."

Usually, the one who leaves, or ends up better off financially, or remarries first, is the winner, the one left is the loser. These simplistic labels are perfect descriptors of the couple's feelings, and all their interactions over the next decades may be influenced by their desire to win. But in reality, if divorce is a contest, both lose. If men "win," they usually establish financial success but at the expense of their relationship with their children. If women "win," it is usually in emotional terms; financially they are still worse off, and their children don't have a father. Both end up more prone to depression.

By making divorce a contest, we deny ourselves the opportunity to do the grief work necessary for giving up on what had been perhaps one of our biggest dreams. Grieving means going through the familiar stages of denial, bargaining, anger, and ending up accepting the loss. Acceptance means achieving a balance in feelings about the lost person; no longer colored by rage or hurt, but tolerant and objective. If we're unable to do this, we go on projecting our misery on our spouse, who is no longer even there to respond. We keep ourselves in a depressed position, unable to digest our grief. If we're going to divorce, we have to commit to going all the way through it — to giving up on the fantasy that our partner is to blame for all our unhappiness, to accepting the sadness of our lost hopes, to taking responsibility for our own lives and our own decisions.

Children and Adolescents

CHILDREN, ONCE THOUGHT to be immune from depression, are now recognized to suffer frequently, though their symptoms may be confusing. Many of the newer syndromes recognized among young people, like ADHD, Asperger's syndrome and other mild autism-spectrum disorders, and childhood bipolar disorder, in my opinion are closely intertwined with depression, and some of the newer medications may be treating depression through the back door. As I said above, it's fashionable now to treat with medication instead of looking closely at the child's experience. These may be stress- or trauma-related disorders, the stress transmitted through the mother *in utero* or by the relation-ship with parents. The more we know about the developing brain, the more we understand how easily it can be changed or damaged by expe-rience. Adolescents have increased their incidence of suicide alarmingly over recent years. They may make their depression painfully obvious, through depressed moods, self-destructive behavior, anorexia, bulimia, or cutting; or they may mask it by adopting a tough, rebellious exterior.

Monkey Depression

When we think of children, we see how both nature and nurture play a part in the development of depression; both the mind as a mental apparatus and the brain as organ of the mind are involved. Before we discuss human children, let's look briefly at monkey babies. Many people probably still remember Harry Harlow's experiments with rhesus monkeys in the fifties and sixties.[1] He was trying to understand how monkeys learn to be monkeys. He took infant monkeys and gave them a choice between two surrogate mothers—one of wire, with a nursing bottle to give food; one of cloth, with a hot water bottle for warmth. The baby monkeys would cling to the warm, soft mother and only leave it to go to the other for food. The conclusion was that primate infants have an innate need for security, comfort, and attachment to a mother figure as well as a need for food.

Scientists have been studying Harlow's monkeys ever since. Rhesus monkeys are interesting because they share 95 percent of human DNA and they live in social groups. Their ability to function, as with humans, is less "hard-wired" than that of lower animals; they depend on what they learn as children in order to get by. Monkeys separated from their mothers at birth and reared by humans appear very disturbed as adults. They don't know how to socialize, are overly aggressive, and are likely to be neglectful or abusive mothers.

Other monkeys who are separated from their mothers for more limited periods show more complex patterns of behavior. They fit more easily into monkey society and in general are hard to distinguish from other monkeys. But if those with this history of brief trauma in childhood are then subjected to stress—social isolation—as adults, they behave differently from normal monkeys. They act as if they are depressed and anxious—they are more passive, they cry, they rock themselves, they engage in excessive self-grooming and other self-stimulating behaviors. If they are repeatedly subjected to the same stress, even as seldom as annually, their behavior continues to deteriorate when compared to normal monkeys.

There are also changes in the brain. The deprived monkeys, when isolated at six months, show changes in levels of cortisol and norepinephrine significantly different from those of normal monkeys under stress. At eighteen months, these changes are stronger, and serotonin levels are also significantly different.

These monkeys appear to be a good analog for depression in humans. Under normal circumstances, they look the same as other monkeys. When something goes wrong, however, they can't respond to stress as well. With repeated stress, their ability to respond deteriorates. It's hard to escape the conclusion that it was the early childhood experience of deprivation that has led to troubled patterns of behavior in adult life that look like depression, and changes in brain functioning that are similar to the brain functioning of depressed humans.

These observations certainly raise interesting questions about the origins of depression: how much in humans is the result of early childhood experience, how much the result of current stress, how much is a biological given. Therapists and researchers tend to hang their hats on a theory that stresses one of the three at the expense of the other two. But just as it doesn't make sense to try to understand world history from an exclusively religious, economic, or political perspective, it doesn't get us very far to be reductionistic in thinking about depression. Rather, we must think of multiple causal factors.

Every patient I've ever known who was depressed had a difficult childhood. Sometimes it was a very critical, demanding father, sometimes a cold, narcissistic mother, sometimes both, sometimes variations on these themes. The death of a parent at an early age or loss of the parental relationship through divorce or separation certainly seems to make people susceptible.

On the other hand, I can't find such evidence in my mother's story. I remember her parents as warm and loving. She was the youngest of three daughters, the baby of the family. My grandfather was a factory worker and they were not well off, but the family seemed happy and stable. Photographs show a happy child and adolescent. She was successful and popular in school.

When we left West Virginia for Chicago, her troubles seemed to start. I was an only child. My growing up deprived her of what had been her major function in life—raising me. She had trouble making friends, and she and my father fought bitterly. She tried working but didn't stick with anything. She started to drink and abuse prescription drugs, and would spend hours watching television, dressed in her nightgown and slippers. The model of the rhesus monkey in isolation, self-stimulating and self-soothing, makes intuitive sense to me.

But I know my perception of my grandparents, who may have been warm, loving, and indulgent with a child who was not their primary responsibility, may have been vastly different from my mother's. It may ultimately be that she experienced her childhood as difficult or depriving for reasons that other people may not be able to understand. It may be that she was genetically predisposed to be unable to respond effectively to stress and isolation.

My case is similar. It's possible that I've inherited some genetic predisposition to depression. I certainly worry about it in my kids. I also know that my childhood experiences, and my mother's death and its aftermath, left me angry at the world, suspicious and reserved, wanting very much to be loved but afraid to trust—a sure setup for depression.

Depression in Children

Until the 1980s, it was generally thought that children could not become depressed. We depended on a psychological theory that said, essentially: depression is the result of a punitive superego; the superego isn't developed until adolescence; ergo, depression is impossible in children. Now researchers recognize that children, like everyone else, are not immune at all. Because they usually lack the capacity to step back and recognize that the way they're feeling isn't normal for them, diagnosis and treatment of depression is more difficult than it is for adults.

Also, the symptom picture of depression in children and adolescents is confusing. Sometimes children will let us know that they feel hopeless, empty, or overwhelmingly sad—the signs we look for in adults. But more often children cannot express their feelings so directly and we must interpret their behavior. Irritability is a key indicator. Children may seem easily frustrated, cranky, or moody. They can't be pleased. Boys may simply appear unusually angry or sullen, girls whiny and easily upset. If this mood is unrelieved for more than a week, and especially if it does not seem to come in response to some real disappointment or loss, the parent should most likely seek help. Other signs of depression in children include changes in appetite or energy level; sleeping a great deal more or less than usual; a drop in school performance; and excessive worrying. Especially troubling is a loss of interest in things that used to give pleasure, as when a child seems not to care any longer for favorite toys or activities. Injuries that seem accidental may have been the result of carelessness. The child may talk about death or thoughts of punishment.

Untreated, depression can be permanently devastating to children. Relationships within the family are impaired, school performance is affected, and peer relations are disturbed. Depressed children tend to have fewer close friends, and their relationships are not long-lasting. They are shyer and get teased more than nondepressed children. They have difficulty concentrating and are easily distracted and fatigued; they score significantly lower than other children on most standardized tests. If these trends continue, the child will not succeed in school and may be "tracked" into programs that really don't allow her to meet her potential.

The actual incidence of depression among children is not known because diagnosis is so difficult. Estimates range from a few tenths of a percent to the 15 to 20 percent that is found in adults. One estimate that seems realistic is that 10 percent of all children will suffer a depressive episode before age twelve. It's well recognized now that suicide, usually a result of depression whether diagnosed or not, is on the increase among teens. But thoughts or wishes of death, and self-destructive behavior (often misinterpreted by adults as risky or dangerous play) are increasingly reported by young children. An eight-year-old child went to school with rope burns on her neck; she had told her mother she only hurt herself playing, but the school nurse wasn't fooled.

The idea that a child might think of taking his or her own life is horrifying. And while we may be able to entertain the idea in theory, in real life when we run across such a child, perhaps in our own family, our denial kicks in. Every child therapist can tell stories about seemingly caring parents who were unable or unwilling to take the simplest concrete steps—locking up medicines, getting rid of guns—to protect a suicidal child or adolescent. Therapists, teachers, physicians, and others who know the child can be fooled as well, so that though a child or teen may sound seriously depressed to a neutral third party, others can be too close to see the forest for the trees.

One recent study found that a high proportion of adults viewed childhood depression as a serious problem requiring intervention, but also found that many were very reluctant to recommend that parents talk to others (except for professionals) about the child's condition.[2] So adults seem to remain very confused and frightened about childhood depression, and see it as a shameful subject to be kept secret. This just fuels denial. It doesn't help that some of the SSRIs, which can be of real help with seriously depressed young people, may at the same time increase suicide risk; but children with depression should be very closely monitored anyhow.

In my adult practice, most patients report that their depression only became a serious problem in college or early adulthood; but most would also say they had depressed episodes as children, and their depressed feelings now are closely connected to how they felt then—hopeless, lonely, worthless, defective. It's very rare for them to report that anyone noticed what was going on when they were children; rather, they were depressed partly because their parents were somehow unavailable to them—preoccupied, working too hard, alcoholic, perhaps depressed themselves.

Children today grow up in a world of fear. The whole society is still reeling from 9/11 and the threat of terrorism, and children are affected too. In kindergarten they are taught about stranger danger;

in fourth grade or earlier they are taught about the dangers of drugs; in junior high, the subject is AIDS. On television, politicians disgrace themselves, sports heroes abuse drugs, Wall Street is a shell game, but no one takes responsibility. No one is to be trusted. Parents don't have neighbors or grandparents to help them with parenting. While it used to be that the whole community was involved in child-rearing, now there is no community. The task falls solely on parents and professionals, who seem to be more and more at odds. Parents and children alike are overwhelmed by mass culture, without a support system to reinforce any alternatives.

But parents must find the ability to step up. Parents' emotional availability to the child is probably the single biggest factor in the later development of depression. Remember that in Chapter 4 we discussed how childhood experience affects adult brain functioning, and that the relationship with parents is the key experience of childhood. This is scary news to parents, but you don't need to know a lot or have any special expertise to be a "good-enough" parent. What you really need is time with your child: time when you aren't distracted by the idea that you should be working or being more "productive." Good parenting is an easy and natural thing. Even if you had lousy parents yourself: if you can remember what you needed and didn't get as a child, give your child that. If you can be undistracted enough to empathize with your child, to understand what he or she is feeling, then you know what to do. The empathy itself may be the most important thing.

One of my best teachers used a bicycle analogy to describe how the child absorbs a healthy sense of self-esteem from the parent. At first, the young child learning to ride a two-wheeler needs a parent literally to hold her up. When the training wheels come off, the parent continues to provide support and direction, running along beside the little bicyclist, at first with a hand on the handlebars to steer and another on the seat to hold the bike up. Very gradually, as the child develops a better sense of balance and understands — unconsciously — the principles of momentum, velocity, and gyroscopic stability, the parent needs to provide less and less support. Eventually, the parent lets go of the handlebars, keeping the other hand on the seat but with a light touch, running along beside and encouraging the child with words and emotions. At some point the parent lets go of the seat but continues to run along, perhaps with arms outstretched to catch the child in case of accident. The child hears the parent's footsteps and does not even realize, at first, that she is now in control. The parent's skill, judgment, and confidence have become a part of the child. The parent and child have engaged in a very complex and unspoken transfer of knowledge and control from one to the other. The needed skills are transferred through shared experience, not through explanation. In much the same way, the parent teaches the child that she deserves love and fairness and that she has a bright future.

But today, the opportunity to be close and empathic with your child is becoming more and more scarce. The economy demands that mothers go back to work far too soon after their child's birth. When they do return, their attention is divided. Women — and men, if they take on a major portion of childcare responsibilities — are expected to balance career and family today, and that's a very stressful thing. It can leave parents distracted and guilty, and make it difficult to find that bonding time that children desperately need. A disturbing recent study found that mothers ranked child care as one of their least preferred, most frustrating activities, right down there with commuting.[3] The researchers noted by way of explanation that these mothers were likely multitasking and found child care distracting. I'm sure we would find the same result for fathers who take a major role in child-rearing. Child care goes on continually in the background while we have to take care of other things; thus child care can become an annoyance when we are too busy and stressed.

When parents do become aware that a child is depressed, they must make some adjustments in the way the family interacts in order to help a child or teen recover. They can't rely on medication or therapy. They have to make a deliberate effort to take more interest, simply to show up — at homework time, at mealtime, at bedtime, at sports and school events. Parents can shake off some of their own depression by finding activities to do together with their children. As far as your child is concerned, it's never too late to start.

Adolescents

Depression among adolescents has become so serious that an influential government panel has recommended that every teen be screened for depression annually. The U.S. Preventive Task Force has concluded that a simple verbal screening procedure is accurate enough, and that treatment, especially talk therapy, is effective enough, that early intervention will prevent teens from developing full-blown major depression and will reduce the risk of suicide.[4]

Depression in teens is often masked, but a professional using a good screening tool can often see what caring adults cannot. I recently re-read *The Catcher in the Rye* and was amazed to see Holden Caulfield, the protagonist I had felt such a bond with, from my now-adult perspective. Though I still felt sympathetic, I was struck by how depressed and self-destructive his behavior seemed. For instance, Holden gets angry at Stradlater, his jock of a roommate, because Stradlater may have seduced a girl Holden liked as a child. Holden's anger is such that he takes a punch at the bigger boy, who wrestles him and pins him:

> *"Holden. If I letcha up, willya keep your mouth shut?"*
> *"Yes."*
> *He got up off me, and I got up too. My chest hurt like hell from his dirty knees. "You're a dirty stupid sonuvabitch of a moron," I told him.... Then he really let one go at me, and the next thing I knew I was on the goddam floor again.[5]*

Holden is like many adolescents, both boys and girls, who appear rebellious, argumentative, in minor legal trouble, or just have a "bad attitude," but are actually depressed. They don't look it because they have learned a set of skills—they can stir things up, get everyone mad, keep the emotional pot boiling—so that they don't have to feel empty inside. They can make others feel responsible for their own behavior, keeping parents and school engaged in a power struggle, so they don't have to start really facing independence. One theorist observes that with delinquent kids, one or both parents are full of rage against society or each other. "The child thus assumes the role of avenger for the parent...releasing the parent from having to own and assume responsibility for his or her own feelings and actions."[6] In other words, a parent is going through life with a grievance, a chip on the shoulder, perhaps feels dominated by the other parent but unable to stand up for herself—and secretly admires and encourages the child's rebelliousness, until it rebounds and becomes directed back at the parent.

Jason was fifteen when I first got to know him. He was on probation after having been caught in some petty vandalism. He was a strong, handsome young man who could have been a popular football player at his high school if he hadn't felt too alienated from the system to take part in things.

His mother was one of the angriest people I've ever met. She seemed to have a grievance against the world. She and her second husband, Jason's stepfather, fought constantly, mostly about money. The stepfather spent every spare penny on adult toys—boats, snowmobiles—which he would gleefully deny Jason access to. Jason's mother would rant and rave about how unfair this was to Jason, but was never able to put her foot down with the stepfather. This was despite the fact that she was the real breadwinner in the family and that her own parents had paid for the house they lived in. They were so prone to grievance that they were suing their neighbors on either side over petty neighborhood disputes.

Jason was quite depressed, though outwardly functional. He was lethargic and absorbed by small bodily concerns. He slept poorly and abused alcohol. He saw absolutely no purpose in living, but was not directly suicidal. He complained about having to come in for treatment but always was on time and talked openly. When his probation was up, he committed another petty offense and got more probation time, which I interpreted to mean that he wanted more counseling. He was bright and could have done well in school, but he never studied. He spent his leisure time either making out with his girlfriend or watching television. He wanted to do more; at times he felt a strong desire to make something of himself, but it was as if he didn't know where to start.

Although Jason was a moderate troublemaker at school, he had so many winning qualities that the authorities never turned against him. His mother was a different story. Several times a week, she would call the school to harangue them about something Jason or his sister had done or failed to do.

One day Jason told me somewhat sheepishly that as he was talking to his mother, he'd taken off his sweater and a bag of marijuana had rolled out and fallen at her feet. He laughed as he told me how he'd gotten her to believe that it wasn't his, he was only holding it for a friend.

Incredibly enough, the exact same scene was repeated a few weeks later. This time I could see that Jason wasn't only laughing at his mother's gullibility. When I said that he must have been disappointed that she didn't seem to care enough to see through his story, he started to cry—the first time I'd seen him admit any pain at all. He poured out all his years of resentment at feeling that he was the true grown-up in the family. He told me that he'd been sexually active since the age of eight, always right under his mother's nose; that he knew he was too young to be involved with older girls like this, but that he had the strange feeling his mother knew about it and approved. He had the same feeling about some of the petty theft and vandalism he committed. He didn't get any joy from these acts, but his mother seemed secretly pleased as she put on a show of disapproval.

Jason clearly needed people he could respect who could give him some guidance, but he would push away anyone who attempted to offer it. If Jason continued to grow up without better role models, he could easily turn into a cynical, bitter man who achieves outward success but feels empty inside. He could be a smooth and successful drug dealer. If so, he'd be living out his depression—doing something every day that increased his hatred for himself.

Jason used his intelligence, charm, and empathic skills both to seek help for himself and reject it. He could outsmart himself— certainly he had no conscious intention of showing the marijuana to his mother—but then outsmart everyone else by talking his way out of difficult situations. As much as he hated it, he could read his mother's mind—she did not want to hear that he might need her help—so he would tell her what she wanted to hear, denying his anger at her and increasing his self-loathing.

Besides this acting-out form of adolescent depression, there are many teens who are simply, overtly, depressed. They may not talk about it to parents or peers, but an experienced eye just has to look at them, their grades, their hygiene, their motivation, their manner of speaking. Anorexia, bulimia, and more subtle weight and body-image problems; covert self-mutilation; substance abuse; unnecessary risks; concentration and focus problems; a drop in performance at school; a withdrawal from friends; a loss of interest in things that used to bring joy—these are some of the indicators that concerned parents need to be watchful for. Unfortunately, it's easy for parents and teachers to be too close to see these patterns in a larger context, which enables them to be blind to the teen's depression. A patient of mine, a woman in her thirties who had her own struggle with self-mutilation in her teens, now an employee at a posh private school, told me about noticing that a female student with fresh cuts on her arms was literally waving her hands in front of the dean—who didn't see the cuts.

Depressed adolescents—overtly depressed or acting out—are usually crying out for help in some such way, but will deny that they are depressed or need help if you ask them directly. When parents can put their foot down and get the teen over the therapist's threshold, quite often the teen will keep coming back voluntarily. Just feeling that someone is listening can be of great help. This process can be a blow to parents, who want to be helpful and don't understand why their child has become alienated from them; but if therapy is working, the child and parent can soon repair their relationship.

I have talked with a surprising number of adults who remember suicide attempts as a teen. They were upset and hurt, felt that no one cared and that life wasn't worth living. They took a bottle of pills and went to sleep, expecting never to wake up. Fortunately, they didn't know how many pills to take, so they woke up the next morning perhaps with nothing more than a bad headache. Because they were convinced that no one cared, they told no one. Things got a little better, and they didn't repeat the attempt. But twenty years later, they are in my office, feeling like unlovable failures. They don't connect that feeling to their adolescent suicide attempt, because the mind doesn't work that way — repression lets us remember the event without the feelings connected with it — but it's clear that this feeling has been with them for so long it's now part of the self.

The incidence of suicide among adolescents has been rising at a frightening rate, and no one knows why. Between 1950 and 2000, the rate among adolescents in the United States tripled, while among adults the rate decreased.[7] Suicide is generally considered to be the second or third most common cause of death among adolescents, even though it is seriously underreported. Sixty percent of adolescents know someone who has made an attempt. Sometimes teens will try to harm themselves to get attention, and unintentionally kill themselves in the process. Taking an overdose of Tylenol will kill you pretty quickly, and a slip of a razor can bleed you out fast.

The major risk factors for suicide among young people are not what one might imagine. Instead of the stereotype of a lonely, romantic teen pining away for lack of love, teens who commit suicide have more often been angry, defiant, and in trouble. Not surprisingly, depression — though it's often disguised — is the primary risk factor.

Other risk factors and warning signs include:

- *Substance abuse.* Some young people who have never expressed a suicidal thought have taken their own lives when they got drunk to ease the pain of a disappointment or loss. But when they got drunk, they felt worse, not better, and they committed a rash, impulsive act which they wouldn't have done sober. About 45 percent of teens who take their lives are intoxicated at time of death.[8]
- *Behavioral problems* — getting in trouble in school or with the law, fighting with parents — are the third risk factor for suicide. We tend to think of potential suicides as sensitive, shy people who are overwhelmed by life. We don't see the cocky, obnoxious adolescent as potentially self-destructive, even though his behavior — continually getting in trouble, keeping the world at arm's length — has exactly that effect.
- *Access to a gun* vastly increases the odds of death from a suicide attempt. People can survive an overdose or a wrist-cutting when they get medical attention, but not often a gunshot wound. Whenever there is a risk of suicide, parents absolutely must lock up the guns, their prescription drugs, and the liquor cabinet. Teens will object mightily, but they are secretly reassured.
- *A history of previous attempts* is the last major risk factor. Half of all teens who have made one suicide attempt will make another, sometimes as many as two a year, until they succeed.

Other factors that influence suicidal potential include a family history of depression or substance abuse, and a recent traumatic event. Look back to the story of Jane and her son (page 25) to see all these risk factors at work.

Some children who take their own lives are indeed the opposite of the rebellious teen. They are anxious, insecure kids who have a desperate desire to be liked, to fit in, to do well. Their expectations are so high that they demand too much of themselves, so are condemned to constant disappointment. A traumatic event, which can seem minor viewed from an adult perspective, is enough to push them over the edge into a severe depression. Being jilted, failing a test, getting into an accident—they have the sense that their life is a delicate balance, and one failure or disappointment seems to threaten the whole house of cards.

Depressed Parents, Depressed Children

Good child therapists know that often when a child has behavior problems, parents are depressed. Though the parents often feel that they are depressed because of the child's defiance, it usually makes more sense to understand that the child is angry because of the parent's depression. I know of extreme cases where the family has somehow "expelled" the troublesome child from the home (through boarding school or placement with relatives; or the child has run away) only to have the next child in age step into the troublemaking role. We often explain to parents that the child is really trying to get a rise out of them, to get them to be parents, to put their foot down, enforce rules, and pay attention. The parent may never have realized that, in reality, he or she is quite depressed and not responding appropriately. When we can treat the depression successfully, the parent has the energy to pay attention, to set limits, to be firm and consistent, and the child's behavior improves.

There is a great deal of research documenting that children of depressed parents are at high risk for depression themselves, as well as for substance abuse and antisocial activities.[9] A series of studies[10] has suggested that depressed mothers have difficulty bonding with their babies; they are less sensitive to the baby's needs and less consistent in their responses to the baby's behavior. The babies appear more unhappy and isolated than other children. They may be difficult to comfort, appear listless, and be difficult to feed and put to sleep. When they reach the toddler stage, they are often very hard to handle, defiant, negative, and refuse to accept parental authority. This, of course, reinforces mother's sense of being inadequate and a failure. Her parenting is likely to remain inconsistent, because nothing she does has any visible effect. At our clinic, we became so used to hearing from single mothers of four-year-old boys (a particularly difficult combination) that we developed a standard treatment plan: get mom some immediate relief (daycare, relatives, camp, babysitters), then treat her depression, teach her to defuse power struggles, and start slowly to rebuild an affectionate bond between mother and child.

When the depressed parent isn't able to get help like this, the outlook isn't good for the child. He grows up with dangerous and destructive ideas about the self—unlovable, uncontrollable, and a general nuisance. Boys don't know how to get attention from adults in positive ways, so they get labeled as troublemakers. Girls look for love in all the wrong places, through a sexual connection. Neither boys nor girls know how to soothe themselves, so they are at risk for substance abuse. They don't know they're worthwhile human beings, so they remain very vulnerable to depression.

Pursuing Your Child into Adolescence

In our culture, separation of child from parent comes earlier and earlier. When children are only four, they're likely to be in preschool or daycare programs where they spend a great deal of time with peers. By third or fourth grade, children may spend every afternoon in lessons or sports and every evening with the TV or homework. By sixth or seventh grade, parent and child may be speaking directly to each other only about chores: *Is your homework done? Did you feed the dog? What time is practice tomorrow?* In actuality, the child is much more strongly influenced by the 95 percent of time he or she spends with peers. And the peer culture, in turn, is influenced by the media, by the desire to fit in, and the fear of being different. Parents may see their children going about their business and be vaguely aware that they don't really know what's going on in the child's head, but decide "If it ain't broke, don't fix it."

This is a fatal assumption. Parents need to be nuisances. It's part of the job description to be intrusive. It's how our children know we love them.

After age five or six, children don't make it easy for us to cuddle them, to display affection directly; they squirm away when we reach out. They get absorbed in the business of growing up and don't like to be treated like "babies" anymore. Some parents feel rejected by this normal developmental stage and withdraw from their children. Parents who are better prepared psychologically just shift their tactics — they pursue the child into this new stage. The questions sound inane, and the child will roll his eyes and act as if you're *so stupid* for asking: "What did you do in school today? What do you think of your new teacher? How are you getting along with your friends? What did you think of that show on television? Did you read the story in the paper about the fossil they dug up in South America? What kind of music do you like now? What's the difference between rap and hip-hop (punk, alternative, techno)? Do you think girls should play Little League? Do you want to go to a movie tonight?"

The child will resist, but keep in mind the distinction between content and process, words and music, in a conversation. Emotionally, content doesn't matter very much; the child hears the music. And the constant refrain is "I care about you. You are an interesting person. What you think and how you feel matters to me." Although the child may need to push away and not respond directly to these parental overtures, he gains in confidence and self-esteem with every encounter. Then you may also find those rare occasions when the child will make himself available for some conversation that goes beyond the superficial — because he knows you're interested.

In adolescence, things get tougher yet, but we have to persevere. Media beamed at adolescents is so powerful that we're all scared of it. When my son was small, I didn't want him to watch a certain television program marketed to boys. I thought it taught violence as a means of solving problems, was sexist, and was more than a little scary — much the way parents today think about video games. For a while I held out, but all Michael's friends at school watched that program every day. It was the major theme of their play. Michael begged, and I relented. When they were adolescents, I wished my children wouldn't watch MTV, or listen to much of the music they seemed to like. The values are so unhealthy: *Buy this, and be cool. Adolescent sex is perfectly fine. Intimidation and violence are how people get what they want. Sex is titillating and casual. The world is divided between winners and losers. Parents know nothing. School is boring. Work is boring. Life is boring.* Alcohol and drugs are a constant subtext. I consider myself lucky that my kids seem to have turned out okay so far.

But we must do what we can to challenge what our children are getting from the media. One suggestion is to barge in and watch television with your kids. You may not even have to say very much. Children will be embarrassed at what's on the screen merely because you're present—you are their chief arbiter of values, their external conscience. Because you're there with them, they see the screen partly through your eyes and they can't get sucked so far into the tube. (By the way, don't let them have a TV in their rooms.) If you do say something, don't make it an obvious put-down. They will feel obligated to defend their culture, and you won't win the argument. Instead, ask questions: *What does it mean that that rapper has five girls in his bed?* Or go back to the subject later, when the television is off—tell your kid what you found disturbing, and why, and ask him how he feels about it.

The painful truth is that youth culture is just an extension of the values of adult culture. We live in a society where we are defined as consumers; we are marketed and manipulated twenty-four hours a day; our leaders don't lead but instead follow the ratings. Older ideas of the dignity of labor seem quaint. Anyone who works hard today is a fool; the smartest person makes the most money with the least effort. Since parenting and making a marriage are also hard work, those who keep at it are also fools. It's easy to walk away from a marriage. When was the last time you heard anyone criticized for divorce?

This is indeed a depressing picture. The popular culture of our time is shallow and narcissistic; those who are immersed in it will become depressed when their sources of narcissistic supplies dry up—when they grow old, when their money or drugs run out, when they wake up alone. Those families who stick together, who make time for each other, who teach communicating and caring, will be in much better shape for the future.

This is another area where the world has changed enormously since the first edition of this book. Now, besides television, adolescents have their own cell phones, they IM or Twitter each other constantly, they're on Facebook, they're watching YouTube and Break.com. It's more and more difficult for parents to remain a part of the adolescent's world, and adolescence starts younger and younger. Personally, I experienced a tremendous feeling of loss as my children made it clear I was no longer very interesting. You have to remember that they'll probably get through it and you can have rewarding relationships with them as adults. But some depressed parents may lose sight of this, feel rejected by their kids, and take it personally. It can lead to bitter fighting that may end up meaning that they won't come back to you. Or the parent may build a new world with a second marriage, a relocation, the development of new interests that leave the adolescent out. The child away at college may find that his bedroom has been converted into something else, but not protest because that would mean admitting he's still attached. Things like this can lead to permanent schisms. We have to remember that our children must prove that they are independent of us—but we should leave the porch light on.

Teach Responsibility by Example

As children grow out of the toddler stage, they leave behind that phase of development in which they unabashedly worshipped mommy and daddy as powerful, beautiful, and wise. Sometimes the rapid shift from idealization to treating you like an embarrassment, an incredibly dense and insensitive failure who can't understand the simplest thing, is hard for parents to take. Often, the child will treat you affectionately one minute and contemptuously a half hour later, and you don't have any idea what caused the change. This stage can last from about age six through sixteen, and can severely undermine parents' self-esteem.

Although children at this time seem to have as their goal driving parents crazy, what they actually need is for parents to demonstrate resilience and dependability. Therapists' offices across the country are full of depressed adults grieving about how their parents let them down, never realizing that their parents were doing what they thought their children wanted. A son, who perceives his father as having inexplicably withdrawn from him as he entered adolescence, never thinks that his father may have been hurt by the son's own withdrawal and gone on with other aspects of his life. A woman whose self-esteem is damaged by promiscuity and drug abuse in adolescence feels that her mother deserted her in her hour of need — not understanding that her mother responded to the daughter's insistence on pushing her away. Although children may treat their parents with evident contempt, there is still a piece inside that needs to feel that mom and dad are reliable, competent, and committed to them. If parents can't project that image despite the child's testing, the child will fail to internalize a sense of himself as safe, reliable, and competent.

Parents need to remember that they are the patterns on which the child builds his personality. To self-consciously try to do the right thing in a difficult situation because we want our children to think well of us is not hypocrisy, it's good parenting. How we deal with anger and frustration, cope with anxiety and stress, communicate intimacy and affection — these are habits our children will learn from us. We don't have to be perfect. They can change their habits as they grow up. But we can change, too. Sometimes wanting to set an example for our children brings out the best in us.

Who wasn't moved by Atticus Finch in *To Kill a Mockingbird*? I've heard Gregory Peck reflecting on the hundreds of attorneys who have told him they chose their profession after seeing that film as children. The image of a strong, kind parent who faces evil and teaches tolerance inspires us to try to be better than we are.

Keep Perspective

The depressed reader who is a parent may now feel more depressed than at the beginning of this section. I've been saying that parental depression is responsible for all kinds of problems in the later life of the children, and I've been holding out very high standards for good parenting to prevent children from developing depression as adults. If the reader who wants help with his or her own depression now feels that it must be a real challenge to be a good-enough parent, I can't blame you for feeling that way. But there's no point avoiding the truth. For those of us who have the opportunity, parenting is the most important thing we do with our lives. It's not easy, and how we are and who we are with our children will affect them until the day they die.

But there are two things I can say that can help. One is that in parenting, coming close counts; effort and desire count more than actual success. Above all, our children need to sense our continual caring and concern. We don't have to be perfect. We can be angry or irritable, even depressed and defeated, and our children can accept that if only we can still show that we love them.

The other point restates the message of this entire book: depression is treatable! People get better all the time. More than 80 percent of people who get just a few months of psychotherapy and medication show great improvement. But if you're a depressed parent, you can't be one of the two-thirds of depressed people who don't seek help. You owe it to yourself and your children to get better. It's not as hard as you think.

Community

THE OTHER DAY I saw a young homeless man with his dog, a
good-looking German Shepherd, asleep in the noonday sunshine
on a grating above the St. Mark's station on the New York subway,
thousands of people passing by. I have to confess, I don't think I
would have noticed except for the dog, which aroused my curiosity.
I looked closer and saw a fairly healthy-looking young man, apparently not yet badly affected by street life, and a clean, healthy dog.
I wondered, *How jaded have I become?* I now pass by homeless
people every day without thinking very much about it. When we first
came to New York, it was a shock. Now that I've traveled around
the country some more, I realize homelessness is everywhere, big
cities, small cities, and out in the country as well. Of course many
of the homeless are veterans, brain-damaged by their wars. Others
are the severely mentally ill, kicked out of state hospitals because we
believed that medications would take care of them — and inciden-
tally save a lot of money.

I grew up in the sixties, a time of optimism for our country. To
many of us, there was a rebirth of caring, of empathy and egalitari-
anism. The federal government had programs to fight poverty and to
build communities — how quaint that seems today. A popular song
referred to the prisoner, the drunkard, the hobo, with the refrain

"There but for fortune go you or I."[1] We assumed that, if things were bad, they could be changed, and we might even trust our government to direct the change.

You don't have to be an expert to see that the mental health of our society has declined since then. Children have to be medicated to be able to attend school. Depression, drug abuse, incarceration rates, and homelessness are all soaring. The number of homeless people is a disgrace, and it's hard not to despair for our country. During the Great Depression, Steinbeck wrote *The Grapes of Wrath* and John Ford made a powerful, touching motion picture of it. Such conditions were just not acceptable in America; they were cause for outrage. Today it seems as if we've given up. The gap between rich and poor is higher than it has been since the "Gilded Age," at the end of the nineteenth century, which eventually led to the rise of powerful revolutionary movements. A presidential candidate is ridiculed by the media when he brings up the idea of redistribution of wealth — but I know many everyday people who feel that the time has come.

While the incidence of depression, homelessness, divorce, and incarceration have been climbing, rates for mania, schizophrenia, and panic disorder — more biologically based illnesses — have stayed about the same, supporting the idea that depression is tied to cultural change. There is too much about our society today that is, simply, depressing. We don't feel optimistic about the future or trust our leaders. Even before the economic meltdown, it was more and more difficult to find careers or meaningful work. Is there anything we can do as a society that might slow down or reverse the epidemic of depression?

Depression has a lot to do with how we treat ourselves. In recent years, there have been essential changes in the ways we live our lives, some of which have gone largely unnoticed. Scientists estimate that our caveman ancestors actually "worked" about four hours per day — as is the norm in so-called primitive societies today.[2] The rest of the time was spent in communal activities — mostly just talking, but also a lot of time spent developing artistic skills, singing and dancing, and performing religious ceremonies. "Work" as we know it—the exchange of labor for pay—was only developed in the eighteenth century, and ever since then workers have been fighting for a fair exchange. Getting the workweek down to forty hours was a triumph of the American labor movement.

But over the past twenty-five years, the average American has increased his working hours from forty to fifty—more than any other country in the world, including Japan.[3] Remember a few years ago when we used to pity the Japanese, those nameless "salary-men" who were supposed to be naïve wage slaves, exploited by their employers? Now you don't hear those remarks so much, because Americans have been working about three and a half weeks longer than the Japanese each year (six weeks more than the British, twelve weeks more than the Germans). We do it because we're afraid not to; even in the years before the recent crash, Americans were taking less vacation time off than we earned, because we were acutely aware that we could be easily replaced. Before the crash, *Americans were working 25 percent more hours, and had 25 percent fewer hours for leisure, just to maintain the same standard of living we had twenty-five years ago*—and that doesn't even take into account that most women had joined the workforce as well. We'd been losing the race for years, and we hadn't even noticed.

Those changes in how we spend our time have been demolishing family life. It's become normal now that both partners in a marriage work, and the children are in daycare. The cultural shift that opened up more opportunities for women outside the home can also be seen as an overall reduction in our standard of living, if it takes two of us to provide what only one provided a few decades ago. Now four out of ten Americans work nontraditional hours, so it's rarer still for both parents to be home at the same time. Only about 5 percent of families are able to have mom at home available for the kids after school.

At the same time, our sense of community has been in decline. In the United States in the past fifty years, visiting among neighbors has dropped off drastically. So has trust in social institutions like education, religion, the media, and government.[4] Those of us who can have been isolating ourselves in air-conditioned homes in gated communities, only going out to drive in our air-conditioned cars to the air-conditioned mall, and back home again with our purchases, but without human interaction. Just at the time when social scientists have demonstrated that intimacy, community, and trust are the basic elements of human security and happiness, those elements are in danger of disappearing from our society.

These social changes get into our brains just like trauma and abuse do. Stressful jobs lead to a marked increase in major depression and anxiety disorders in previously healthy young people.[5] Instead of a cooperative world where your life's value is defined by how well you contribute to your community, we have a competitive society that tries to measure your value by your income and possessions. Instead of a world of social ties and ritual that provides security in virtually every aspect of your life, we have a world of me-first. Instead of the sense of belonging to a community, we have the anxiety of unemployment and homelessness. So for the past twenty-five years in both the United States and Europe, rates of anxiety, depression, and stress-related disorders have been accelerating every year; in 2006, Americans spent an estimated $76 billion a year on antidepressants.[6] Now health authorities predict that soon depression will be the world's second largest public health concern.[7]

Consumerism and materialism have been a big part of the problem. Since advertising and television have flourished, we've been brainwashed into materialistic values, taught that happiness and success in life comes from working harder and harder so we can be better off than our neighbors, so we can buy the right things and wear the right clothes. We spend all our money on consumer goods, go into debt, leave our families and friendships behind to pursue careers, rely on alcohol and prescription drugs to make us happy, don't do anything to build a sense of meaning or purpose into our lives. We become mindless, full of stress hormones that wear out our brains and bodies, pushing ourselves all the time. Some of us crash and burn, some of us just gradually wear out, and some of us change our values. A lot of psychotherapy for depression involves helping people see that they need to change direction. Medication holds out the hope that you don't have to change, you can keep on doing what you've been doing—which I think is the stress that leads to depression in the first place. It's usually a vain hope.

It's going to be very interesting to see what happens to the individual American psyche as a result of the global economic meltdown. No doubt there will be pain and stress for many, but if it means giving up on materialistic values and refocusing on relationships of mutual support, that may be a positive change. Happiness researchers have known for some time that the more materialistic your goals, the less happy you are, and that the richest nations are not the happiest.[8]

The Risk of Caring

It's hard not to wish the problems would just go away. It's very hard to feel, "There but for fortune go you or I." That kind of empathy, letting down the walls we put up to keep ourselves snug and secure, can be very painful. In the case of the young man who wrote the song with that refrain, it may have cost him his life.

Phil Ochs sang "There but for fortune" at the Newport Folk Festival in 1964, and Joan Baez made something of a hit of it a year later. Ochs was one of the leading lights of the folk-protest movement of the late sixties. He showed up at the Chicago convention in 1968 and led the crowd in "I Ain't Marchin' Anymore" and "The War Is Over," two anthems of the peace movement that he had written. His guitar was entered into evidence at the trial of the Chicago Seven. Pete Seeger said, "Phil was so likable, so earnest. And good golly, he was prolific. He'd have a new song every two or three days. And they were good, too." [9]

But after 1968, Phil's candle started to flicker. His marriage ended in divorce; his recordings, though respected, were never the hits he wanted; he started drinking more and composing less. He developed a mysterious stomach ailment that had him believing he was dying for almost a year. When it was diagnosed and cured, he went on a manic drinking spree. He took on another personality, calling himself John Train. John Train was loud, obnoxious, and violent. He became paranoid and started carrying weapons. He got thrown out of the clubs he used to headline. Once he was arrested after running up a limousine bill he couldn't pay. The police allowed him to call his lawyer, and Ramsey Clark, the former Attorney General, showed up at the precinct station.

By December 1975, Phil was past the manic episode, worn out, depressed, and broke. He went to live with his sister on Long Island and spent his days watching television and playing cards with her children. In April 1976, he hanged himself with his belt from the back of her bathroom door. He didn't leave a note.[10]

This was a gifted and beloved young man who threw his life away. I can't help thinking that part of the reason was the pain his vision cost him—the pain of putting yourself in the place of the other guy, of not allowing yourself to feel safe and superior to a faceless, anonymous other, but knowing that except for a few lucky breaks you might be in that position yourself. The best, the most compassionate, of psychotherapists live with that every day. We have to temper it with our professional skills, but it's what enables us to engage people, it's what enables those in trouble to trust us in the first place. Of course many other good people retain the same empathy, but you don't see much of it in public.

It's possible that today we might do more for someone like Phil Ochs. His friends tried to get help for him, but nothing worked. Today we have some different medications and, I think, a better understanding of the psychological treatment of depression. But the truth is, with our still limited abilities we can't force treatment on people who don't want it, and that's probably for the best.

A Time of Hope and Peril

The community bears a great responsibility in preventing depression and other mental illness. Every time the school system treats a child unfairly, every time the wealthy and powerful get preferential treatment, every time adults are not able to respect each other's differences, we lose a little of our community mental health. Children learn that their self-esteem is vulnerable because truth and fairness don't always work. On the other hand, when a group of unconnected people meet on the Internet to volunteer for something they believe in, when a neighbor takes in a foster child, when the ambulance squad drops everything to respond to an emergency, we gain a little bit in terms of caring, giving opportunities and hope, showing a belief in social justice.

Consider mental health through the life cycle of the individual. The child is born with a unique combination of innate strengths and deficits, into a family that may operate out of love, respect, and fairness, or out of abuse, abandonment, and blame—more likely a combination of some of the positive qualities, some of the negative. The family's ability to nurture and support the child is not fixed or innate. It changes in response to stress, to success, to bad luck. As our children grow, some of the more vulnerable break. Does the community deny them, or own them? Do they get sent out of state, or into special classrooms, or into long-term-care facilities? As those who grow up more or less successfully enter the life of the community as adults, what's the community's responsibility in terms of offering opportunities to earn a living, marry, raise a family? If they choose an alternative lifestyle, how tolerant will the community be? The community decides how people in trouble are to be treated. Are they to be helped, by whom, to what extent?

True mental health comprises healthy but realistic self-esteem, a basic liking for one's self that recognizes both abilities and limitations. This self-esteem has its roots in the experience of being loved as an infant, owes something to the child's innate endowment and temperament, and is affected by the fit between the child and the parents' abilities. After maturity, it is something that isn't threatened by the usual ups and downs of life. This affection for the self grows in two directions:

1. A wish for mastery — to have an impact on the world — coupled with an objective view of one's unique assets and handicaps.

2. The desire to gain intimacy through relationships based on caring and trust, balanced against the need to maintain one's independence.

Mental health is dependent on society; the culture must give parents the opportunity to love their children; must honor justice and fair play; must provide hope through opportunities available to all. Thus the world of work, the family, and the larger community all affect not only the current state of mind of the individual but the ability of the individual ever to achieve a state of emotional health.

I enjoy living in a community that's small enough so that people know each other and are not just faceless strangers, and small enough so that many people, if not most, feel that their presence and participation makes a difference. People are now finding ways to make these connections work on a big scale, in our cities. Maybe we can do some things to help the whole nation feel a sense of mutual responsibility. We can't ignore society's failures, but neither is it enough to send them away, to pity them, and to throw money at them as long as they stay at a distance. Nor can we blame them and turn away. We are all *interdependent;* it takes us out of our comfort zone to recognize this — but it costs us more to ignore it.

Taken to the extremes we've done, avoidance of social problems and belief in our powerlessness to do anything about them doesn't really get us off the hook. Remember unconscious guilt? Having been told from childhood on that we are our brother's keeper, we can't abandon that burden without feeling that we have failed. But when it comes to our social problems, we've built elaborate rationalizations for giving up, and big walls to keep the problems out of view. We've lost faith in political leaders and bought the idea that government hurts more than it helps — we've accepted the convenient excuse that there are no real solutions for social problems. Too many of us gave up on the idea that a health care system should be accessible to all, turning a blind eye to the truly offensive profits that are being sucked out of the system.

Just as I write this, it's Inauguration Day for a new administration in Washington. There is no argument that a great deal of Mr. Obama's appeal has been that he can rouse the better angels of our nature, giving us hope, finally, for meaningful change. My hope is that he will be able to inspire us to a new commitment to shared responsibility, to mutual support, to less cynicism and greater trust. At the same time, however, the economy has collapsed around us and we are certainly in for a rough ride, of dreams disappointed, of less security and more anxiety. But happiness isn't a product of material success. Around the world, people who live in societies where mutual support and cooperation are high, where trust in the government is high, and who know how to celebrate and dance, are happier than their richer cousins who live in more materialistic societies.[11] So even if economic recovery is slow, there is the possibility of social change that can make much more difference to those at risk for depression. I urge my readers to put aside their skepticism and hope for the best.

Depression is a disease that hits us both as individuals and as a society. Let's expand our vision: the paranoid, self-centered "I've got mine" outlook leads to depression; the expansive, inclusive "Let's work together" attitude, though uncomfortable and challenging, is life-affirming and joyful. If each of us could do something regularly to make a contribution to the larger good by taking the trouble to get involved, on a personal level, in a way that challenges our comfort, it will help shake us out of depression individually and collectively.

Part 4

A New Synthesis

The Rest of the Story

FOR MANY YEARS, I was haunted by the belief that I wouldn't live past my thirty-eighth birthday. That was my mother's age when she took her life, and I was obsessed with the idea that I couldn't outlive her, that whatever drove her over the edge would catch up with me. I've since learned that this is not an uncommon belief with the children of suicides—witness Ted Turner, mentioned earlier.

After my mother died, what I felt, consciously, was anger. I blamed her for being selfish, and I could not believe that she had ever really cared about me. My father and I grew apart; he quickly remarried and I had a new family before I was ready. Rather than let myself feel rejected by my parents, I rejected them. I developed an icy armor. I threw myself into the one thing I knew I could do well, school. I got terrific grades and SAT scores. I won a scholarship to a college a thousand miles away from home. I told myself I'd never look back.

But I was unprepared for the fact that there would be lots of people as bright as I at college. It turned out everything I'd accomplished in high school was easy; now that I didn't stand out, things were tough. I got scared. I learned to drink. I became desperate to fit in. My grades were lousy. I wasted four years of college and a few years afterward, scared and depressed. I still had this self-image of a tragic hero who was going to write the great American novel, or accomplish something else earth-shaking. But I didn't write or do anything else constructive. My idea of myself as a misunderstood genius was a pitiful attempt not to need anyone. I didn't recognize my real fear, that if I let myself depend on someone again, I could lose them again—and of course it would be my fault, because deep down inside I was truly unlovable. *I started mixing alcohol and pills, the same sleeping pills my mother had used. There were nights when I didn't care if I woke up the next morning.*

Something motivated me to get help. I went to see a therapist a friend recommended. It turned out to be a husband-and-wife team, practicing some of the gimmicky Transactional Analysis–type stuff so popular in the seventies. They passed me back and forth between them and had me join a group they were running. It was pretty hokey, but very helpful. They helped me realize I needed to change my life—to stop hanging back and embrace living. During this time, I changed careers and got married.

I went to graduate school and did pretty well, but I had a problem with stage fright; I couldn't speak up in class. I told one of my professors about it, and also a little about my background. She recommended that I see a colleague of hers who was a psychiatrist. I thought I was moving up in the world. I had learned enough in graduate school to look down on the therapy—that I had thought had helped me—as not scientifically respectable. The husband-and-wife team were social workers, and the new guy was a psychiatrist. Despite the fact that I was in training to be a social worker myself, I caught both the profession's own doubts about its own self-worth, and its perception of the pecking order in mental health.

What happened next wasn't the psychiatrist's fault. Just after our first appointment, he came down with a serious illness that laid him up for several months. When he came back, he seemed weak and frail. In his office on the twenty-third floor, he sat between me and the window. I had a full-blown anxiety attack in his office, feeling that something was drawing me out that window. It was devastating, the worst feeling that I ever remembered, and it happened every session after that for three years. I was trying to mourn my mother's death, but I didn't feel safe; all I could feel was panic, not grief.

This is what we call an iatrogenic problem—a problem induced by the treatment. Perhaps if the psychiatrist hadn't been sick, or if he hadn't presented himself as so gentle and tentative, I would have felt safe. As it was, I couldn't feel comforted in his presence. This was despite the fact that I consciously liked and respected him. My life on the outside went along pretty well. We had children, and I discovered I was a good father. I did well in graduate school and began to enjoy my work. But every week, I would be sweating bullets in his office, convinced I was doomed. My phobia generalized; soon I couldn't go up in any tall buildings, or cross bridges.

Perhaps this helped me by confining my depression, as it were, to this one symptom and letting me get on with my life. Even if this were true, though, it's not how therapy is supposed to work. Besides, these weekly episodes of pure terror were eating away at my self-esteem, making me feel as if there were a demon inside me I couldn't control. It seems incredible to me now that both the psychiatrist and I let this drag on for so long. I hope that if I were the therapist in this situation, I would say, Look, this is crazy. Let's try something different. Let's try some medication, or behavior therapy, or let me refer you to a colleague for a fresh start.

I was thirty-five and still believed time was running out for me, and that I wasn't getting the help I needed. I extricated myself from the situation by getting accepted as an analytic subject at the Chicago Institute for Psychoanalysis—I knew this was something my psychiatrist couldn't argue with. We parted company.

When I met my analyst, I was somewhat disappointed that he wasn't much older than I was—how much could he know? But he had good credentials and had already published with some high-powered thinkers. I rather liked him—he was pretty unstuffy for an analyst, had a quirky sense of humor, and seemed to respect me. I stayed with him for another five years, getting through my thirty-eighth birthday unscathed, with a real sense of relief. We worked on my phobia together, and I felt comforted and supported. I enjoyed the analytic process, and recommend it highly as a growth experience.

I was finally able to talk about the bind I was in regarding my mother. It seemed to me that either she had correctly perceived the futility and meaninglessness of life, or she didn't love me. Neither alternative was acceptable to me. But somewhere along the line, I learned to understand her better and to forgive her a little. She knew what her choices were. She had seen her older sister impoverished by divorce, finally forced into another abusive marriage as an economic necessity. Isolated from her family, stuck in a loveless marriage, my mother could see no alternatives. Her suicide was both a result of despair and a gesture of defiance. She was so far down in the well, her vision so distorted, that her choice made sense at the time.

I'm not symptom-free, but I haven't felt the need for regular treatment. I still have periods of depression. I have a psychiatrist I trust to help me with medication when I need it, and a therapist I know who I can turn to when I need to. I'm still working on all this; in discussing this book with my father before his death, he gave me still another perspective on my mother. He reminded me of how guilty she felt about being depressed, the horrible debt that the cost of her treatment had placed upon the family. In a sad, twisted way, her suicide was also a self-sacrifice. She saw herself as a burden on us; removing that burden was, in her mind, a gift to us. This point of view certainly helps me feel less anger toward her, but I can't help feeling a little guilty now, and the terrible implicit sadness is something I can take only in small doses.

A while ago, my analyst sent me a copy of a paper he was writing. He used an incident in my therapy to illustrate a point he wanted to make. In doing so, he had to summarize my background and treatment. I was knocked for a loop. There was so much in the analysis that I had repressed. I had repressed all the times I spent on his couch, writhing in terror and anxiety, trying not to hear what he had to say. We had gotten past my height phobia; there were times when I felt very safe with him and times when I didn't feel safe at all. And seeing my case history laid out in objective clinical terms, I was overwhelmed with feeling for my self: pity, but not self-pity in the usual sense; more the kind of objective empathy we might feel for a stranger. Some of that compassionate curiosity. Also, I could see that while my analyst had a particular theoretical point of view about my problems, I had a different one. This wasn't news. During the analysis, we had often disagreed on this subject, but both felt we were in good agreement as far as the practical implications for me. It got me thinking about how doctrinaire I used to be, and how I seem to have gotten away from that.

What all this has made me realize is that therapy—and probably medication—doesn't really work for the reasons professionals think it does. My first therapists, with their naïve enthusiasm, helped me greatly using methods that no one takes seriously now. My second, with all his expertise, did me more harm than good. My analyst helped me a great deal—but I think he did it by acting like a caring, respectful friend I could lean on, and he thinks he did it by helping me get in touch with repressed impulses. Most psychopharmacologists believe sincerely in their pills, even though they can't explain how they're supposed to work. The therapists at the clinic I directed—from a variety of training, backgrounds, and disciplines—were usually quite helpful with their clients, but all had different explanations for how therapy works.

So it doesn't matter how you get better, as long as you get better. The wiser, warmer, more experienced therapists can probably help you more reliably, but I think it's like teaching a child how to ride a bicycle. You can explain how to steer and how the pedals work, but you can't explain balance and momentum. You have to hold the bicycle up while the child learns these things for himself.

A good psychotherapy is in essence a creation, a change in the patient's way of being, crafted by the patient and the therapist in a mutual process. For many patients, it may be their first creative effort since kindergarten.

A Program for Recovery

DEPRESSION IS a disease and a social problem, an illness to be treated professionally and a failure to adapt to stress that we must overcome through self-determination. These days, with managed care and medication so dominant, I'm concerned that professional help usually doesn't go far enough. I already referred to the studies showing that long-term therapy achieves much better results than the treatment-as-usual studies. Further, medication and brief treatment don't reduce the likelihood of future depression. The grim truth is that if you have one episode of major depression, the odds are that you'll have more. But I believe very strongly that a self-directed program of recovery such as I am recommending can reduce those odds and can increase our satisfaction with our selves and our lives.

In this chapter, I want to distill our previous discussion into some general principles for recovery. I worry that trying to express the complexities of psychological observations in simple language reduces them to the level of self-evident platitudes. But on the other hand I look at the success of AA, based on only twelve steps and twelve traditions, and realize that it is the thought, digestion, meditation, discussion, even arguing over the meaning and application of basic principles that brings them to life. The weekly meetings become a forum to practice new mental skills. With the warning, then, that these ideas are meant to serve as the stimulus for work on the reader's part, not to be the summary of wisdom on depression, I will describe what I think are basic principles for a program for recovery.

Remember: depression forces us into certain ways of thinking, feeling, and behaving that come to feel natural to us, and we have trouble imagining alternatives. These habits get engraved in our brains, becoming the default neural pathways that dictate what we see, think, feel, and do. But diligent, focused practice can change the brain again, teaching us even more constructive ways of living than we had ever known before. It takes longer than we want it to, but each time we are successful in using a new skill, we make it easier to do it again. Follow these steps, practice mindfulness every day, and you will get better.

PRINCIPLE ONE: *Feel Your Feelings*

Depression is an effort to avoid feeling. A great deal of what we depressives assume is our character and personality is the result of years of using self-destructive defense mechanisms — adopted in an effort to insulate ourselves from painful or upsetting emotions. But emotions are important signals to us about life; to try to avoid experiencing them wastes mental energy and deprives us of vital information. Besides, we don't seem to be able to avoid only unpleasant emotions; we miss out on the good things in life too. We numb ourselves; we develop acedia.

There is really nothing to fear about feelings. They are self-limiting. Our most intense joy, our most intense pain, never lasts, while depression can last a lifetime. With normal feelings, eventually we get distracted, we wear ourselves out, or some new event changes the way we feel. We're like a buoy on the water; waves may knock us over, but we have a balance, a ballast, which means we eventually will return to a stable position. We have to trust that we can ride the waves.

The expression of suppressed feelings, when it's done in the right environment, can lift a depressed mood. A good cry, a healthy argument, an appropriate assertion of our rights, a careful exploration of hidden feelings—these help us feel better. But pick your environment. Make sure that you will have the support and understanding you need.

Remember that there is an important difference between feeling emotions and expressing them. We can, and should, control how we express feelings; in a way, that's what growing up is all about. But we can't control how we experience feelings; the idea that we shouldn't feel the way we do is dangerous nonsense that eats away like acid on our self-esteem.

PRINCIPLE TWO: *Nothing Comes Out of the Blue*

When we feel our mood change, there is always a reason; something has happened to make us feel this way. Even when we are sliding into a major depressive episode and we know that the depth of our depression is far out of proportion to the event that caused our change in mood, we can take comfort in the fact that there was an event. We have reasons to feel the way we do; we are not crazy.

If you don't believe this, or if you can't identify the precipitants to your changes in mood, use the Mood Journal regularly. It won't take long for you to begin to penetrate your own defenses and see that, for instance, the depression that took you down for no apparent reason yesterday evening probably has something to do with a difficult conversation with your mother yesterday morning. In the evening, you "forget" about the conversation, but the Mood Journal reminds you.

Sometimes the event is obvious: a loss, a disappointment, a setback. Sometimes the event will be obvious to others; we attempt to deny its importance, but we still feel the hurt. This is where friends, loved ones, and a support system can help. Sometimes the event is a memory, a dream, an association sparked by something we read or heard. This is where a private journal can help.

Knowing what's made us feel bad is the first step toward recovery. When we understand what's causing us distress, remember there are only three choices: Alter, avoid, accept. Try to change the situation, try to avoid the situation in the first place, and if you can't do either, work on accepting it.

PRINCIPLE THREE: *Practice Mindfulness*

Remember that regular mindfulness meditation practice can reprogram your brain so that you can stop your obsessive worrying and
self-focus. It can reset the thermostat within you so that you can
experience more happiness than ever. And learning the skills of
mindful living means you can be in thoughtful, deliberate control
of yourself, not the phony control that depends only on obsessive
thinking. Your mind, brain, and body can work together to make
you slow down and pay attention to the joys of life that you're missing. You learn to see how you've always judged your experience in
black-and-white terms, and how to see beneath that and appreciate
life in all its beauty and complexity. Seeing the world and yourself
objectively, without the distortions of depression, you will naturally
make better decisions, which will help you gain greater satisfaction
with your life.

We spend far too much time and effort trying to control things
we can't, and mindfulness will help us know when we're spinning
our wheels. When we're in a stressful situation and feeling upset,
we need to ask ourselves two questions: How much does this really
matter in the context of my life, and what can I realistically do about
it? We can find that many things that worry us are really not all that
important; we've just gotten caught up in emotional contagion and
lost our bearings. Or we're making ourselves miserable trying to
change something we can't.

"God, grant me the serenity to accept the things I cannot change,
the courage to change the things I can, and the wisdom to know
the difference." This is the AA Serenity Prayer. It's a good mantra
for depression, too. Consistent mindfulness, and the serenity that
accompanies it, are not easy to achieve. They are goals that we must
strive for through mental discipline. We have to learn to stop ourselves, to halt the adrenaline rush that makes us feel there is a crisis
we have to take care of right now.

We're on a roller coaster. The ride will take us up and down, spin
us around and scare us and thrill us. We don't have any steering

or brakes and we can't get out. We're better off to look around and enjoy the experience, because we don't get a second ride.

PRINCIPLE FOUR: *Keep Practicing*

The brain doesn't merely store our experiences, it embodies them. Every new experience, including our thoughts and feelings, changes the brain, structurally, electrically, and chemically. The brain becomes the experience. In order to recover from depression, we need to build our brains through practicing the new skills I've been describing: mindfulness, clear thinking, direct communication. When we're depressed, our minds can damage our brains by building and cementing connections that support depressed habits. But we can deliberately use the power of our minds to engrave on our brains the new skills we need to learn. Unfortunately, just thinking about getting better doesn't do it. Insight, new understanding of how we got to this place, doesn't do it. It's not sufficient to *get* mindfulness, you have to *do* mindfulness. It's only by *practicing* new behavior—including internal behavior like stopping obsessive thought patterns or deliberately changing our perspective—repeatedly, day after day, even when it seems like you're not going anywhere, that you can build a healthy brain.

It's not your fault that you're depressed, but you still have to help yourself. That feels inherently unfair, and I don't want to dismiss the anger and frustration that you might feel as a result of that unfairness. I've felt that way, too. Therapy can help with those feelings. But you can't let them get in the way of your recovery. The only choice you have is to stagnate, or practice what's good for you, right now, in the present moment. Choice is not in the past or the future. But if you practice now, it will get easier in the future. If you don't, it won't. That's your choice. That's your free will in action.

PRINCIPLE FIVE: *Rise Above Depressed Thinking*

Try to keep in mind that your basic assumptions about life and yourself are colored by your disease. You see the world through brown-colored glasses.

You are a pessimist. You expect bad events to be permanent, pervasive, and personal (your fault), while you think good things are temporary, limited in scope, and simply the result of chance, certainly not caused by anything you did. This probably means that you don't prepare adequately, give up too easily, and thus aren't as successful as someone whose thinking isn't dominated by depression.

Most tragically, you probably turn this depressive thinking on yourself. You remember all the times you failed and all the times the other guy succeeded; you literally can't remember your own successes. You probably think of yourself as different from others: weaker, damaged, shameful. You don't consider that you can't get inside another person's skin. The confidence you envy may be just a front; the skill you wish for is just practice and hard work; the success you covet may be bought at a high price.

These ways of thinking are only bad habits, and they can be changed. But changing any habit is hard work. Use the Daily Record of Dysfunctional Thoughts, or any similar tool, to help you identify your own particular depressed thinking habits. Identify that Inner Critic, and stop listening to him. Every time you hear that voice, remind yourself: this is a bad connection in my brain; this is an inserted thought, left over from childhood; this is not me and not the truth about me.

PRINCIPLE SIX: *Establish Priorities*

The more of your time on earth you can spend doing things that will help you get what you really want out of life, the happier you will feel every day; the more time you have to spend doing things that are trivial or unimportant, the more miserable you will feel. But you can't do everything you want. You can't please everyone. You have to make choices.

Go back to Exercise 5, where you identified your key values (page 247). Think about how you use the skills of depression to keep yourself from pursuing them. How you think pessimistically and give up too soon. How you let yourself get distracted by anger and fear, so you can't focus. How your unassertive behavior means you let others interfere with achieving what you want. How good you are at procrastination so that you never really get around to trying to change. Get a little mad at yourself, like Howard Beale: *"I'm as mad as hell, and I'm not going to take this anymore!"* Stop letting yourself be pushed around by your own bad habits, and make a serious effort to follow your own priorities.

PRINCIPLE SEVEN: *Take Care of Your Self*
We need to learn to enjoy ourselves. Most of us have not experienced much happiness. When occasionally we stumble on it, it scares us. We have to approach it with care.

One way to get used to enjoying ourselves is to work on feeling proud. This is an uncomfortable feeling, but one we can get more comfortable with through practice. Take a few minutes each day and jot down in a notebook a list of three things you've done that you feel good about. These may be things you thought you couldn't do, or difficult tasks you had to force yourself to do, or just spontaneous acts of generosity or intimacy. After a week, look through the notebook at all the things you can feel good about. If you start to feel a little proud of yourself, you will probably be a little uncomfortable with that feeling. Never mind all the theorizing about why it's hard for you to feel proud; just ride out the discomfort for a few minutes, and you'll see that it soon recedes a little. With practice, before long you may start feeling a little good about yourself.

Another way is to pay attention to small pleasures. Most of us depressives are not good at being "in the moment"—instead of paying attention to what's actually going on around us, we're worried about what's going to happen next, or we're feeling bad about what happened before. We can change this habit, too. Cultivate a better awareness of how your mind takes you away from the present; when you notice it, bring yourself back. Pay more attention to your senses than your thoughts. Attend to the taste of your food, the sounds in the evening with the TV off, the colors around you. Do what you can to make things more pleasant for yourself.

Find opportunities for flow, the experiences that take us out of our preoccupation with time. Practice activities that are a mild challenge, that occupy your mind and body, that require a high degree of concentration, that have clear rules and prompt feedback. Practice concentration, making a deliberate effort to focus your attention on the task at hand. Forget yourself; lose the observing eye that is always evaluating you critically. Even at work, even if you hate your job, you will like yourself better if you find ways to make it challenging and stimulating. If this means you work harder and the boss will be pleased with you, that's just a risk you've got to take.

Learn to relax. Play whenever you get a chance. Take a course in yoga, or T'ai Chi, or join a group to sing or dance. Exercise, aerobically, for a half hour at least three times a week. Take care of your body, and learn to listen to it. Eat healthy but delicious meals. Don't drink to excess. When we neglect or abuse our bodies, we're only being passive-aggressive with ourselves. We're treating ourselves as if we're unworthy of love.

PRINCIPLE EIGHT: *Communicate Directly*

We have to give up the wish that our loved ones understand us merely because they love us. If we don't tell people what we want, we can't expect to get it. If we don't tell people how we feel, we can't expect them to understand us. We have to learn to speak in direct, unambiguous language, and we have to learn to match what we say with how we say it. We also have to be responsible for listening carefully to what others say to us. If we don't understand, we have to ask for clarification.

Remember that we depressives tend to give up too easily. We withdraw from conversation when it seems that we can't get our point across. We feel tongue-tied and exasperated. We retreat into feeling misunderstood, put-upon, and hopeless. Instead, try slowing down. Focus on your feelings and express your feelings as "I" statements. Ask the other person for help in making yourself understood: "Please ask me questions."

We have to learn the power of metacommunication, of talking

about how we're talking: *Do I understand you correctly? Am I making myself clear? You seem to be giving me mixed messages, and I don't know how to respond.* We tend to think communication is just about the subject of the conversation; on the contrary, all communication is about the relationship between the parties involved. Being direct and open shows respect and caring, and invites the same treatment in return. Being shy or withdrawn can easily be misunderstood as disrespect or unfriendliness.

Practice extraversion. Reach out to people. Smile. Talk more. Extraverted people are much more likely to experience themselves as happy. Or is it that happier people are more extraverted?—we don't know, and it doesn't matter. A study of both types of college students found that everyone was happiest when they were acting extraverted, but even the introverted students were happiest when pretending to be extraverted, "implying that anyone who musters the will to be outgoing will be happy as a result."[1]

PRINCIPLE NINE: *Look for Heroes*

When we have no one to look up to, we are impoverished. We live in an age of cynicism and exposé, and we are all lesser for it. But there are people who take risks because of their beliefs, who stand up to oppressors, who can serve as models of courage and kindness. Look around your own community. Ask people who they admire—perhaps a teacher, a civic leader, a clergyman, a fireman, an intellectual figure. Find people for yourself to admire, and strive to be like them. If there are people like this at work in your community, perhaps you can help them in their work.

If there doesn't seem to be anyone around, read biography. You don't have to go back too far in time to find real heroes: Eisenhower, Truman, Franklin and Eleanor Roosevelt, Gandhi, Mother Teresa, and Martin Luther King. My heroes of depression, Lincoln, Churchill, and Freud. These are all people who had faults, who could be petty and human and yet more than human, too. When there are people we can admire, we are elevated and enriched through our admiration. We construct our selves on models we derive unconsciously from our experiences with our parents and with popular culture. When our models are people we truly respect, we respect our selves.

PRINCIPLE TEN: *Be Generous*

You can't cure depression by giving all your money away; but if you can cultivate a true generosity of spirit, you can't be depressed. I can't count the number of times I saw someone in a therapy group reach out to another member in great pain. Maybe they would tell some of their own story to show they understand, or maybe just to express their sympathy and support. Often it was the tone as much as the words—somehow an emotional connection is established with someone who is feeling ashamed, alone, and afraid. You could feel the electricity in the air.

The sufferer is comforted, but the person who took a risk and reached out is enriched. She's learned that she, just by virtue of being herself, has something valuable to share.

There are probably people close to you who could benefit if you make an unselfish gift of your love, attention, time, respect; whatever it is they need, you have the power to give it. If there's no one like that close to you now, there are opportunities to volunteer in your community.

Charity is big business now. We have United Ways and community trusts and arts councils that vouch for the worthiness of their causes; but you can't get much good feeling about yourself just by writing a check. I think, if you're going to donate money, you ought to get something out of it, too. Get to know the people in your charity; get a taste of the problems they're trying to solve; get to feel what it's like to reach out and care. Paradoxically, the Internet has created all kinds of new ways of bringing strangers together, to organize and volunteer.

This is a time to apply "fake it till you make it." Smile at strangers, and they'll likely smile back at you, and you'll feel a little better. Go out of your way to be courteous and thoughtful, give away your spare change, and donate generously to causes you believe in, even if you feel grumpy and begrudging. Soon these habits of generosity will get under your skin and you will start to feel better about yourself. Remember that depression means being all wrapped up in yourself, so make a real effort to break out.

PRINCIPLE ELEVEN: *Cultivate Intimacy*

Intimacy means laying oneself bare to another, to let the other see you, warts and all. It's what we both desire and fear most in relationships. It's more a process than an event or state. We've talked about the universal need for balance between intimacy and autonomy, but everyone I've ever known with depression needs more intimacy. It's curative.

Depressives fear intimacy more than most people. We put on masks for the world, because we believe our true selves to be shameful, unworthy. With practice, we can keep our masks up all the time, so no one ever knows what we think we're really like inside. We can fool everybody into thinking we're loyal, honest, generous, and caring when deep inside we are convinced it's an act.

But if you keep up an act like this all your life, who are you fooling? Who is the real you? Is it the one that people love, or is it the secret self inside? I submit that the real you is the self you present to the world; this is the self you are responsible for. The inside self is an artifact of depression, guilt, and shame, no more than a trick of the mind, but one that can dominate our life unless we let people know about it.

If we just open up and let our loved ones know about our secret fears, our doubts, our inadequacies, we can grow through the corrective emotional experience of being loved and accepted despite our guilty secrets; as we do this, the gap between our public self and our secret self diminishes; eventually it may disappear altogether so that we are just one congruent person. No secrets, no shame.

PRINCIPLE TWELVE: *Get Help When You Need It*

Learn to identify the signals that can tell you when you're slipping into depression. These early signs vary from individual to individual.

You may have trouble sleeping; you may realize you're having trouble concentrating; you may be cranky or irritable. You may just have a lump in your throat or a knot in your stomach. Earlier I mentioned the patient who stopped seeing colors; your warning signs may be just as unique. But when you see them, get help. Don't tell yourself it will pass. Don't tell yourself you should be tougher. Just going for a one-time visit to your therapist may be enough to arrest your downward slide.

Set up a support system in advance. Develop a relationship with a therapist you can trust who understands depression. Develop a relationship with a psychiatrist or APRN who stays informed about the latest developments in medication. If medication is helping you, don't stop just because you feel it's a sign of weakness; that's your critical, self-destructive self talking. Join, or form, a support group and attend it regularly. Enlist your loved ones in your plans; consider "advance directives" that they should follow if you really get bad.

Remember that being ashamed of needing help is a symptom of your disease. Be smarter than your depression.

Living your life according to these principles will not be easy. It requires a total commitment to change. It means accepting that much of what you take for granted about yourself contributes to your depression, and that you, and no one else, have to devote a lot of time and energy to a continuous self-examination. Then it means that you will have to self-consciously practice new skills to replace your old habits of depression. Learning new skills is not easy, but it can be done. Be patient. Remember that it took three months of daily juggling practice for the researchers to see brain growth—and even then, three months doesn't make you a good juggler. You'll have to practice your new skills for a long time. As you are doing this, you are likely to feel anxious and uncomfortable. Remember this is the way you feel when you try anything new; with enough practice, the new skills become part of yourself. And you will begin to recover from depression.

Beyond Recovery

UNFORTUNATELY FOR MOST people with depression, "recovery" has always meant return to the same comfortable state of misery we endured before the depression became unbearable. Research shows that feeling genuinely good again is the very last step of recovery, and most people never get that far. Those who do, however, are much less likely to have future episodes than those who have only an incomplete recovery. They've learned new skills that insulate them from depression, and they've rewired their brains so that they're no longer subject to the floods of depression and stress hormones that make relapse so easy.

Experiencing Joy

Remember that all your struggles with depression have caused brain damage, especially in the parts of the brain that have to do with experiencing joy and pleasure. We stop producing the chemical messengers of happiness, and the nerve centers that are designed to receive them disappear. It's not just that we believe life is dull and bleak; that is actually how we experience it. And this, of course, has ramifications beyond our brains. If we can't express happiness when it's appropriate, people will start to avoid us or resent us. We'll lose motivation, because we won't want anything. We have to make a deliberate effort to undo that damage, and we do that by seeking out positive experiences and developing our awareness of the feelings that they bring.

Practicing mindfulness meditation regularly has been shown to help rewire the brain in this way. Applying better mindfulness skills in everyday life will also help mightily, teaching us to focus our attention, to see things as they really are, to stop judging, and to learn to attend to things like natural beauty, our sensual experiences, and the beauty in other people. It turns out that we all have our own individual set points on the thermostat for happiness, which we return to after each positive or negative experience.[2] Depressed people have had their set points pushed to the gloomy side, but they can be reset. The Positive Psychology movement has recently begun to investigate whether psychological principles can be used to help people feel good, instead of only relieving distress, and has had some success on this.[3] Chris Peterson's book, *A Primer in Positive Psychology*, is full of practical tips and methods designed to help us see more joy in living.

These are some of my ideas about achieving a more mindful state:

• Make sure you get some time every day when you can be alone and get into a reflective state, whether it's in deliberate meditation, on a long walk, in a hot bath, in church—somewhere where there are no distractions. As you do, try to maintain that attitude of compassionate curiosity toward yourself; look at yourself as a wise and loving friend might do.

• Watch where your mind goes when you leave it alone. Learn to develop an observing eye that notices where your thoughts go when you're not paying attention. When you're driving, or walking, or falling asleep, does your mind dwell on successes or failures? Do you keep returning to instances of shame or humiliation? Do you constantly worry about whatever is the next item on your mental list? Are you afraid to think too deeply about the future? If this is so, no wonder you're depressed. Work on observing your thoughts, not being commanded by them.

• If you find that you're constantly judging yourself, try to get your mind around the idea that the judging is the depression. You have an inner bully who is constantly putting you down and beating you up. Instead of reacting defensively, mindlessly, when that bully shows up, try to remember that he doesn't speak the truth, only a distorted version of reality that goes out of its way to find fault with you. If you've ever dealt with a bully, you know you can't reason with him, argue, or defend yourself. Whatever you say will be thrown back in your face. You need a *deus ex machina,* a skyhook, to suddenly appear and lift you out of the confrontation. Your skyhook is mindfulness, and the detachment that goes with it. As you rise away, the judging and bullying seem smaller and smaller, weaker and weaker.

• If you are worrying too much, are constantly reacting to fears, consider that what you do about fear may be the problem. If you try to stuff it and forget about it, the fear will just come back later, perhaps in another form. If you're afraid to look too closely, it will just move closer to you. There's probably a basic fear there, that you're simply incompetent and inadequate, that you have to work so hard at life that you have no hope of happiness. One big secret I know from my patients is that everyone, no matter how successful or accomplished, has that kind of fear at times. Drag that fear out into the light of day and look at it with compassionate curiosity. No one who is able to read this book is completely incompetent or inadequate. You probably got that idea from some old, bad experiences, but they're not happening now. If you can face your fears about yourself, they lose all power over you.

• Pay attention to your dreams. Keep a pad of paper by your bedside and write down whatever you can remember when you first wake up. Look for themes. Are you lost, or trapped? Fighting or fleeing? Is there a childhood scene that keeps reappearing? Dreams like these often represent your attempts to solve a problem that's been pushed into your unconscious.

• Look for patterns in your life. Do you always feel exploited? Disappointed? Rejected? Do your relationships always end badly? Do you keep finding overly critical bosses, unfaithful lovers, coworkers who take advantage of you? Maybe some of this is baggage you carry with you. If so, try to let it go and leave it behind. Approach every new situation with no expectations, expect that it might be an opportunity for something good to happen.

• Where does it hurt? Sometimes there is a symbolic meaning to physical symptoms. Digestive problems may mean you're trying to swallow something you shouldn't. A backache can mean you're carrying too heavy a load. Chronic fatigue can be a way of saying you're scared and overwhelmed. Breathing problems may mean someone is cutting off your air supply.

• Talk to your intimates. Are there things your best friend would tell you about yourself if you gave permission? Are there ways you keep shooting yourself in the foot, which others can see but you can't?

• Think back over the course of your life. At what point did things start to go wrong? When did you begin to be afraid, or feel that you were different or defective? What was going on around you at that time? Were your parents having trouble, or was there trouble in school? Were you ill? Did something harm you or scare you and you got no help for it?

• If you can identify a hurt or injury like that, think about how you adapted to it. Our adaptations are really most of the trouble. If you started feeling defective, for instance, what did you do to cover that up?

If you can't quite convince yourself that all this is going to work, pretend. "Fake it till you make it" is good advice from AA. You're trying to change some basic things about yourself, and of course you're going to have doubts. But keep practicing anyway. You don't have to believe everything I'm telling you. Practice will lead to changes that eventually may let you believe. Or you may arrive at a different explanation for how it is that you're getting out from under your depression. The point is to practice.

Here is one exercise that is so easy there's no excuse for not doing it, yet the research shows that it can have lasting positive benefits:[4]

Exercise 6: Three Good Things

• *When you turn out the light to go to sleep, clear your mind of other thoughts and focus on three good things that happened during the day. These can be very small things, like what you had for lunch, an attractive person you saw on the street, an old song you heard. Sometimes there will be a bigger thing, something you accomplished or a really enjoyable experience, but small things work just as well.*

• *Focus on the subtleties of your good feelings. Do you feel proud, excited, nostalgic, loving, satisfied? Does the memory make you want to smile? Focus attention on the muscles on your face as they form a smile. Where else in your body do you feel these feelings? Do you feel warm? Where? Do you feel a pleasant lump in your throat? Do you feel tension flowing out of you? Are you settling down more comfortably in bed?*

• *Visualize the neurons in your brain forming new happiness circuits—tiny little bulldozers widening the channels to happiness. Remember that brain cells form new circuits just because we're remembering. Visualize endorphins flowing to those withered joy receptors like fresh streams of water refreshing desert plants. Remember that doing this exercise regularly will change your happiness set point; you'll feel more joy, more easily, more often.*

• *Let yourself go to sleep as you continue to focus on these good feelings.*

One test of this exercise found that people who participated felt more happy and less depressed for the entire six months of the study period, although participants had been asked to do it for only a week. It turned out that many of the participants continued the exercise entirely on their own.[5] Perhaps you will want to continue this habit for the rest of your life. It might be interesting, if you start getting depressed or cranky at some point in the future, to notice whether you've forgotten to practice.

This exercise will help you "be in the moment" more often and more easily during the day, by stimulating you to pay attention to experiences of beauty, pleasure, and pride. *What a pretty sunset! I'll have to remember that tonight.* Depressed people have a lot of trouble being in the moment, present and fully aware, because they're distracted by their own suffering. This will help shift your attention away from your suffering.

Maturity and Wisdom

People who are prone to depression seem to need more from other people to feel whole, hopeful, and competent. However, they rarely seek what they need in a straightforward manner. Instead they distort their needs, presenting them in a variety of self-defeating ways, largely because of their use of immature defense mechanisms that distort reality. These defenses merely reinforce a depressed position.

Defenses are ways of dealing with conflict between parts of our selves that want different things; defenses serve to keep the conflict out of consciousness. Conflict is always between a wish and a fear, an impulse and the forces in our mind that constrain our impulses. That's why repression is a defense mechanism. We "forget" about what made us feel bad, even though we still feel bad. The defense is not against emotion, but against awareness of conflict. A loved one hurts us, and for some reason we don't want to feel our anger or look at what that means about the relationship. The bottom drops out of our mood, and we don't know why.

I hope I've made it clear that defense mechanisms are not bad things in and of themselves — they are necessary to life — but some defenses are less healthy than others. Defenses like acting out and passive-aggression can mask reality and expose us to real danger or blow up in our faces. Other defenses, like denial and projection, which can dramatically and perhaps permanently interfere with our ability to accept reality, are crippling when compared to those that allow us to perceive reality more correctly. These immature defenses may keep our feelings or impulses out of consciousness, but one of the great cosmic ironies is that we can still feel guilty about feelings we're not aware of. We feel guilty, undeserving, and false without knowing why. That is why I've suggested using the Mood Journal to track the connections between the mood shifts we experience and the external events that cause them. We need a tool to get around our defenses, to see that a depressed mood is a response to an external event that has stirred up feelings we try not to feel.

There are alternatives to these immature defenses. These are also ways of protecting ourselves from awareness of uncomfortable conflict, but they distort reality much less. When we are able to perceive reality more correctly, our actions are much more likely to have the effect we desire. One excellent review and guide to understanding how our defenses work is George Vaillant's *The Wisdom of the Ego*. Vaillant lists five mature defenses:

1. *Altruism* involves seeing that others have some of the same needs I do, and feeling better about myself by taking care of their needs. The paranoid looks at the big houses of the rich and considers himself cheated. The altruist takes care of the poor and considers himself blessed. In so doing, he also opens himself up to the love and respect of others.

2. *Sublimation* takes our out-of-control feelings and allows them to be expressed directly but in a socially acceptable way. Sublimation is the defense of poets, novelists, and playwrights. When Eugene O'Neill puts his own tortured family on stage, he is transforming his interior experience into high art. When I come home from a frustrating meeting and watch *The Terminator,* I'm sublimating my rage by vicariously watching someone else act it out.

3. *Suppression* is the conscious decision to delay action. There is an awareness of the conflict—an unacceptable desire, or a change in our world that we will eventually have to address—but a decision

to take no action, to let things cook for a while. We may deliberately decide that waiting is wise, or we may just feel confused and uncertain. But if we can tolerate remaining aware of the conflict— perhaps by buying ourselves some time through intimate conversation about it, through dreaming, through finding other outlets to release the anxiety—we are suppressing, and that usually leads to better decisions.

4. *Anticipation* means taking the anxiety over a conflict and dealing with it in advance, a little at a time. It is like inoculating ourselves against a future stress. As in suppression, the conflict is there in consciousness, but we deal with it in drips, not buckets. Vaillant refers to Chuck Yeager and other test pilots with "the right stuff": "To have underestimated danger would have been fatal. To have exaggerated danger would have been incapacitating. Thus, they worried in advance, made lists, practiced, and then, appreciating that they had prepared as well as they could, they relaxed. So easy to say, so difficult to do."[6]

5. *Humor* is the hardest to define. Somehow mature humor takes the conflict, our dilemma of being caught between the rock of our desires and the hard place of reality, and makes us take a step back out of the picture and see the absurdity of our situation. It doesn't push the conflict, or even the anxiety, out of consciousness; but it defuses it, robs it of some of its energy by letting us see that, even when things are rotten, we might as well enjoy. Depressed people have a real affinity for black humor, and most of the best comedians are depressed. Learning to laugh at the absurdities of life is a lot better than tilting at windmills. If we let others in on the joke, we strengthen our bonds.

The lay reader may object that these are not skills, defenses, or personality styles, these are conscious choices. Religion teaches us altruism. Suppression is just the mature delaying of gratification. Everyone is capable of seeing the humorous side of a situation. But it is not that easy. If we could all choose to suppress our impulses, we wouldn't have jails. If we could all practice true altruism by conscious choice, we wouldn't need institutional charity. If we could all anticipate reality, we would floss regularly. We want to believe we can bootstrap ourselves into these abilities, because we want to be able to look down on those who seem to be unable to. But if we're honest with ourselves, we'll acknowledge that we've tried many times, and failed. We have to try again, using the methods in this book to maximize success.

On the other hand, many of my professional colleagues will object that it's pointless to suggest people practice mature defenses or cultivate empathy. In the therapeutic community, there has been a general feeling that patients can overcome deep-seated problems only through intensive psychotherapy. In the medical community, the perception is that the problematic behavior that accompanies depression is only a result, not a cause, of a chemical imbalance. Both believe that expecting the patient to make much progress through self-conscious attempts to change behavior is futile, if not cruel.

I disagree. The more I learn about people, the more I believe their problems stem from not knowing alternatives, rather than from pathology or resistance. It's the old philosophical debate of free will versus determinism. Do we have the power to choose between courses of action, or does it only seem as if we do? Is everything that happens to us preordained, perhaps the logical consequence of a chain of events that goes right back to when the Prime Mover set the universe in motion? I don't mean to duck legitimate scientific questions, but it also seems reasonable to point out that scientists take positions on questions like these not only because of their science but also because of their personal values and beliefs. I've also learned that true change comes from practice, not from the insight of psychotherapy or the effects of medication. Both may help us get ready to change, but it takes dedicated practice to move us to a different place. Meanwhile, the pragmatic answer is that we must behave as if we have the power to control ourselves, because if we don't, we have no hope.

The optimistic observation is that there is such a thing as wisdom.

As we grow older, if we allow ourselves to learn from our experiences, we develop a better perspective on what really matters. We grow wiser. We don't lose sleep over details. We learn to value what we have. We learn to let go of what we can't control. We can laugh at the ironies of life a little more easily. Altruism, humor, and the other mature defenses are qualities that life teaches us; we just have to pay attention to the lessons.

A Creative Life

To Vaillant's list of mature defenses I would add one more quality—the capacity for creativity—as essential for recovery from depression.

We tend to think of creativity as something only for artists—"creative types" who write, paint, dance, make music, or sculpt for a living. But a sense of creativity is something we all need in our lives. Creativity is the antithesis of depression. It is a way of saying that what I think and feel matters. Everyone whose work enables them to express themselves or accomplish something meaningful; parents who are devoting themselves to raising their children; those whose leisure activities offer them opportunities for self-expression or for making a difference—all are involved in a creative pursuit.

Depression is not just an illness but a failure of creativity. Depression tells us there is no meaning; to recover means we have to create meaning for ourselves. We need to make a deliberate effort to make the self fertile; if we're depressed, that effort is essential to life. The developmental challenge of adulthood is to generate more life and serve a purpose somehow, or else to stagnate. The challenge is to find ways to grow, produce, and create after we realize that life is short and that we can't do everything we want; the fear is of rotting, growing self-absorbed and putrescent.

One of my group members once spoke of the satisfaction of depression. We all looked at her in surprise; this was not a subject that was on our minds at the time. "I'm serious," she said. "Sometimes I feel entitled to be depressed. I feel like I've suffered a lot of crap in my life, and if anyone deserves to feel sorry for themselves, it's me. Depression feels safe and comfortable. I can wrap it around me like a big old blanket. Keep myself warm at night with all my grievances. I may be lonely but I'm sure self-righteous." I never heard anyone put the seductive side of stagnation any better. Stagnation implies something easy, quiet, and unchallenging. We can stay home, watch TV, and feel sorry for ourselves. It's easier than working our way out of depression. The problem is that stagnation isn't static. Once you start rotting, you don't stop. You may be able to stay in your bathrobe and watch a few weeks of TV safely, but any more than that and you will be doing yourself harm. Your self-esteem, ambition, humor, and juices will dry up. Before long you'll have trouble leaving the house at all. You'll stop answering the phone. Pretty soon you'll put your head in the oven.

Because our only choice is to grow or die. The long-term cure for depression doesn't come from anything other than living right— being productive, generous, caring, other-centered. Happiness is something we achieve through our own effort, not something we can buy or acquire, not something anyone else can give us. It's a by-product of living a certain kind of life that helps us feel good about ourselves. It comes from being fully engaged in life, from paying attention to the present moment, to the process of living.

But living the right kind of life doesn't mean only being dutiful. It implies having some fun along the way. It means learning how to be creative as well as responsible. Creativity requires an element of play. It suggests taking what seems mundane and seeing it from a new perspective, from a child's eyes that have not been trained to see things as they are generally defined, but instead can see new combinations that lead to new solutions. A new whole is created that is greater than the sum of the parts. It requires an appreciation of humor and paradox. Creativity is also a synthesis of reason and emotion. In visual arts, literature, and music, for instance, the artist creates a product that expresses emotions—it engages the emotions of the audience—through a discipline. We admire the skill and technique, but without emotional engagement we are unmoved. In science and engineering, the creative person is moved by his own emotional engagement in the problem to go beyond the ordinary, to search for unique solutions. He is challenged and stimulated by the problem; solving it becomes an exercise in flow.

Creativity is a mastery of anxiety. There is a recognized process to creativity that starts with hard work. You immerse yourself in the problem or the project. You seek out all the information you can find that might be helpful; the more open you can be to new information, fresh points of view, the more likely you are to come up with new solutions. But doing this creates stress. We hear conflicting ideas and advice about a subject that is important to us, and we get confused. We have a hard time retaining all this information. We can feel frustrated; why isn't there a simple answer? We turn our frustration on ourselves; what's wrong with us that we can't we find the answer? We continue to seek more and more information until we become overloaded. Our anxiety becomes intolerable, and we put the problem aside.

If we're depressed, that's probably the end of the creative process, because we will self-censor the next phase, during which our unconscious mind works on the problem. If we're not depressed, our unconscious will play with the problem, combining and recombining information in ways that our conscious mind doesn't permit. Eventually, while we're jogging or showering or falling asleep, the pieces fall into place and we have the *Aha!* experience. The solution is clear and obvious. We forget about all the hard work and anxiety that preceded the solution.

We need to think of ourselves as capable of creativity in all aspects of our lives, not just the artist's studio or the research lab. We can apply the same principles to all the challenges we face: raising our children, making a living, getting along with difficult people. We have to work on the problem, and we have to play with it as well.

Most of us are familiar with the concept of the vicious circle. Most of our patients in psychotherapy are caught in one or another. One bad event elicits a response that engenders other bad events, eliciting more negative responses, and so on down into the well. The patient who is depressed at her mother's death has trouble concentrating on the job, irritates her boss and gets fired, loses her health insurance and can't get help for the kids when they are sick, and becomes even more depressed as a result. A concept that is not so familiar is the *adaptive spiral*. It's not as dramatic and vivid as the vicious circle but, thankfully for all of us, it happens a lot more often. It's when our response to a single good event makes it more likely that other good things will happen to us. A husband and wife make love and, as a result, the next morning the wife smiles a little more than usual. Her boss notices her cheerful attitude and gives her a special assignment. Pleased with the expression of confidence in her, she continues to feel especially good and eventually earns a promotion.

To feel truly good about ourselves, we must feel challenged. Here at the end of the book is my challenge to you: consider that your job is your self. You are in charge of rebuilding your self. Take all the help you need, but remember that in the end we are all responsible for ourselves. Remember that if we set our goals too high, we get anxious and discouraged, and if we set our goals too low, we get bored and apathetic. So practice self-constructive behavior at a pace that challenges you. Get to know your own feelings. Question your assumptions. Cultivate mindfulness and humor. Practice altruism. Smile more. It doesn't matter that these things will seem phony and forced at first. That is simply how you feel learning anything new, and the feeling of phoniness wears off quickly. I hope I've made clear by now that our brains and minds are highly malleable; that what feels like "me" is the result of a gradual accretion of habits, some healthy, some not. It's quite possible to change "me," that basic nature, and to make of ourselves what we want, someone stronger and more resilient, someone who can fight off depression without even having to think about it. Because, with enough practice, these new, healthy skills become established in the brain, part of ourselves.

Appendix: Organizations Promoting Recovery

Organizations that provide advocacy, information, and support about depression and other mental illnesses:

National Foundation for Depressive Illness
www.depression.org

National Alliance for the Mentally Ill
www.nami.org

American Foundation for Suicide Prevention
www.afsp.org

Depression and Bipolar Support Alliance
dbsaalliance.org

Mood Disorders Support Group of New York City
www.mdsg.org

Lawyers with Depression
www.lawyerswithdepression.org

Recommended Reading

Alberti, R. E., and M. L. Emmons. *Your Perfect Right: A Guide to Assertive Living*. Ninth edition. Atascadero, CA: Impact, 2008.

Antony, Martin M., Michelle G. Craske, and David H. Barlow. *Mastering Your Fears and Phobias*. New York: Oxford, 2006.

Antony, Martin M., and Richard P. Swinson. *The Shyness and Social Anxiety Workbook*. Oakland, CA: New Harbinger, 2000.

Barlow, David H., and Michelle G. Craske. *Mastery of Your Anxiety and Panic: A Workbook*. New York: Oxford, 2006. Barlow is the great authority on anxiety disorders.

Bass, Ellen, and Laura Davis. *The Courage to Heal: A Guide for Women Survivors of Child Sexual Abuse*. New York: Harper Perennial, 1993.

Beck, Aaron T., A. John Rush, Brian F. Shaw, and Gary Emery, *Cognitive Therapy of Depression*. New York: Guilford, 1987.

Begley, Sharon. *Train Your Mind, Change Your Brain*. New York: Ballantine, 2007.

Benson, Herbert. *The Relaxation Response*. New York: Outlet, 1993.

Black, Claudia. *It Will Never Happen to Me*. New York: Ballantine, 1987. One of the first books to explain codependency, still a classic.

Bourne, Edmund J. *The Anxiety and Phobia Workbook*. Fourth edition. Oakland, CA: New Harbinger, 2005. Very detailed, practical information; lots of helpful exercises to practice alone or use in a group.

Bower, S. A., and G. H. Bower. *Asserting Yourself: A Practical Guide for Positive Change*. Reading, MA: Addison-Wesley, 1991.

Burka, Jane B., and Lenora M. Yuen. *Procrastination: Why You Do It, What to Do About It*. Reading, MA: Addison-Wesley, 1990. A very thorough, thoughtful treatment of this subject.

Burns, David. *Feeling Good.* New York: Harper, 1996. Cognitive treatment of depression in a clear, readable self-help framework.

Burns, David. *The Feeling Good Handbook: Using the New Mood Therapy in Everyday Life.* New York: Plume, 1999.

Casey, Nell. *Unholy Ghost: Writers on Depression.* New York: Harper, 2002. A series of excerpts and essays from authors about their own experiences with depression.

Copeland, Mary Ellen, and Matthew McKay. *The Depression Workbook.* Second edition. Oakland, CA: New Harbinger, 2002. This is real self-help, a long compendium of exercises and advice meant to be used as an individual workbook.

Cronkite, Kathy. *On the Edge of Darkness: Conversations about Conquering Depression.* New York: Dell, 1994. Celebrities and others describe their experiences. Very well written, with good dramatic examples that will lend you courage and inspiration.

Csikszentmihalyi, Mihaly. *Flow.* New York: Harper and Row, 1990. Psychological research of peak experiences — how to access a creative state of mind. Very readable, very helpful with depression.

Davis, Martha, Elizabeth R. Eshelman, Matthew McKay, and Patrick Fanning. *The Relaxation and Stress Reduction Workbook.* Sixth edition. New York: New Harbinger, 2008.

Dowling, Colette. *You Mean I Don't Have to Feel This Way? New Help for Depression, Anxiety, and Addiction.* New York: Bantam, 1991. Very readable, persuasive, helpful. Describes her own family experience well.

Dreikurs, Rudolf. *Children: The Challenge.* New York: Plume, 1991. A classic. Despite its dated examples, an excellent resource for building families.

Ellis, Albert, Robert A. Harper, and Melvin Powers. *A Guide to Rational Living.* Los Angeles: Wilshire, 1975. Some people love Ellis and others hate him, but he will certainly challenge your perspective.

Faber, Adele, and Elaine Mazlich. *How to Talk So Kids Will Listen and Listen So Kids Will Talk.* New York: Avon, 1982. Very good concrete advice about communicating with children.

Fiore, Neil A. *The Now Habit: Overcoming Procrastination through Quality Work and Guilt-Free Play.* New York: J. P. Tarcher, 1989.

Frankl, Victor. *Man's Search for Meaning: An Introduction to Logotherapy.* Boston: Beacon, 1992. Frankl, an Auschwitz survivor, addresses the meaning of life in a very inspiring book.

Gilbert, Daniel. *Stumbling on Happiness.* New York: Knopf, 2006. Why it's so difficult for us to be happy.

Goleman, Daniel. *Emotional Intelligence.* New York: Bantam, 2006.

Hayes, Steven C. *Get Out of Your Mind and Into Your Life.* New York: New Harbinger, 2005. How conventional thinking maintains misery. Will challenge some of your most basic assumptions.

Healy, David. *Let Them Eat Prozac: The Unhealthy Relationship Between the Pharmaceutical Industry and Depression.* New York: NYU Press, 2006. There are many alarmist books about Big Pharma and depression. Healy's, by contrast, is well-grounded in good science.

Herman, Judith. *Trauma and Recovery.* New York: Basic, 1992. I recommend this to every patient who is a trauma victim, and all feel Herman understands. She explains what trauma and long-term stress do to the brain, mind, and relationships.

Hyatt, Carole. *When Smart People Fail.* New York: Simon and Schuster, 2009. An analysis of self-destructive behavior and the effects of disappointment on self-esteem.

James, John W., and Russell Friedman. *The Grief Recovery Handbook.* Second edition. New York: Collins Living, 1998.

Jamison, Kay Redfield. *Night Falls Fast: Understanding Suicide.* New York: Vintage, 2000. Not pleasant reading but eye-opening.

Jamison, Kay Redfield. *An Unquiet Mind.* New York: Knopf, 1995. A respected researcher reveals her own struggle with bipolar disorder. Well written and interesting.

Kabat-Zinn, Jon. *Full Catastrophe Living: Using the Wisdom of Your Body and Mind to Face Stress, Pain, and Illness.* New York: Delacorte, 1990. A great book about mindfulness.

Karen, Robert. *Becoming Attached.* New York: Warner Books, 1994.

Karp, David. *Speaking of Sadness.* New York: Oxford University Press, 1996. Karp is a sociologist and a sufferer from depression. His book is a fascinating analysis about the social effects and meaning of depression.

Kasser, Tim. *The High Price of Materialism.* Cambridge, MA: MIT Press, 2002.

Klein, Donald F., and Paul H. Wender. *Understanding Depression: A Complete Guide to Its Diagnosis and Treatment.* Second edition. New York: Oxford University Press, 2005. Klein is a leading researcher in the pharmacological treatment of depression.

Kübler-Ross, Elizabeth. *Death: The Final Stage of Growth.* New York: Touchstone, 1986. The most accessible book from the originator of current understanding on death, dying, and grief.

Kushner, Harold S. *When Bad Things Happen to Good People.* New York: Avon, 1983. Very readable and comforting.

Layard, Richard. *Happiness: Lessons from a New Science.* New York: Penguin, 2005. The new brain science and behavioral economics.

Lerner, Harriet Goldhor. *The Dance of Anger: A Woman's Guide to Changing the Patterns of Intimate Relationships.* New York: HarperCollins, 1989.

Manning, Martha. *Undercurrents.* San Francisco: Harper, 1994. A therapist's diary of two years' struggle with depression, leading to ECT.

Martin, Philip. *The Zen Path Through Depression.* New York: Harper, 2000.

McManamy, John. *Living Well with Depression and Bipolar Disorder.* New York: Collins Living, 2006. From the host of a popular website, very objective and very practical.

Milam, James, and Katherine Ketcham. *Under the Influence: A Guide to the Myths and Realities of Alcoholism.* New York: Bantam, 1984.

Miller, Alice. *The Drama of the Gifted Child (Prisoners of Childhood).* New York: Basic, 1981. Misleading title: it really concerns the creation of depression in the child.

Moore, Thomas. *Care of the Soul.* New York: HarperCollins, 1992. Coming to terms with the differing needs of parts of our selves, especially the spiritual side.

Nettle, Daniel. *Happiness: The Science Behind Your Smile.* Oxford, UK: Oxford University Press, 2005. Another look at the new science of happiness.

Neuman, Frederic. *Rising Above Fear: Healing Phobias, Panic, and Extreme Anxiety.* New York: Simon and Brown, 2008. A self-help guide to exposure therapy.

Norem, Julie K. *The Positive Power of Negative Thinking.* New York: Basic, 2001. The benefits of depressive realism.

O'Connor, Richard. *Happy at Last: The Thinking Person's Guide to Finding Joy.* New York: St. Martin's, 2008.

O'Connor, Richard. *Undoing Perpetual Stress: The Missing Connection Between Depression, Anxiety, and Twenty-First-Century Illness.* New York: Berkley, 2006.

O'Hanlon, Bill. *Do One Thing Different.* New York: Harper, 2000. O'Hanlon is a master at challenging you and changing your perspective.

Peck, M. Scott. *The Road Less Traveled.* New York: Simon and Schuster, 1978. A wise, classic book, very helpful for the depressive in recovery.

Peterson, Christopher. *A Primer in Positive Psychology.* New York: Oxford USA, 2006.

Peurifoy, Reneau Z. *Anxiety, Phobias, and Panic.* Revised edition. New York: Grand Central Publishing, 2005.

Pittman, Frank S. *Man Enough: Fathers, Sons, and the Search for Masculinity.* New York: Putnam, 1993. Highly recommended.

Ratey, John J. *Spark: The Revolutionary New Science of Exercise and the Brain.* New York: Little, Brown, 2008.

Ratey, John J. *A User's Guide to the Brain.* New York: Pantheon, 2001.

Salzberg, Sharon. *Insight Meditation: A Step-by-Step Course in How to Meditate.* Boulder, CA: Sounds True Publications, 2006. Also look for her CDs and workshops; a very popular and respected teacher.

Sapolsky, Robert M. *Why Zebras Don't Get Ulcers: An Updated Guide to Stress, Stress-Related Diseases, and Coping.* Third edition. New York: W. H. Freeman, 2004. A guide to stress from a brilliant, irreverent scientist.

Scaer, Robert C. *The Body Bears the Burden: Trauma, Dissociation, and Disease.* New York: Haworth, 2007.

Scarf, Maggie. *Intimate Partners: Patterns in Love and Marriage.* New York: Ballantine, 1988. This is a very helpful and accessible book that popularizes much of what family therapy understands about love and marriage.

Schuchter, Stephen R., Nancy S. Downs, and Sidney Zisook. *Biologically Informed Psychotherapy for Depression.* New York: Guilford, 1996.

Segal, Zindel V., Mark Williams, and John Teasdale. *Mindfulness-Based Cognitive Therapy for Depression.* New York: Guilford, 2002.

Seligman, Martin E. *Authentic Happiness.* New York: Free Press, 2002. The introduction to positive psychology.

———.*Learned Optimism.* New York: Pocket Books, 1992. An excellent resource; surprisingly interesting, personal, and readable.

Sheffield, Anne. *How You Can Survive When They're Depressed.* New York: Three Rivers Press, 1999. A wonderful support for spouses and family members.

Sher, Barbara. *I Could Do Anything If I Only Knew What It Was.* New York: Dell, 1994. Witty, practical advice on getting your life prioritized.

Siegel, Daniel J. *The Developing Mind.* New York: Guilford, 2001. A great introduction to brain science.

Siegel, Daniel J., and Mary Hartzell. *Parenting from the Inside Out.* New York: Tarcher, 2004. Simply the best new resource for parents who want to raise emotionally healthy children.

Smith, Hyrum W. *The Ten Natural Laws of Successful Time and Life Management.* New York: Warner, 1994.

Smith, Manuel. *When I Say No, I Feel Guilty.* New York: Bantam, 1985.

Solomon, Andrew. *The Noonday Demon: An Atlas of Depression.* New York: Scribner, 2001. Vivid, harrowing account of his own experience, and his search for understanding.

Sternberg, Esther. *The Balance Within: The Science Connecting Health and Emotions.* New York: W. H. Freeman, 2001.

Styron, William. *Darkness Visible: A Memoir of Madness*. New York: Random House, 1990. Styron's account of his struggle with depression at the height of his fame.

Tannen, Deborah. *You Just Don't Understand: Women and Men in Conversation*. New York: Ballantine, 1991. Understanding hidden communication patterns. See her other books as well.

Tavris, Carol. *Anger: The Misunderstood Emotion*. New York: Touchstone, 1989.

Taylor, Shelley E. *Positive Illusions*. New York: Basic, 1989. How unrealistic positive thinking pays off, and how it doesn't.

Vaillant, George E. *The Wisdom of the Ego*. Cambridge, MA: Harvard University Press, 1993. The best guide to understanding how our defenses work.

Viorst, Judith. *Necessary Losses*. New York: Free Press, 1998. Loss, change, and growth.

Williams, Mark, John Teasdale, Zindel Segal, and Jon Kabat-Zinn. *The Mindful Way Through Depression*. New York: Guilford, 2007. Mindfulness and depression, a step-by-step guide, with a meditation CD.

Winston, Stephanie. *Getting Organized: The Easy Way to Put Your Life in Order*. New York: Warner, 1991. Reducing chaos in your life.

Woititz, Janet Geringer. *Adult Children of Alcoholics*. New York: Health Communications, 1990.

Wolf, Anthony E. *Get Out of My Life, But First Could You Drive Me and Cheryl to the Mall? A Parent's Guide to the New Teenager*. Revised edition. New York: Farrar, Straus, & Giroux, 2002.

Zimbardo, Philip. *Shyness: What It Is, What to Do About It*. New York: Addison-Wesley, 1977. A classic of self-modification.

Acknowledgments

WRITING THIS BOOK has been a wonderful exercise in remembering experiences and people who have helped me over the years. Any attempt to acknowledge them all is bound to be incomplete, but there are some teachers and colleagues who stand out: Bill Reid, Laura Epstein, Bernece Simon, Mary Gyarfas, Joe Palombo, Frank Lachmann, Susan Buckman, Florence Forshey, Rob Mardirossian, Kathy Fox, Ann Schreiner, Irwin Hoffman, Paul Lippmann.

I also owe a tremendous debt to Arthur Rosenthal, for his wise advice, and to Sally Ellsworth, for her friendship and unwavering support. My agent, Jim Levine, and editor Jennifer Josephy at Little, Brown were both instrumental in making the first edition into a readable book. Two friends and colleagues, Jeanne Russo and Helen Bray-Garretson, were kind enough to read early drafts and make encouraging and helpful suggestions. For this second edition, Tracy Behar, my new editor at Little, Brown, has been a great help in improving my language and helping me integrate the new with the old.

A therapist learns most from his patients, and I've been lucky to know some brave and inspiring people. I hope I've been able to portray them here with the affection and admiration I feel for them. I particularly want to thank my old Tuesday group for all the support they provided, as well as serving as a catalyst while some of these ideas were in the process of development.

I have to mention Max, our big goofy dog, who was the embodiment of love and joy. He left us too soon but he gave us a lot.

My children, Sarah and Michael, have not only put up with my moods over the years but have come out of it as pretty admirable human beings, which warms my heart. Most of all, my wife, Robin, has always lent me her confidence and given me her love and support. I know I wouldn't be writing this today if I hadn't been able to lean on her when I needed to.

Notes

Chapter 1: Understanding Depression

1. Gerald Klerman, "Evidence for Increases in the Rate of Depression in North America and Western Europe During Recent Decades," in H. Hippius, G. Klerman, and N. Mattusek (eds.), *New Results in Depression Research* (Berlin: Springer Verlag, 1986).
2. Paul Waraich, Elliot M. Goldner, Julian M. Somers, and Lorena Hsu, "Prevalence and Incidence Studies of Mood Disorders: A Systematic Review of the Literature," *Canadian Journal of Psychiatry* 49:2 (2004).
3. U.S. Department of Health and Human Services, Public Health Service, Agency for Health Care Policy and Research, *Clinical Practice Guideline: Depression in Primary Care: Vol. 1. Detection and Diagnosis.* (Washington, DC: U.S. Govt. Printing Office, 1993).
4. Gerald M. Klerman and Myrna Weissman, "Increasing Rates of Depression," *Journal of the American Medical Association* 261, 2229–2235 (1989).
5. Daniel Goleman, "A Rising Cost of Modernity: Depression," *New York Times,* Dec. 8, 1992. Cross-National Comparative Group, "The Changing Rate of Major Depression," *Journal of the American Medical Association* 268:21, 3098–3105 (1992).
6. Christopher J. L. Murray and Alan D. Lopez (editors), *The Global Burden of Disease: A Comprehensive Assessment of Mortality and Disability from Disease, Injuries, and Risk Factors in 1990 and Projected to 2020* (World Health Organization, World Bank, Harvard University, 2006).
7. Ibid.

8. Paul E. Greenberg, R. C. Kessler, H. G. Birnbaum, S.A. Leong, et al., "The Economic Burden of Depression in the United States: How Did It Change Between 1990 and 2000?" *Journal of Clinical Psychiatry* 64:12, 1465–1475 (2003).

9. American Association of Suicidology (http://www.suicidology.org), data for 2005. "Avert" website: http://www.avert.org/statsum.htm, data for 2006.

10. Michael E. Thase, "The Long-Term Nature of Depression," *Journal of Clinical Psychiatry* 60, 3–35 (1999).

11. James H. Kocsis, Alan J. Gelenberg, Barbara Rothbaum, Daniel N. Klein, et al., "Chronic Forms of Major Depression Are Still Undertreated in the 21st Century: Systematic Assessment of 801 Patients Presenting for Treatment," *Journal of Affective Disorders* 110, 55–61 (2008).

12. Mark Olfson, Steven C. Marcus, Benjamin Druss, Lynn Elinson, et al., "National Trends in the Outpatient Treatment of Depression," *Journal of the American Medical Association* 287, 203–209 (2002).

13. T. J. Moore, "No Prescription for Happiness," *Boston Globe*, E1 (Oct. 17, 1999).

14. Shankar Vedantam, "Antidepressant Use by U.S. Adults Soars," *Washington Post* (Dec. 3, 2004).

15. Mark Olfson and Stephen C. Marcus, "National Patterns in Antidepressant Medication Treatment." *Archives of General Psychiatry* 66(8), 848–856 (2009).

16. Ernst R. Berndt, Lorrin M. Koran, Stan N. Finkelstein, Alan J. Gelenberg, S. G. Kornstein, et al., "Lost Human Capital from Early-Onset Chronic Depression," *American Journal of Psychiatry* 157, 940–947 (2000).

17. Luhrman has a fascinating, well-written, though bleak, book about this schism in psychiatry. T. M. Luhrman, *Of Two Minds: The Growing Disorder in American Psychiatry* (New York: Knopf, 2000).

18. See, for example, J. M. Schwartz, P. W. Stoessel, L. R. Baxter, K. M. Martin, and M. E. Phelps, "Systematic Changes in Cerebral Glucose Metabolic Rate After Successful Behavior Modification Treatment of Obsessive-Compulsive Disorder," *Archives of General Psychiatry* 53, 109–113 (1996); Kimberly Goldapple, Zindel Segal, Carol Garson, Mark Lau, et al., "Modulation of Cortical-Limbic Pathways in Major Depression: Treatment-Specific Effects of Cognitive Behavior Therapy," *Archives of General Psychiatry* 61, 34–41 (2004).

19. Alice Miller, *The Drama of the Gifted Child (Prisoners of Childhood)* (New York: Basic, 1981).

20. William Styron, *Darkness Visible: A Memoir of Madness.* (New York: Random House, 1990).

21. Daniel Goleman, "Depression in the Old Can Be Deadly, but the Symptoms Are Often Missed," *New York Times,* C10 (Sept. 6, 1995).

22. J. A. Egeland and J. N. Sussex, "Suicide and Family Loading for Affective Disorders," *Journal of the American Medical Association* 25, 4915–4918 (1985). David B. Cohen, *Out of the Blue: Depression and Human Nature* (New York: Norton, 1994). American Association of Suicidology (http://www.suicidology.org), data as of 2005.

23. Robert N. Anderson and Betty L. Smith, "Death: Leading Causes for 2002," *National Vital Statistics Reports* 53 (2005). http://www.cdc.gov/nchs/deaths.htm.

Chapter 2: The Experience of Depression

1. Jane Brody, "Personal Health: Myriad Masks Hide an Epidemic of Depression," *New York Times* (Sept. 30, 1992); National Mental Health Association, "NMHA Survey Finds Many Americans are Poorly Informed About Depression, Slow to Seek Help," *Hospital and Community Psychiatry* 43:3, 292–293 (March 1992).

2. Miller, *Drama of the Gifted Child.*

3. Ibid. Emphasis added.

Chapter 3: Diagnosing Depression

1. American Psychiatric Association, *Diagnostic and Statistical Manual of Mental Disorders, Fourth Edition* (Washington, DC: APA, 1994).

2. U.S. Department of Health and Human Services, *Clinical Practice Guideline.*

3. Ibid.

4. Ibid.

5. Martin B. Keller, R. M. Hirschfeld, and D. Hanks, "Double Depression: A Distinctive Subtype of Unipolar Depression," *Journal of Affective Disorders* 45, 65–73 (1997).

6. Lewis I. Judd, H. S. Akiskal, J. D. Maser, P. J. Zeller, et al., "A Prospective 12-Year Study of Subsyndromal and Syndromal Depressive Symptoms in Unipolar Major Depressive Disorders," *Archives of General Psychiatry* 55, 694–700 (1998).

7. Lewis I. Judd, H. S. Akiskal, J. D. Maser, P. J. Zeller, et al., "Major Depressive Disorder: A Prospective Study of Residual Subthreshold Depressive

Symptoms as Predictor of Rapid Relapse," *Journal of Affective Disorders* 50, 97–108 (1998).

8. U.S. Department of Health and Human Services, *Clinical Practice Guideline.*

9. See *Time*'s profile on Ted Turner by Priscilla Painton, *Time*, p. 12, Jan. 6, 1992.

10. Madhukar H. Trivedi, A. John Rush, Stephen R. Wisniewski, et al., "Evaluation of Outcomes with Citalopram for Depression Using Measurement-Based Care in STAR*D: Implications for Clinical Practice," *American Journal of Psychiatry* 163, 28–40 (2006).

11. Jules Angst, "Major Depression in 1998: Are We Providing Optimal Therapy?" *Journal of Clinical Psychiatry* 60, 5–9 (1999, Suppl. 6).

12. P. W. Lavori, M. B. Keller, T. I. Mueller, and W. Scheftner, "Recurrence After Recovery in Unipolar MDD: An Observational Follow-Up Study of Clinical Predictors and Somatic Treatment as a Mediating Factor," *International Journal of Methods in Psychiatric Research* 4, 211–229 (1994).

13. Angst, "Major Depression."

14. Ronald C. Kessler, Katherine A. McGonagle, Shanyang Zhao, Christopher B. Nelson, et al., "Lifetime and 12-month Prevalence of DSM-III-R Psychiatric Disorders in the United States: Results from the National Comorbidity Study," *Archives of General Psychiatry* 51, 8–19 (1994); Ronald C. Kessler, Christopher B. Nelson, Katherine A. McGonagle, J. Liu, et al., "Comorbidity of DSM-III-R Major Depressive Disorder in the General Population: Results from the U.S. National Comorbidity Study," *British Journal of Psychiatry* 18, 17–30 (1996, Suppl. 30).

15. Maurizio Fava, A. John Rush, Jonathan E. Alpert, et al., "Difference in Treatment Outcome in Outpatients with Anxious versus Nonanxious Depression: A STAR*D Report," *American Journal of Psychiatry* 165:3, 342–351 (2008).

16. Gavin Andrews. "Comorbidity and the General Neurotic Syndrome," *British Journal of Psychiatry* 168, 76–84 (1996, Suppl. 30).

17. These are reviewed in Richard O'Connor, *Active Treatment of Depression* (New York: Norton, 2001).

18. Charles B. Nemeroff, "Comorbidity of Mood and Anxiety Disorders: The Rule, Not the Exception?" *American Journal of Psychiatry* 159:1, 3–4 (2002).

19. Richard O'Connor, *Undoing Perpetual Stress: The Missing Connection Between Depression, Anxiety, and Twenty-First-Century Illness* (New York: Berkley, 2006).

20. Ibid.

21. I'm happy to see that someone as eminent as David Barlow is thinking along the same lines: see Laura B. Allen, R. Kathryn McHugh, and David Barlow,

"Emotional Disorders: A Unified Protocol," in David H. Barlow (ed.), *Clinical Handbook of Psychological Disorders* (New York: Guilford, 2008).

22. Robert M. Sapolsky, "Foreword," in Bruce S. McEwen, *The End of Stress as We Know It* (Washington, DC: Joseph Henry Press, 2002).

23. H. Sadowski, B. Ugarte, I. Kolvin, C. Kaplan, and J. Barnes, "Early Family Life Disadvantages and Major Depression in Adulthood," *British Journal of Psychiatry* 174, 112–120 (1998).

24. Donald F. Klein at Columbia is the principal researcher on atypical depression and MAOIs. See, for instance, M. R. Leibowitz, F. M. Quitkin, J. W. Stewart, P. J. McGrath, W. M. Harrison, J. S. Markowitz, J. G. Rabkin, E. Tricamo, D. M. Goetz, and D. F. Klein, "Antidepressant Specificity in Atypical Depression," *Archives of General Psychiatry* 45:2, 129–137 (1988).

25. Michael W. O'Hara and Annette M. Swain, "Rates and Risk of Postpartum Depression—A Meta-analysis," *International Review of Psychiatry* 8:1, 37–54 (1996).

26. Michael F. Greene, "Teratogenicity of SSRIs—Serious Concern or Much Ado About Little," *New England Journal of Medicine* 356:26, 2732–2733 (June 28, 2007).

27. Raymond W. Lam, Anthony J. Levitt, Robert D. Levitan, Murray W. Enns, et al., "The Can-SAD Study: A Randomized Controlled Trial of the Effectiveness of Light Therapy and Fluoxetine in Patients with Winter Seasonal Affective Disorder," *American Journal of Psychiatry* 163, 805–812 (May 2006).

Chapter 4: Explaining Depression

1. Re: the hippocampus shrinking with repeated episodes of depression. See, for example, Yvette I. Sheline, M. H. Gado, and H. C. Kraemer, "Untreated Depression and Hippocampal Volume Loss," *American Journal of Psychiatry* 160:8, 1516–1518 (2003); Meena Vythilingam, Christine Heim, Jefffrey Newport, Andrew H. Miller, et al., "Childhood Trauma Associated with Smaller Hippocampal Volume in Women with Major Depression," *American Journal of Psychiatry* 159:12, 2072–2080 (2003); Jennifer Keller, Lin Shen, Rowena G. Gomez, Amy Garrett, et al., "Hippocampal and Amygdalar Volumes in Psychotic and Nonpsychotic Unipolar Depression," *American Journal of Psychiatry* 165, 872–880 (2008); Robert M. Sapolsky, "Foreword," in Bruce S. McEwen, *End of Stress*; Poul Videbech and Barbara Ravnkilde, "Hippocampal Volume and Depression: A Meta-Analysis of MRI Studies," *American Journal of Psychiatry* 161, 1957–1966 (2004).

2. Kimberly Goldapple, Zindel Segal, Carol Garson, Mark Lau, et al., "Modulation of Cortical-Limbic Pathways in Major Depression: Treatment-Specific Effects of Cognitive Behavior Therapy," *Archives of General Psychiatry* 61, 34–41 (2004).

3. Joel A. Posener, Lei Wang, Joseph L. Price, Mokhtar H. Gado, et al., "High-Dimensional Mapping of the Hippocampus in Depression," *American Journal of Psychiatry* 160, 83–89 (2003).

4. Mario Liotti, Helen S. Mayberg, Scott McGinnnis, Stephen L. Brannan, and Paul Jerabek, "Unmasking Disease-Specific Cerebral Blood Flow Abnormalities: Mood Challenge in Patients with Remitted Unipolar Depression," *American Journal of Psychiatry* 159, 1830–1840 (2002).

5. Robert M. Post, "Transduction of Psychosocial Stress into the Neurobiology of Recurrent Affective Disorder," *American Journal of Psychiatry* 149, 999–1010 (1992).

6. Eleanor A. Maguire, David G. Gadian, Ingrid S. Johnsrude, Catriona D. Good, et al., "Navigation-Related Structural Change in the Hippocampi of Taxi Drivers," *Proceedings of the National Academy of Sciences* 97, 4398–4403 (March 14, 2000).

7. Thomas Elbert, Christo Pantev, Christian Wienbruch, Brigitte Rockstroh, and Edward Taub, "Increased Cortical Representation of the Fingers of the Left Hand in String Players," *Science* 270, 305–307 (1995).

8. Bogdan Draganski, Christian Gaser, Volker Busch, Gerhard Schuierer, Ulrich Bogdahn, and Arne May, "Neuroplasticity: Changes in Grey Matter Induced by Training," *Nature* 427, 311–312 (2004).

9. Daniel Goleman, *Emotional Intelligence* (New York: Bantam, 1995).

10. A. Bertelsen, B. Harvald, and M. Hauge, "A Danish Twin Study of Manic-Depressive Disorders," *British Journal of Psychiatry* 130, 330–351 (1977).

11. Bradley S. Peterson, Virginia Warner, Ravi Bansal, Hongtu Zhu, Xuejun Hao, Jun Liu, Kathleen Durkin, Phillip B. Adams, Priya Wickramaratne, and Myrna M. Weissman, "Cortical Thinning in Persons at Increased Familial Risk for Major Depression," *Proceedings of the National Academy of Sciences* 106, 6273–6278, 2009.

12. Allan N. Schore, *Affect Regulation and the Origin of the Self: The Neurobiology of Emotional Development* (Hillsdale, N J: Erlbaum, 1994): Allan N. Schore, *Affect Deregulation and Disorders of the Self* (New York: Norton, 2003a); Allan N. Schore, *Affect Regulation and the Repair of the Self* (New York: Norton, 2003b).

13. Vincent J. Felitti, Robert F. Anda, Dale Nordenberg, David F. Williamson, et al., "Relationship of Childhood Abuse and Household Dysfunction to Many of the Leading Causes of Death in Adults: The Adverse Childhood

Experiences (ACE) Study," *American Journal of Preventive Medicine* 14:4, 245–258 (1998); Vincent J. Felitti, "Reverse Alchemy in Childhood: Turning Gold into Lead," *Family Violence Prevention Fund Health Alert* 8:1, 1–8 (2001); Valerie J. Edwards, George W. Holden, Vincent J. Felitti, and Robert F. Anda, "Relationship Between Multiple Forms of Childhood Maltreatment and Adult Mental Health in Community Respondents: Results from the Adverse Childhood Experiences Study," *American Journal of Psychiatry* 160:8, 1453–1460 (2003).

14. Robert J. Waldinger, George E. Vaillant, and E. John Orav, "Childhood Sibling Relationships as a Predictor of Major Depression in Adulthood: A 30-Year Prospective Study," *American Journal of Psychiatry* 164, 949–954 (2007).

15. Robert F. Musson and Lauren Alloy, "Depression and Self-Directed Attention," in Lauren Alloy (ed.), *Cognitive Processes in Depression* (New York: Guilford, 1988), pp. 193–220.

16. Stephen R. Schuchter, Nancy Downs, and Sidney Zisook, *Biologically Informed Psychotherapy for Depression* (New York: Guilford, 1996), p. 86.

17. C. Thomas Gualtieri, Lynda G. Johnson, and Kenneth B. Benedict, "Neurocognition in Depression: Patients On and Off Medication versus Healthy Comparison Subjects," *Journal of Neuropsychiatry and Clinical Neuroscience* 18, 217–225 (2006).

18. Christoph Herrmann, Sigrid Brand-Driehorst, Britta Kaminsky, Eric Leibing, Hermann Staats, and Ulrich Rueger, "Diagnostic Groups and Depressed Mood as Predictors of 22-Month Mortality Among Medical Inpatients," *Psychosomatic Medicine* 60, 570–577 (1998).

19. For example, P. M. Lewinsohn, "A Behavioral Approach to Depression," in R. J. Friedman and M. M. Katz (eds.), *The Psychology of Depression*, (Washington, DC: Winston, 1974) pp. 157–177; Sandor Rado, "The Problem of Melancholia," in Willard Gaylin (ed.), *Psychodynamic Understanding of Depression* (Northvale, NJ: Jason Aronson, 1994) (Reprinted from *International Journal of Psycho-Analysis* 9, 420–438 [1928]); Paul Wachtel, *Therapeutic Communication: Knowing What to Say When* (New York: Guilford, 1993).

20. Judith Herman, *Trauma and Recovery* (New York: Basic, 1992).

21. Schore, *Origin of the Self, Disorders of the Self, and Repair of the Self.*

22. O'Connor, *Undoing Perpetual Stress.*

23. Martin Seligman, *Learned Optimism* (New York: Pocket Books, 1990).

24. Randolph M. Nesse, "Is Depression an Adaptation?" *Archives of General Psychiatry* 57:1, 14–20 (2000).

Chapter 5: The World of Depression

1. Dan Blazer, *The Age of Melancholy: "Major Depression" and Its Social Origins* (New York: Routledge, 2005).
2. Jerome Frank, *Persuasion and Healing: A Comparative Study of Psychotherapy* (New York: Schocken, 1974).

Chapter 6: Emotions

1. George E. Vaillant, *The Wisdom of the Ego* (Cambridge: Harvard University Press, 1993).
2. A very helpful resource on anger is Carol Tavris, *Anger: The Misunderstood Emotion* (New York: Simon and Schuster, rev. ed. 1989).
3. Michael Fellman, *Citizen Sherman* (New York: Random House, 1995), pp. 105–106.
4. Geoffrey C. Ward, *The Civil War: An Illustrated History* (New York: Knopf, 1990).
5. Shelby Foote, *The Civil War: A Narrative,* vol. 3, *Red River to Appomattox* (New York: Random House, 1974), p. 996.
6. Robertson Davies, "The Deadliest Sin of All," in *One Half of Robertson Davies* (New York: Viking, 1977), pp. 62–68. Martin E. Seligman *(What You Can Change and What You Can't)* deserves credit for emphasizing this concept and discovering this essay. One source says the term survives in common speech in Appalachia as *acidie* (by folk etymology, a sour mood). Edwin R. Wallace, "Psychiatry and Its Nosology," in John Z. Sadler et al., *Philosophical Perspectives on Psychiatric Diagnostic Classification* (Baltimore: Johns Hopkins University Press, 1994).
7. Shelley E. Taylor, *Positive Illusions: Creative Self-Deception and the Healthy Mind* (New York: Basic, 1989).
8. O'Connor, *Undoing Perpetual Stress.*
9. Richard O'Connor, *Happy at Last: The Thinking Person's Guide to Finding Joy* (New York: St. Martin's, 2008).

Chapter 7: Behavior

1. Jane B. Burka and Lenora M. Yuen, *Procrastination: Why You Do It, What to Do About It* (Reading, MA: Addison-Wesley, 1983).
2. Sidney J. Blatt, "The Destructiveness of Perfectionism: Implications for the Treatment of Depression," *American Psychologist* 50, 1003–1020 (1995).

3. Aaron T., Beck, A. John Rush, Brian F. Shaw, and Gary Emery, *Cognitive Therapy of Depression* (New York; Guilford, 1987).

4. David Burns, *The Feeling Good Handbook: Using the New Mood Therapy in Everyday Life* (New York: Plume, 1999).

5. Vaillant, *Wisdom of the Ego,* p. 52.

6. Andrew Solomon, *The Noonday Demon: An Atlas of Depression* (New York: Scribner, 1992).

7. O'Connor, *Happy at Last.*

8. Styron, *Darkness Visible,* pp. 40–43.

9. F. Scott Fitzgerald, *The Crack-Up* (New York: New Directions, 1945).

10. Michael Argyle, *The Psychology of Happiness* (New York: Routledge, 2002).

Chapter 8: Thinking

1. Beck et al., *Cognitive Therapy;* David Burns, *Feeling Good: The New Mood Therapy* (New York: Harper, 1999).

2. Beck et al., *Cognitive Therapy.*

3. Albert Ellis, *Reason and Emotion in Psychotherapy* (New York: Birch Lane, 1994).

4. Jon Kabat-Zinn, *Full Catastrophe Living* (New York: Delacorte, 1990); Jon Kabat-Zinn, *Wherever You Go, There You Are* (New York: Hyperion 1994).

5. Seligman, *Learned Optimism.*

6. From Beck et al., *Cognitive Therapy.*

7. Lauren B. Alloy, "Depressive Realism: Sadder but Wiser?" *Harvard Mental Health Letter,* 4–5, April 1995.

8. Donald J. Martin, Lynne Y. Abramson, and Lauren Alloy, "The Illusion of Control for Self and Others in Depressed and Nondepressed College Students," *Journal of Personality and Social Psychology* 46, 125–136 (1984).

9. Lauren B. Alloy and Lynne Y. Abramson, "Judgment of Contingency in Depressed and Nondepressed Students: Sadder but Wiser?" *Journal of Experimental Psychology: General* 108, 441–485 (1979).

10. Julie K. Norem, *The Positive Power of Negative Thinking.* (New York: Basic, 2001).

Chapter 9: Stress and Depression

1. Harold A. Sackheim and Barbara L. Steif, "Neuropsychology of Depression and Mania," in Anastasios Georgotas and Robert Cancro (eds.), *Depression and Mania* (New York: Elsevier Science, 1988).

2. Pearl H. Chiu and Patricia J. Deldin, "Neural Evidence for Enhanced Error Detection in Major Depressive Disorder," *American Journal of Psychiatry* 164, 608–666 (2007).

3. See, for example: Zindel V. Segal, J. Mark G. Williams, and John D. Teasdale, *Mindfulness-Based Cognitive Therapy for Depression* (New York: Guilford, 2001); Jon Kabat-Zinn, "An Outpatient Program in Behavioral Medicine for Chronic Pain Patients Based on the Practice of Mindfulness Meditation: Theoretical Considerations and Preliminary Results," *General Hospital Psychiatry* 4, 33–47 (1982); Jon Kabat-Zinn, M. D. Massion, J. L. Kristeller, L. G. Peterson, et al., "Effectiveness of a Meditation-Based Stress Reduction Program in the Treatment of Anxiety Disorders," *American Journal of Psychiatry* 149, 936–943 (1992); J. L. Kristeller and C. B. Hallett, "An Exploratory Study of a Meditation-Based Intervention for Binge Eating Disorder," *Journal of Health Psychology* 4, 357–363 (1999); Jon Kabat-Zinn, E. Wheeler, T. Light, Z. Skillings, et al., "Influence of a Mindfulness-Based Stress Reduction Intervention on Rates of Skin Clearing in Patients with Moderate to Severe Psoriasis Undergoing Phototherapy UVB and Photochemotherapy PUVA," *Psychosomatic Medicine* 50, 625–632 (1998); D. L. Goldenberg, K. H. Kaplan, M. G. Nadeau, C. Brodeur, S. Smith, and C. H. Schmid, "A Controlled Study of a Stress-Reduction, Cognitive-Behavioral Treatment Program in Fibromyalgia," *Journal of Musculoskeletal Pain* 2, 53–66 (1994); I. Kutz, J. Leserman, C. Dorrington, C. Morrison, J. Borysenko, and H. Benson, "Meditation as an Adjunct to Psychotherapy," *Psychotherapy and Psychosomatics* 43, 209–218 (1985); M. Speca, L. E. Carlson, E. Goodey, and M. Angen, "A Randomized, Wait-List Controlled Clinical Trial: The Effect of a Mindfulness Meditation-Based Stress Reduction Program on Mood and Symptoms of Stress in Cancer Outpatients," *Psychosomatic Medicine* 62, 613–622 (2000); S. L. Shapiro, G. E. Schwartz, and G. Bonner, "Effects of Mindfulness-Based Stress Reduction on Medical and Premedical Students," *Journal of Behavioral Medicine* 21, 581–599 (1998).

4. Richard J. Davidson, Jon Kabat-Zinn, Jessica Schumacher, Melissa Rosenkranz, et al., "Alterations in Brain and Immune Function Produced by Mindfulness Meditation," *Psychosomatic Medicine* 65, 564–570 (2003); Linda E. Carlson, Michael Speca, Kalama D. Patel, and Eileen Goodey, "Mindfulness-Based Stress Reduction in Relation to Quality of Life, Mood, Symptoms of Stress, and Immune Parameters in Breast and Prostate Cancer Outpatients," *Psychosomatic Medicine* 65, 571–581 (2003).

5. Daniel Goleman, *Destructive Emotions: How Can We Overcome Them? A Scientific Dialogue with the Dalai Lama* (New York: Bantam, 2003b).
6. Kabat-Zinn, *Full Catastrophe Living.*
7. O'Connor, *Happy at Last.*
8. Steven C. Hayes, Kirk E. Strosahl, and Kelly G. Williams, *Acceptance and Commitment Therapy* (New York: Guilford, 2003); Steven C. Hayes, *Get Out of Your Mind and Into Your Life* (New York: New Harbinger, 2005).
9. Segal et al., *Mindfulness-Based Cognitive Therapy.*
10. Susan Nolen-Hoeksma, "Sex Differences in Control of Depression," in Daniel Wegner and James Pennebaker (eds.), *Handbook of Mental Control* (Englewood Cliffs, NJ: Prentice-Hall, 1993).
11. O'Connor, *Happy at Last.*

Chapter 10: Relationships

1. David Karp, *Speaking of Sadness* (New York: Oxford University Press, 1996), p. 28.
2. Cynthia Fu, Steve Williams, Michael Brammer, et al., "Neural Responses to Happy Facial Expressions in Major Depression Following Antidepressant Treatment," *American Journal of Psychiatry* 164, 599–607 (2007).
3. Kramer, in *Listening to Prozac* (New York: Penguin, 1993), pp. 87–107, has a thoughtful discussion of this subject, summarizing the work of Donald F. Klein, a research psychiatrist.
4. F. Scott Fitzgerald, *The Great Gatsby* (New York: Charles Scribner' Sons, 1925), p. 119.
5. Some resources for learning assertiveness include Edward J. Bourne, *The Anxiety and Phobia Workbook,* fourth edition (Oakland, CA: New Harbinger, 2005); Martin M. Antony and Richard P. Swinson, *The Shyness and Social Anxiety Workbook* (Oakland, CA: New Harbinger, 2000); Robert E. Alberti and Michael L. Emmons, *Your Perfect Right: A Guide to Assertive Living*, ninth edition (Atascadero, CA: Impact, 2008); Sharon and Gordon Bower, *Asserting Yourself* (Reading, MA: Addison-Wesley, 1991); Manuel Smith, *When I Say No, I Feel Guilty* (New York: Bantam, 1985).
6. I saw a wonderful illustration of this in, of all places, *The Magnificent Seven.* Chris (Yul Brynner) is trying to convince Frank, the greedy one, that there is no gold in the village. Frank, assuming that everyone else is as greedy as he is, thinks that Chris is just putting on an act for the benefit of the villagers. "Don't understand me so fast," says Chris.

Chapter 11: The Body

1. Michael F. Scheier, Karen A. Matthews, Jane F. Owens, Richard Schulz, et al., "Optimism and Rehospitalization After Coronary Artery Bypass Graft Surgery," *Archives of Internal Medicine* 159:8, 829–835 (1999).
2. Schore, *Origin of the Self, Disorders of the Self,* and *Repair of the Self.*
3. Felitti et al., "The Adverse Childhood Experiences (ACE) Study."
4. O'Connor, *Undoing Perpetual Stress.*
5. Cristina Fortes, Sara Farchi, Francesco Forastiere, Nera Agabiti, et al., "Depressive Symptoms Lead to Impaired Cellular Immune Response," *Psychotherapy and Psychosomatics* 72:5, 253–260 (2003).
6. Lawson R. Wulsin and Bonita M. Singal, "Do Depressive Symptoms Increase the Risk for the Onset of Coronary Disease? A Systematic Quantitative Review," *Psychosomatic Medicine* 65, 201–210 (2003).
7. Nancy Frasure-Smith, François Lespérance, Martin Juneau, Mario Talajic, and Martial G. Bourassa, "Gender, Depression, and One-Year Prognosis After Myocardial Infarction," *Psychosomatic Medicine* 61, 26–37 (1999).
8. C. Herrmann, S. Brand-Driehorst, B. Kaminsky, E. Leibing, H. Staats, and U. Rueger, "Diagnostic Groups and Depressed Mood as Predictors of 22-Month Mortality Among Medical Inpatients," *Psychosomatic Medicine* 60, 570–577 (1998).
9. Maurice M. Ohayon and Alan F. Schatzberg, "Using Chronic Pain to Predict Depressive Morbidity in the General Population," *Archives of General Psychiatry* 60, 39–47 (2005).
10. Michael C. Miller, "The Benefits of Positive Psychology," *Harvard Mental Health Letter* 18, 6 (December 31, 2001).
11. Deborah D. Danner, David A. Snowdon, and Wallace V. Friesen, "Positive Emotions in Early Life and Longevity: Findings from the Nun Study," *Journal of Personality and Social Psychology* 80, 804–813 (2001).
12. Robert M. Sapolsky, *A Primate's Memoir* (New York: Scribner, 2002).
13. Vedantam, "Antidepressant Use."
14. Dowling, Colette, *You Mean I Don't Have to Feel This Way?* (New York: Bantam, 1991).
15. Ellen McGrath and Gwendolyn P. Keita, *Women and Depression: Risk Factors and Treatment Issues* (Washington, DC: American Psychological Association, 1990).
16. U.S. Census Bureau, "Expectation of Life at Birth and Projections," http://www.allcountries.org/uscensus/116_expectation_of_life_at_birth_and.html.
17. Bruce P. Dohrenwend, Itzhak Levav, Patrick E. Shrout, Sharon Schwartz, et al., "Socioeconomic Status and Psychiatric Disorders: The Causation-Selection Issue," *Science,* 946–951 (Feb. 21, 1992).

18. Steve Herman, James A. Blumenthal, Michael Babyak, Parinda Khatri, et al., "Exercise Therapy for Depression in Middle-Aged and Older Adults: Predictors of Early Dropout and Treatment Failure," *Health Psychology* 21:6, 553–563 (2002).
19. James A. Blumenthal, Michael A. Babyak, P. Murali Doraiswamy, et al., "Exercise and Pharmacotherapy in the Treatment of Major Depressive Disorder," *Psychosomatic Medicine* 69, 587–596 (2007).
20. O'Connor, *Happy at Last.*
21. Tal Ben-Shahar, remarks, Conference on Meditation and Psychotherapy, Boston, MA, June 1, 2007.
22. O'Connor, *Happy at Last.*

Chapter 12: The Self

1. John Bradshaw, *Healing the Shame That Binds You* (Deerfield Beach, FL: Health Communications, 1988).
2. Robert Karen, "Shame," *The Atlantic*, pp. 40–70 (Feb. 1982).
3. "NMHA Survey Finds Many Americans Are Poorly Informed About Depression, Slow to Seek Help," *Hospital and Community Psychiatry* 43:3, 292–293 (1992).
4. Charles L. Whitfield, *Boundaries and Relationships* (Deerfield Beach, FL: Health Communications, 1993).
5. Thomas F. Fogarty, "The Distancer and the Pursuer," *The Family* 7:1, 11–16 (1979).
6. Tavris, *Anger.*
7. Peter Kramer, *Listening to Prozac* (New York: Penguin, 1993).

Chapter 13: Treating Depression Medically

1. Mark Olfson and Stephen C. Marcus, "National Patterns."
2. Goldapple et al., "Modulation of Cortical-Limbic Pathways."
3. Jack M. Gorman, *The Essential Guide to Psychiatric Drugs* (New York: St. Martin's Griffin, 2007).
4. I. M. Anderson and B. M. Tomenson, "The Efficacy of Selective Serotonin Reuptake Inhibitors in Depression: A Meta-Analysis of Studies Against Tricyclic Antidepressants," *Journal of Psychopharmacology* 8, 238–249 (1994).
5. Agency for Health Care Policy and Research, "Treatment of Depression: Newer Pharmacotherapies," http://www.ahcpr.gov/clinic/deprsumm.htm. Posted March 1999.

6. Joanna Moncrieff and David Cohen, "Do Antidepressants Cure or Create Abnormal Brain States?" *PLoS Medicine* 3:7, 240 (July 2006).

7. "Top 5 Reasons to Forget About Pristiq," *Carlat Psychiatry Blog* (March 1, 2008).

8. "Antidepressants and Bipolar Disorder: An Update," *The Carlat Psychiatry Report* 6:7 and 8 (July/August 2008).

9. My resources for this section are all known for being free of drug-industry sponsorship. An essential guide for anyone dealing with bipolar disorder is John McManamy, *Living Well with Depression and Bipolar Disorder* (New York: Collins, 2006). Also see his website at http://www.mcmanweb.com. Other sources here include: "Novel Anticonvulsants: An Update on Efficacy," *The Carlat Psychiatry Report* 6:2 (Feb. 2008); and Gorman, *Essential Guide.*

10. Anne Berghöfer, Martin Alda, Mazda Adli, Christopher Baethge, et al., "Long-Term Effectiveness of Lithium in Bipolar Disorder: A Multicenter Investigation of Patients with Typical and Atypical Features," *Journal of Clinical Psychiatry* 69:12, 1860–1868 (November 18, 2008).

11. Kessler, McGonagle, et al.; Kessler, Nelson, et al., "Comorbidity."

12. R. J. Goldberg, "Diagnostic Dilemmas Created by Patients with Anxiety and Depression," *American Journal of Medicine* 98, 278 (1995).

13. Olfson et al., "National Trends in the Outpatient Treatment of Depression."

14. I summarized this research in *Active Treatment of Depression.* See also Lewis L. Judd, Hagop S. Akiskal, Jack D. Maser, et al., "A Prospective 12-year Study of Subsyndromal and Syndromal Depressive Symptoms in Unipolar Major Depressive Disorders," *Archives of General Psychiatry* 55, 694–700 (1998); David A. Solomon, Martin B. Keller, Andrew C. Leon, Timothy I. Mueller, et al., "Multiple Recurrences of Major Depressive Disorder," *American Journal of Psychiatry* 157:2, 229–233 (2000); and Michael E. Thase, "The Long-Term Nature of Depression," *Journal of Clinical Psychiatry* 60, 3–35 (1999, Suppl. 4).

15. Daniel N. Klein, Joseph E. Schwartz, Suzanne Rose, and Julie B. Leader, "Five-Year Course and Outcome of Dysthymic Disorder: A Prospective, Naturalistic Follow-Up Study," *American Journal of Psychiatry* 157:6, 931–939 (2000).

16. Thase, "Long-Term Nature."

17. Irving Kirsch, Thomas J. Moore, Alan Scoboria, and Sarah S. Nicholls, "The Emperor's New Drugs: An Analysis of Antidepressant Medication Data Submitted to the U.S. Food and Drug Administration," *Prevention and Treatment* 5 (article 23) http://journals.apa.org/prevention/volume5/pre0050023a.html. 2002.

18. W. A. Brown, "Placebo as a Treatment for Depression," *Neuropsychopharmacology* 10:4, 265–288 (1994).

19. Madhukar H. Trivedi, A. John Rush, Stephen R. Wisniewski, et al., "Evaluation of Outcomes with Citalopram for Depression Using Measurement-Based Care in STAR*D: Implications for Clinical Practice," *American Journal of Psychiatry* 163, 28–40 (2006).

20. Catherine J. Harmer, Nicholas C. Shelley, Philip J. Cowen, and Guy M. Goodwin, "Increased Positive Versus Negative Perception and Memory in Healthy Volunteers Following Selective Serotonin and Norepinephrine Reuptake Inhibition," *American Journal of Psychiatry* 161, 1256–1263 (2004).

21. Brian Knutson, Owen M. Wolkowitz, Steve W. Cole, Theresa Chan, et al., "Selective Alteration of Personality and Social Behavior by Serotonergic Intervention," *American Journal of Psychiatry* 155, 373–379 (1998).

22. Adam Opbroek, Pedro L. Delgado, Cindi Laukes, et al., "Emotional Blunting Associated with SSRI-Induced Sexual Dysfunction: Do SSRIs Inhibit Emotional Responses?" *International Journal of Neuropsychopharmacology* 5, 147–151 (2002).

23. Peter Kramer, *Listening to Prozac*.

24. Marlene P. Freeman, Joseph R. Hibbeln, Katherine L. Wisner, et al., "Omega-3 Fatty Acids: Evidence Basis for Treatment and Future Research in Psychiatry," *Journal of Clinical Psychiatry* 67:12, 1954–1967 (2006).

Chapter 14: Psychotherapy, Self-help, and Other Means to Recovery

1. Tomas Furmark, Maria Tillfors, Ina Marteinsdottir, et al., "Common Changes in Cerebral Blood Flow in Patients with Social Phobia Treated with Citalopram or Cognitive-Behavioral Therapy," *Archives of General Psychiatry* 59, 425–433 (2002).

2. Amit Etkin, Christopher Pittenger, H. Jonathan Polan, and Eric R. Kandel, "Toward a Neurobiology of Psychotherapy: Basic Science and Clinical Applications," *Journal of Neuropsychiatry and Clinical Neurosciences* 17, 145–158 (2005).

3. Sidney J. Blatt et al., "Characteristics of Effective Therapists," *Journal of Consulting and Clinical Psychology* 64:6, 1276–1284 (1996).

4. Beck et al., *Cognitive Therapy*.

5. Gerald M. Klerman, Myrna Weissman, Bruce J. Rounsaville, and Eve S. Chevron, *Interpersonal Psychotherapy of Depression* (New York: Basic Books, 1984).

6. Falk Leichsenring and Sven Rabung, "Effectiveness of Long-term Psychodynamic Psychotherapy: A Meta-Analysis," *Journal of the American Medical Association* 300, 1551–1565 (2008).

7. Zac E. Imel, Melanie B. Malterer, Kevin M. McKay, and Bruce E. Wampold, "A Meta-Analysis of Psychotherapy and Medication in Unipolar Depression and Dysthymia," *Journal of Affective Disorders* 110, 197–206 (2008); Pim Cuijpers, Annemieke van Straten, Patricia van Oppen, and Gerhard Andersson, "Are Psychological and Pharmacologic Interventions Equally Effective in the Treatment of Adult Depressive Disorders? A Meta-Analysis of Comparative Studies," *Journal of Clinical Psychiatry* 69:11, 1675–1685 (2008).

8. Imel et al., "A Meta-Analysis."

9. Segal et al., *Mindfulness-Based Cognitive Therapy.*

10. Mark Williams, John Teasdale, Zindel Segal, and Jon Kabat-Zinn, *The Mindful Way Through Depression* (New York: Guilford, 2007).

11. S. Helen Ma and John D. Teasdale, "Mindfulness-Based Cognitive Therapy for Depression: Replication and Exploration of Differential Relapse Prevention Effects," *Journal of Consulting and Clinical Psychology* 72, 31–40 (2004).

12. A helpful resource is Anne Sheffield, *How You Can Survive When They're Depressed* (New York: Three Rivers Press, 1999).

Chapter 15: Work and Sense of Purpose

1. Philip Brickman, Erik J. Coates, and Ronnie Janoff-Bulman, "Lottery Winners and Accident Victims: Is Happiness Relative?" *Journal of Personality and Social Psychology* 36:8, 917–927 (1978).

2. Tal Ben-Shahar, *Happier* (New York: McGraw-Hill, 2007).

3. Ibid.

4. Mihaly Csikszentmihalyi, *Flow: The Psychology of Optimal Experience* (New York: HarperCollins, 1990).

5. Ibid., p. 158, et seq.

6. John P. Robinson and Steven Martin, "What Do Happy People Do?" *Social Indicators Research*, 89:3 565–571 (2008).

7. Argyle, *Psychology of Happiness.*

8. There is now a lot of literature on time management, personal efficiency, and self-improvement, which can be helpful in recovering from depression. Steven Covey's books (*The Seven Habits of Highly Effective People,* etc.) are not bad, though I enjoyed more Hyrum Smith's *The Ten Natural Laws of Successful Time and Life Management.* With both of these, you have to put aside any prejudice you might have against Babbitry and boosterism.

Stephanie Winston's books (*Getting Organized,* etc.) are very practical and helpful. Martin Seligman has made a good contribution with *What You Can Change and What You Can't.* None of these is the answer if you're really depressed; they are to help you as you recover.

9. M. Scott Peck, *The Road Less Traveled* (New York: Simon and Schuster, 1978).

Chapter 16: Living, Together and Apart

1. Deborah Tannen, *You Just Don't Understand: Women and Men in Conversation* (New York: Ballantine, 1991).

2. Jennifer Senior, "Is Urban Loneliness a Myth?" *New York Magazine,* Nov. 23, 2008.

3. See Maggie Scarf, *Intimate Partners: Patterns in Love and Marriage* (New York: Random House, 1987), and *Intimate Worlds: Life Inside the Family* (New York: Random House, 1995). Two of the most reliable and readable books available on the struggle for intimacy and the need for autonomy.

4. See, for example, Bill O'Hanlon, *Thriving Through Crisis* (New York: Perigee, 2005).

5. G. Pirooz Sholevar and Linda Schwoeri, *The Transmission of Depression in Families and Children: Assessment and Intervention* (Northvale, NJ: Jason Aronson, 1994).

6. Judith S. Wallerstein and Sandra Blakeslee, *Second Chances: Men, Women, and Children a Decade After Divorce* (New York: Ticknor and Fields, 1989).

Chapter 17: Children and Adolescents

1. Harry F. Harlow and Robert Zimmerman, "Affectional Responses in the Infant Monkey," *Science* 130, 421–432 (1959).

2. Brea L. Perry, Bernice A. Pescosolido, Jack K. Martin, Jane D. McLeod, and Peter S. Jensen, "Comparison of Public Attributions, Attitudes, and Stigma in Regard to Depression Among Children and Adults," *Psychiatric Services* 58:632–635 (2007).

3. Daniel Kahneman and Alan B. Krueger. "Developments in the Measurement of Subjective Well-Being," *Journal of Economic Perspectives* 20, 13–24 (2006).

4. U.S. Preventive Services Task Force, "Screening and Treatment for Major Depressive Disorder in Children and Adolescents," *Pediatrics* 123:4, 1223–1228 (2009).

5. J. D. Salinger, *The Catcher in the Rye* (New York: Little, Brown, 1951).
6. Samuel Slipp, *Object Relations: A Dynamic Bridge Between Individual and Family Treatment* (New York: Jason Aronson, 1984), p. 181.
7. Alan L. Berman, David A. Jobes, and Morton M. Silverman, "The Epidemiology of Adolescent Suicide," in Alan L. Berman, David A. Jobes, and Morton M. Silverman (eds.), *Adolescent Suicide: Assessment and Intervention*, 2nd ed. (Washington, DC: American Psychological Association, 2006).
8. Harry M. Hoberman and Barry D. Garfinkel. "Completed Suicide in Children and Adolescents," *Journal of the American Academy of Child and Adolescent Psychiatry* 27:6, 689–695 (1988).
9. G. Pirooz Sholevar and Linda Schwoeri, *The Transmission of Depression in Families and Children: Assessment and Intervention* (Northvale, NJ: Jason Aronson, 1994).
10. Jane E. Brody, "Sorrow's Web: Depressed Mother and Difficult Child," *New York Times,* C12, Nov. 2, 1994.

Chapter 18: Community

1. Phil Ochs, "There but for Fortune," © 1963, Appleseed Music, Inc.
2. Robert M. Sapolsky, *Why Zebras Don't Get Ulcers: An Updated Guide to Stress, Stress-Related Diseases, and Coping*, 3rd ed. (New York: W. H. Freeman, 2004).
3. Steven Greenhouse, "Report Shows Americans Have More 'Labor Days,'" *New York Times*, Sept. 1, 2001.
4. See, for instance, Robert E. Lane, *The Loss of Happiness in Market Democracies* (New Haven: Yale University Press, 2000); Richard Layard, *Happiness: Lessons from a New Science* (New York: Penguin, 2005); Robert D. Putnam, *Bowling Alone* (New York: Simon and Schuster, 2000).
5. Maria Melchior, Avshalom Caspi, Barry J. Milne, Andrea Danese, Richie Poulton, and Terrie E. Moffitt, "Work Stress Precipitates Depression and Anxiety in Young, Working Women and Men," *Psychological Medicine* 37:8, 1119–1129 (Aug 2007).
6. Richard Handler, "20 Weeks to Happiness," *Psychotherapy Networker* (Jan/Feb, 2006).
7. Murray and Lopez, *Global Burden*.
8. Tim Kasser, *The High Price of Materialism* (Cambridge, MA: MIT Press, 2002).
9. John Berendt, "Phil Ochs Ain't Marchin' Anymore," *Esquire*, p. 132, August 1976.

10. Michael Schumacher, *There but for Fortune: The Life of Phil Ochs* (New York: Hyperion, 1996).
11. Eric Weiner, *The Geography of Bliss* (New York: Twelve, 2008).

Chapter 20: A Program for Recovery

1. William Fleeson, Adrian B. Malanos, and Noelle M. Achille, "An Intra-individual Process Approach to the Relationship Between Extraversion and Positive Affect: Is Acting Extraverted as 'Good' as Being Extraverted?" *Journal of Personality and Social Psychology* 83:6, 1409–1422 (2002).
2. O'Connor, *Happy at Last*.
3. Martin E. Seligman, *Authentic Happiness* (New York: Free Press, 2002); Christopher Peterson, *A Primer in Positive Psychology* (New York: Oxford USA, 2006).
4. Martin E. Seligman, Tracy A. Steen, Nansook Park, and Christopher Peterson. "Positive Psychology Progress: Empirical Validation of Interventions," *American Psychologist* 60, 410–421 (2005).
5. Ibid.
6. Vaillant, *Wisdom of the Ego*.

Index

medications. *See also* drug industry
  antidepressants, 16–17, 56, 99, 158, 194–95,
    198, 215, 226
  anxiolytic drugs, 56, 209–10
  atypical antipsychotic drugs, 208–9, 210
  benzodiazepines, 210
  doctors who prescribe, 211–12
  duration of treatment, 213
  effectiveness of, versus psychotherapy, 220,
    225–26
  informational resources on, 199
  lithium, 48, 50, 206–7
  MAOIs, 55, 199–200
  mood stabilizers, 58, 206–8
  overuse of, 197
  Remeron (mirtazipine), 205
  reversal of brain damage, 198
  SNRIs, 203, 211
  SSRIs, 16, 49, 58, 201–4, 214–15, 279
  stimulants, 210–11
  tranquilizers, 56, 209–10
  Trazodone (Desyrel), 204
  tricyclics, 200–201
  Wellbutrin (buproprion), 205
meditation. *See* mindfulness and mindful
    meditation
metacommunication, 160–62, 319–20
mindfulness and mindful meditation
  awareness of positive experiences, 115, 195,
    325–27
  being in present moment, 81, 145, 318, 329
  detachment and suspension of judgment,
    81, 128–29, 144, 149
  Mindful Walking exercise, 183–84
  perseverance in practice of, 150
  perspective on thought processes, 155–56,
    315, 325–26
  relaxation and stress reduction, 81, 121,
    143–46, 182
  reversal of brain damage, 61, 81,
    143–44
  Simple Mindfulness Meditation exercise,
    146–48
  Three Good Things exercise, 328–29
  as way of life, 144–45
Mindfulness-Based Cognitive Therapy for
    Depression (MBCT), 226–28
Mindfulness-Based Stress Reduction
    (MBSR), 143, 144
Mindful Way Through Depression, The
    (Williams, et al.), 227

monoamine oxidase inhibitors (MAOIs), 55,
    199–200
mood
  hormonal influence, 179
  Mood Journal, 91–93, 314, 330
  music and, 122–23
  omega-3 treatment, 217–18
  pets and, 123
  understanding changes in, 314
  unfelt feelings and, 90–91
mood stabilizers, 58, 206–8
music, 122

National Institute of Mental Health, STAR*D
    study, 51, 52, 214
negativity. *See* thought patterns
Noonday Demon, The (Solomon), 110
Norem, Julie, 136–37
Nuns of Mankato study, 174

obsessive and compulsive behaviors, 34
obsessive thinking, 115, 151–53, 315, 316
Ochs, Phil, 299–300
O'Connor, Richard
  blog, 213
  detachment during stressful situation, 154
  experience with depression, 6–8, 276–77,
    307–11
  play, 192
  stress in marriage, 267–68
omega-3 (fish oil), 217–18
optimism, 131–32, 134, 172

panic attacks, 55–56
passive-aggression, 35–36, 108–9
passivity, 34
perfectionism, 19, 80, 97, 104–5
personalization, 131–32
pessimism. *See* thought patterns
Peterson, Chris, 325
pharmaceutical industry. *See* drug industry
phobias, 56, 62, 63, 309
physical concerns. *See* body
play, 192–94, 334
pleasure. *See* happiness
Positive Power of Negative Thinking, The
    (Norem), 136–37
postpartum depression (PPD), 57–58
post-traumatic stress disorder (PTSD),
    70–72
pride, 82, 97–99, 194, 240, 318